# THE EASTER JESUS AND THE GOOD FRIDAY CHURCH

George and Evie —
All God's best.
Greg Athnos
10/11/14

To Contact:
gregathnos.com/contact

# THE EASTER JESUS AND THE GOOD FRIDAY CHURCH

Reclaiming the Centrality of the Resurrection

**Gregory S. Athnos**

**Outskirts Press, Inc.**
**Denver, Colorado**

The Easter Jesus and the Good Friday Church
Reclaiming the Centrality of the Resurrection

Outskirts Press, Inc.
http://www.outskirtspress.com

ISBN: 978-1-4327-7450-9

PRINTED IN THE UNITED STATES OF AMERICA

*For those who rejoice in the risen Lord,*
*and desire to live in the power of His resurrection.*

*The Easter Jesus and the Good Friday Church:*
*Reclaiming the Centrality of the Resurrection*

*Gregory S. Athnos*

# Table of Contents

# Acknowledgements

MY THINKING ON this subject began to take shape in 1974 when I began studying the art of the Roman catacombs. Dawning slowly was the realization that there seemed to be an enormous disconnect between what the early Christians viewed as their only hope, that is, the resurrection of Jesus, and our own emphasis on Jesus' sacrifice, often to the detriment of his resurrection. It was difficult to reconcile my growing awareness of that disconnect with those practices of the Christian faith I had observed throughout my entire lifetime. How could I be right if the Christian community's living out of its faith was indeed a reflection of the theology in place for centuries? I soldiered on. I asked questions. I read between the lines. One year followed another until finally I became more certain of the rightness of my path. This book is the culmination of my quest aided by the support of many people.

Sister Maria Francesca, the diminutive nun who was my mentor in the archives of the catacombs in Rome, was the first to encourage me. She lives daily with the thousands of catacomb images of 'resurrection' and 'deliverance' that had sustained those suffering under Roman persecution. Her commitment to keeping their resurrection faith alive continues to be an inspiration to me.

The late Dr. Glenn Anderson, Dean of North Park Seminary in Chicago, dissuaded me from becoming a seminary student. His counsel was to continue my quest without being influenced by current practices, as he also saw the need for some fresh thinking. After his passing, his wife gave me an illuminated manuscript page from a 15<sup>th</sup> century Spanish monastery's liturgical chant book. Set to music were the words from the Apostle's Creed: '…was resurrected on the third day.' It hangs in my home as a reminder not only of that powerful act of God, but also as a constant thanksgiving for Glenn and his encouragement.

I owe much to many hundreds of people who have attended my *Resurrection Seminars*. In their conversations with me they encouraged my continued pursuit of a biblical justification for what I believed, as they had begun to see for themselves a need for balance between the death and resurrection of Jesus in our daily life as well as our worship practices. They will never know how much their support was critical to my journey, and I wish I could remember all their names.

A group of Japanese ministers and seminary students from the Covenant Church of Japan wept through an entire day as I presented my *Resurrection Seminar* in Tokyo. Their tears flowed, they said, because for the first time it became clear the resurrection of Jesus is the one distinctive that sets the Christian faith apart from all the false religions they struggle against every day. What a confirmation that was, and it propelled me to continue.

Perhaps the most important person in my venture is my beloved wife Doy. She has been with me at every stage of my development since my second sojourn in the catacombs in 1983. She believes in my research, but it isn't her belief in my journey that's important. Above all, Doy has kept me grounded. Her wisdom has influenced my writing more than any other person. I trust her judgments without hesitation. What I began to embrace from her counsel is that if the crucifixion of Jesus is no great sacrifice, then the resurrection of Jesus is no great victory—the power of the resurrection is only in proportion to the profundity of the sacrifice. Seeking to establish the authority of the resurrection I was challenged to hold fast and not let go of the immense sacrifice Jesus paid; union and fusion became the goals. Thank you, Doy, for your persistent encouragement. I hope your wise counsel will be wonderfully reflected in what we're about to undertake in this book.

# Preface

I AM A musician by profession. How then, you might ask, did I get involved with the theology of Resurrection? Of one thing I am certain: God's hand was guiding me, perhaps on occasion shoving me through a circuitous route until I had no choice but to proceed. When some doors closed, others opened. It wasn't clear initially, but as the journey progressed I began to see a very definite plan at work—not my plan, but looking back, a plan most marvelous.

Here is how the path unfolded. In 1973 I was granted a Sabbatical leave from my university teaching position in order to continue studying the music of Edvard Grieg and its relation to Norwegian folk music. I had begun that work in the summer of 1967 at the University of Oslo, working with several members of the Grieg Committee of Norway who were at that time on the faculty of the University's International Summer School. When I wrote to them about my leave and my intentions to return to Norway I assumed they would welcome my continuing research into their most famous composer. To my surprise the Grieg committee decided not to let me have access to the archives, presumably because I was no longer a student of theirs, nor was I a Norwegian citizen. Without that permission it was futile to go to Norway. This was a dilemma—my academic leave had been granted, but now I had no project!

I asked myself why I had wanted to go to Norway in the middle of the winter? Why not a place with a warmer climate? Greece immediately came to mind. I had been to my ancestral homeland once before in 1965, and had fallen in love with it. My father had come from Greece as a sixteen year old, by himself, in 1906; all of my distant relatives still live there. This, I thought, would be the perfect place to blend work and pleasure. But what work? There has been little significant classical music from Greece. Why not study something else, I thought, something that was important in Greek history and would also appeal to my growing interest in religious art? Byzantine art, the art of the Greek Christian world from 400 AD to 1400 AD came to mind. I knew very little about it, but was challenged and intrigued by the project. Adding spice to the mix, one of my father's brothers, my uncle Clonos, whom I had never met, had become a Greek Orthodox monk icon painter on Mt. Athos—Agios Oros, the Holy Mountain. Perhaps I would have the privilege to travel to that most sacred of places to find him. My new project gained approval from the Sabbatical Committee and I was on my way. (I received permission from all the authorities and visited Mt. Athos twice, but never found my uncle Clonos, though I visited many of the monasteries located in those mountains of northern Greece. I later discovered that he had been alive when I was there. Not meeting him was a great disappointment to me.)

In January 1974, I flew to Athens, moved into my third cousin's apartment and began to study. For three months I read in the Gennadion Library and examined Byzantine icons in the Byzantine Museum and in significant churches throughout the Greek world of the first one and a half millennia AD. It was an exciting time.

But April was rainy, and with the dampness came an unsettled feeling. I felt that an important ingredient in my study of early Christian art was being missed. Byzantine art was beautiful, the study was fascinating, but the art was too highly developed and stylized. I had been hoping to discover something of the evolution of Christian art, and it appeared to me that Byzantine art was too far along the developmental scale. I wanted to get to the actual beginnings of the

Christian visual aesthetic. Greece was not the place. I assumed Rome would provide some answers.

In May I flew to Rome. I had no idea where to begin, nor did I have a letter of introduction or credentials of any kind. My first attempt was to speak to the director of the Vatican Museum; I figured it was better to start at the top and work my way down! Who knows, I might get lucky! And I did!

I was granted an appointment with the museum director, the late Professor Enrico Josi. I didn't know it at the time, but he was a renowned scholar of early Christian art. I was honest with him. I explained that I was a novice with no background in early Christian art. Two things I brought to the study, I said, were a deep curiosity and a deep commitment to the Christian faith. To my amazement Professor Josi welcomed me and made arrangements for me to work in the Paleo-Christian collection of the Vatican Museum, not then open to the public, on the condition that he accompany me on every visit. What an offer! I was going to be introduced to early Christian art by the world's leading expert! I was also introduced to Vatican archeologists, and was given access to the Vatican Library. It was an incredible experience to show my pass and walk by the Swiss Guards every day on my way into the Vatican State. But most important of all, I was granted the privilege of studying in the archives of the Roman catacombs housed in the Priscilla Convent on Via Salaria, the ancient salt road leading into the city. The convent was built over the oldest Christian catacomb yet discovered. Sister Maria Francesca, chief Archivist of the Catacombs was to be my host and mentor. At this point I began to sense that a force greater than I was at work in my life, moving me in directions beyond my comprehension. Music, the area of my life where I had contacts, credentials and expertise had led nowhere, but in this study where I was a stranger and a novice with nothing going for me but curiosity, every door imaginable was thrown open, doors I wouldn't even have thought of. My journey thus far had seemed like a long maze of frustrations and dead-ends. Now I began to sense a purposeful and direct leading into an arena of study intended by God to have significance in my life.

I arrived at the Priscilla Convent with some trepidation. What was it going to be like to be ushered into the inner sanctum of a monastic order of nuns? I think they had a few trepidations as well. What would it be like for them to have a non-clerical male, and a Protestant to boot, invading their very private sanctuary? My concerns were quickly alleviated. The sisters were gracious, though reserved, and tiny Sister Maria Francesca had an immediate warm smile that made me feel completely welcome. Communication was going to be a challenge; she spoke only a little English, and I spoke no Italian. But seeing we were both driven by a common interest the challenge was met with ease.

I entered into the catacomb archives with certain predispositions. What I knew of the early Christians led me to believe that art would have very little importance to them. Generally speaking they were, at least in the early years, imported slaves from the Greek-speaking world and the unskilled working class of Rome. They labored under the threat and occasionally the brutal realities of persecution from day to day, working from sun-up to sundown seven days a week. What inclination or time, not to mention ability, would such people have to produce works of art? For that matter, why should anyone expect to see art of any kind in burial places? Cemeteries are the last place one would look for aesthetic inspiration!

My second predisposition was that if there were art of any type it would be dark and despairing, with a sense of melancholy in keeping with what I perceived to be the nature of their lives. Living and suffering as they did under Roman persecution I expected death themes and crosses—especially crosses. If the cross is an important symbol today, I thought, ubiquitous as it is throughout our churches and cemeteries, what must it have been in that traumatic age?

I began studying the albums of photographs, the entire collection of known catacomb art works. I was stunned! My first predisposition couldn't have been more wrong. There were thousands of works or fragments of works, from crude scratching in the plaster sealing the graves, to frescoes of meager artistic merit, to elegantly carved burial sarcophagi. If one were to count all the extant works and fragments of works it would amount to two or three artistic expressions every week for the entire 250 year history of art in the catacombs, totaling in the thousands.

Even more astounding than the number of works was the absence of any subject matter having to do with death! Both of my predispositions were wrong! Before the legalization of Christianity in 313 AD not a single death theme exists anywhere in catacomb art. Not only is the theme of death absent, there is no work which is despairing, or dark, or melancholy, or morose. This fact stands in stark contrast to what has been suggested to me many times as the 'death-fixation' of the Christian world over the last fifteen hundred years. While the resurrection of Jesus is part of every true Christian's faith, one cannot help but observe that our greater energies are spent on the suffering and death of Jesus. Every aspect of our worship confirms that emphasis, from hymns to testimonies, prayers, sermons, and the particular catch phrase so much a part of Christian vocabulary: "Jesus died so that I could have forgiveness for sins and eternal life." Such a statement places the emphasis exclusively on the sacrifice of Jesus, as if to suggest that is all we need. Such a statement renders the resurrection of Jesus of less importance, less significance, and almost—if you think about it—superfluous. That isn't what we claim to believe, nor is it the truth of Scripture, but it is the way we generally comport ourselves in our Christian communities and places of worship.

The early phases of my research triggered numerous questions. Where does the resurrection fit? What role does it play, if all we really are professing is our need for the sacrificial and atoning death of Jesus? Was our hope both initiated and brought to completion through the sacrifice of Jesus on the cross? Is the resurrection merely 'frosting on the cake' rather than pregnant with salvific import? These are not hollow questions, nor should they be taken lightly. Whether or not we are fully aware of the problem, one certainly exists. Resurrection preaching and witness, though acknowledged as part of what we believe, play little role in our ongoing relationship with the faith we profess—except on Easter and funerals. On the basis of my own life in the Church I too had come to regard the Church's emphasis on suffering and death as mandated by the Scriptures. What kind of theology was this I was confronting for the first time in the Roman catacombs? What kind of theology was this that portrayed nothing of death even though it had every reason to?

And what about crosses? Shocking as it may seem, only three crosses exist prior to the mid-4th century and none before the legalization of Christianity in 313 AD! One of the three, a simple inscription, appears to be dated after the reign of Emperor Constantine in the fourth century, but the sarcophagus on which it was carved was found in an earlier chamber of the Callixtus catacomb. The other two crosses appear on frescoes in Domitilla and Novitiano catacombs, but were apparently painted or scratched into the corners of those frescoes sometime after that 313 AD date. Imagine it: at most only three crosses and no death themes out of thousands of Christian works!

The standard argument in response to this is one I've heard many times: for the early Church the cross was a symbol of shame and humiliation. For this reason they refused to portray it. I don't agree, for three reasons. The fact that there are no themes of death or suffering of any kind would tend to indicate it was Death itself that was being scorned, not just Jesus' death on the cross. The absence of the cross was no more unusual than the absence of any other death related symbols.

Second, one of the common means by which the early Christians were put to death during the Roman persecutions was crucifixion. It was not considered by them to be a shameful death; rather, it was the moment at which the faithful martyr received the victor's crown of life. If one were to be put to death for one's faith, surely to die the death of the Savior was high honor. Even Peter, perhaps the most prominent and vocal of Jesus' disciples, was crucified. But he insisted that he be crucified upside down, as he felt unworthy to imitate the sacrifice of his Lord.

Last, the cross could only be a sign of humiliation if it had been victorious. But it wasn't. Prior to Jesus, crucifixion was reserved for the lowest of criminals, and indeed was a shameful experience leading to a painful death for the victim and a lasting stigma for the victim's family. Jesus' death was carried out for the same purposes: shame, humiliation, and death. However, his resurrection turned the tables on all three. No stigma could attach itself to a cross over which the One who is the Resurrection and the Life had been the victor.

The Old Testament deliverance stories of Daniel, the Hebrew young men in the fiery furnace, Abraham and Isaac, Noah, and Jonah were painted hundreds of times in the catacombs. The intention was to show God's power of restoring life in situations that without his intervention would have led to certain death. Why wouldn't the same intention reveal itself in depictions of Jesus' sacrificial act? Good question!

Every story in catacomb art is a tale of salvation, a tale of the powerlessness of death and the certainty of the resurrection. God delivers us from the consequences of death situations and gives us life instead. Isn't it interesting that all these acts of God's intervention are portrayed thousands of times in catacomb art, but the one act of intervention in which the Christian Church for the last thousand years has placed so much weight and significance—the cross, the crucifixion— appears at most three times, and then in crude form!

The entire collection of catacomb art demands that we ask the difficult question: did the sacrifice of Jesus on the cross hold greater significance than his resurrection for the early Christians, as it appears to do for us? Or was it the opposite?

This is the point at which I began. I had to get to the bottom of this chasm between the Good Friday emphasis of the contemporary Church and the centrality of the Easter Jesus that seemed to be at the heart of the early Church. If there is no Scriptural evidence to support the resurrection emphasis on display in catacomb art, then that art has little validity and should be considered theologically suspect. If, on the other hand, Scripture supports what catacomb art portrays—an almost exclusive focus on the resurrection power of God in response to his son's willing sacrifice (and notice the order: resurrection, then the sacrifice)—the Church stands in need of correction. I believe the latter is true.

We live on this side of the resurrection, yet we act as if we are on the far side of the crucifixion. Staring into the cross from the Good Friday perspective makes it difficult to see beyond it. It consumes us. It blocks our vision. Even though we understand in our minds there was a Sunday we continue to stand in our hearts on Friday. Living in the post-resurrection era it would seem that the avenue, the road map to the cross would guide our way through the event of God's power made manifest in the raising of his son. That seems not to be the case in the way we direct our activities to the cross while circumventing, or detouring around the event that gave it meaning. What I saw in the catacombs jarred me into a new reality. Reclaiming the power of Jesus' resurrection became the single, fervent challenge of my study and, even more, the challenge of my life.

I believe contemporary Christianity places an unbalanced emphasis on the 'theology of the Cross', to the detriment of a 'theology' of the resurrection. We assume the cross is and has always been the central standard of the Christian faith. We act as though the sacrifice of Jesus stands as the supreme declaration of the New Testament.

In our view of the history of Christian art it appears the crucifixion of Jesus does hold the highest place. When we look back fifteen hundred years it indeed does. Notice I said fifteen hundred years, not two thousand. We haven't looked back far enough. We need to go back to the beginning, those first five centuries after Jesus walked among us. We need to go to Rome and walk the dark corridors of those subterranean burial chambers of the persecuted Christians. There we find a much different theology at work: a theology with resurrection hope and power at the center. I examined those treasures of the catacombs, and it has been life changing and exciting.

For the last thirty-seven years I have been reading, studying, and asking questions about theology, and about early Christian history. I have shared my questions and my research with several hundred groups of people across North America, Europe and Japan. I have found thousands of people who are yearning for a greater sense of the power of the resurrection of Jesus in their churches and in their lives.

I believe ample scriptural evidence is available to support our desire to be centered on the resurrection of Jesus without abandoning or downplaying his sacrificial crucifixion. There was another time, another place, and another view. It was the art of the Roman catacombs that brought me closer to the truth of the New Testament than any of my previously held traditions and practices. I now believe that over the discourse of the centuries we have unknowingly allowed a distortion and disfiguration of that wonderful linkage between the death and resurrection of Jesus intended by the New Testament writers. The *Acts of the Apostles* and the Epistles of Paul strikingly portray that linkage. Furthermore, the Epistle writers go beyond the mere joining of them by declaring the resurrection of Jesus to be the supreme event that, alone, gives any significance to his sacrifice on the cross. Without the resurrection the sacrificial death of Jesus would mean nothing; our faith would be 'null and void', and—if we dare to believe the Apostle Paul—we would still be in our sins (I Corinthians 15).

This is a not a book about catacomb art, though art it was that brought me to ask the great question addressed in my writing. I saw the entire collection of Christian art created during the first three centuries mirroring the truth of resurrection promise declared gloriously by the authors of the New Testament Epistles. It is fair to say that if catacomb artistic images were all we had of Christian theology and practice from the first three centuries AD—no Scriptures—we would have no choice but to conclude that the first message of the Christian faith was the Easter Gospel.

It is precisely this joyful and hopeful promise that sustained the early Christians through their sufferings and martyrdoms and, through their willing sacrifices, brought the Roman Empire literally to its knees before the risen Christ. This book, then, is intended as a testimony to the resurrection faith of the early Christians. Our task will be to confirm the early Christians' resurrection focus by seeing in our Scriptures the very same emphasis that inspired them in their hour of trial; that is, the resurrection power of God at work in our world and in our lives.

One more word is necessary: repetition. A number of Scripture passages will be used several times, but in different contexts. Because of our thirteen hundred year emphasis on the cross, often to the detriment or diminishment of the resurrection, repetition is necessary to confirm our new disposition: the balance between the death of Jesus and his resurrection in thought and practice. The word 'resurrection' will occur hundreds of times throughout the book, often multiple times on a single page. Resurrection is, after all, the theme of this treatise, the highest calling of our hearts, and our only hope for eternity.

CHAPTER **One**

# Predisposition

PREDISPOSITION, OR CONDITIONED mindset, often is responsible for our missing the truth of a situation or experience. I have been amazed at how this works. For example, if I am considering the purchase of a particular new car it is remarkable how many of that model I see on the road. I find myself thinking that all of a sudden more people are purchasing that car than any other. The truth is, there had always been a great number of those vehicles on the road, but because I had not been considering one for myself I wasn't aware of them. In other words, I saw what I was predisposed to see. I conditioned myself. I was programmed by the circumstance I had created.

We can also be programmed, conditioned, or predisposed through the influence of others. Anyone who understands marketing and advertising knows this. My son Trifon, when he was eight years old, rarely watched commercial television, yet he knew dozens of television jingles by heart, much to my chagrin. The power of marketing is enormous. The news media, society, cultural organizations and institutions of either a secular or religious nature all have the power to create positive or negative predispositions regarding circumstances, events, styles, taste, and, yes, even religious practice.

Over the course of my thirty-seven year journey back into the mind and heart of the early Christians two questions have plagued me: first, how can I be right about what I consider our lopsided emphasis on the death of Jesus in the crucifixion, to the detriment of the resurrection, when there is little or no evidence in the last thirteen hundred years of Christian thinking and practice to suggest that it was ever different? Second, if the New Testament really says what I think it says—resurrection is the event that validates the sacrifice on the cross, and therefore stands as the supreme event of history—why have I never heard it in any of the churches I've attended?

One of my biggest obstacles has been my own personal doubt. I'm an artist, a musician, not a theologian. I've never taken a single course in theology. So then, if theologians were more convinced of the centrality of the crucifixion than the supremacy of the resurrection I must be wrong. If, on the other hand, they too were convinced of the supremacy of the resurrection, what could account for the chasm that exists between their thinking and our practice? Either way I looked at the problem my thinking seemed to be out of step with theological positions and/or practices. Whenever I raised my voice in support of a greater emphasis on the resurrection of Jesus it was like shouting into a gale force wind. People would nod their heads vigorously and enthusiastically to the resurrection words I spoke, only to revert back to their time-honored 'cross-centered' clichés and practices when I left. Either that, or people would say my assessment was correct to a degree, but their church certainly was doing it right—the resurrection of Jesus was at the heart of their practices. I knew by these comments that they really didn't understand the magnitude of the problem. It wasn't that I was accusing churches of eliminating the resurrection from their spiritual endeavors; it was that while we say we believe the resurrection of Jesus to be important, it is receiving far less attention than it deserves, far less than is called for by the entire New Testament. My most difficult task seemed to be to convince people that a serious problem really did exist. In other words, our biggest problem is that we don't realize we have a problem. Was tradition really that much stronger than the complete and balanced truth of the New Testament or was I speaking a distortion or a lie?

In spite of my doubts I continued on. There seemed to be just enough positive responses to encourage me when I became discouraged. One response in particular stands out in my memory. I was sharing my research at a Family Camp in Nebraska. During our four days there my wife and I made the acquaintance of a young couple soon to become parents for the second time. They related to us how five years earlier they had lost a baby to Sudden Infant Death Syndrome, or crib death, and how deeply that loss had affected them. Now, after five years they were ready to begin again. They had lived with fears and doubts and still had them. At the end of the workshop I invited those in attendance to join me in celebrating a Eucharist based upon the post-resurrection meals Jesus had with his followers, a Eucharist for which fragments of very early liturgical models exist. We had been working with the power of the resurrection in New Testament thought—why not experience a Eucharist of the same thought, one in which the elements were symbols of the body of believers whose faith was centered in the risen Christ and in new life with him. It was a beautiful service and a spiritually moving experience for all of us. When it was finished a number of people came to thank me for the workshop. The young expectant mother was one of them. When I reached out to shake her hand she threw her arms around me and began sobbing uncontrollably. Her husband stood behind her, the tears welling up in his own eyes. After a long moment she began to speak. Between sobs and sighs, falteringly and hesitatingly, she related how this service, which culminated our attempt to recapture the essence of early Christian resurrection thought, was the first time in the five years since her baby died that she had been able to feel and experience real joy in her life. Her husband nodded in agreement through his tears.

If the resurrection of Jesus has the power to cut through five years of sorrow—which no amount of counseling had been able to touch—then there must be something to it. God's power manifested in the resurrection of Jesus is enormous. It is Truth with a capital 'T'. Maybe not the only truth of the New Testament, but at least an equal truth to that of the crucifixion of Jesus, and a truth which I was and still am convinced is woefully underplayed or nearly absent in Christian worship and experience.

I have come to believe that our unbalanced emphasis on the cross is a distortion due to neglectful omission rather than willful commission. Most Christians do not willfully deny the resurrection power of God. It simply doesn't get the play the New Testament demands for it because, for whatever reasons, we are predisposed to see the cross at the center of the Gospel. If the cross is at the pinnacle of Christian thought, then that is what we'll see as we read the New Testament. We find whatever it is we are looking for, whatever it is remains focused at the forward edge of our thinking.

A thirteen hundred year ingrained, inbred habit or tradition is difficult to break, for it has permeated every fiber of Christian thought and practice. We cannot escape its manifestations. Every hymn we sing (and there are many) which states that through the death of Jesus we have eternal life profoundly reinforces the imbalance that is the concern of this book. Every time we create a stained glass window, mosaic or fresco of a suffering or dying Jesus without a companion symbol of the resurrection we reaffirm the centrality of Good Friday in our spiritual pilgrimage at the expense of the resurrected Christ. Every time we 'Thank God that Jesus died for us so we could have forgiveness for sins and eternal life', and leave the resurrection out of the equation, we recommit ourselves to the false notion that through the death of Jesus the process of salvation was both initiated and completed. Oh, we're willing to admit there was a resurrection, but somehow it appears we feel salvation would be the same with or without it. In essence our practice suggests Easter is just frosting on the Good Friday cake. Predisposition! We are predisposed to the sacrifice of Jesus in all facets of Christian life and worship. Resurrection unfortunately has become merely a lovely afterthought.

In this book ample scriptural evidence will be given to support the position that the sacrifice of Jesus alone, by itself, is not at the center or the heart of the Gospel. What *is* there is a two-faceted event: Death-Resurrection, with supremacy given to the latter facet, the miracle or power of God revealed in the Easter event—the New Testament fervently and without deviation proclaims this truth.

Even the art of the Roman catacombs, which I have studied extensively for thirty-seven years, is not predisposed to the idea of death or sacrifice, for not a single work of the thousands that exist reflects those themes. The complete corpus of early Christian art has as its theme the intervention of God, deliverance from death, and the resurrection. The predisposition of catacomb art is 'Life'. It was this study that turned the tables on my thinking and caused me to reconsider the role the resurrection of Jesus played in early Christian thought. On the basis of this catacomb evidence can we in good conscience suggest that the first predisposition in Christian thought and practice was in favor of the Easter Gospel rather than Good Friday? The answer is an emphatic 'yes'!

Having been convinced by catacomb art that a theology different from that which I knew and experienced existed in the first three centuries, I began to try to read the New Testament with that early Christian resurrection mindset, or predisposition. I attempted to assume, for starters, that everything being said had its roots in the event of the resurrected Christ, not in the event of Jesus' sacrifice. I felt justified in doing this because it would be reasonable to believe that not a single word of the New Testament would have been written if Jesus had only died.

Reading the New Testament with 'resurrection eyes' was not as easy as I thought it would be. The predisposition of the 'cross' continued to invade my sensibilities. Predispositions and traditions died hard; they fought for survival and continuation even against my desire to change. They attacked my mind at its most vulnerable point—because of my lack of theological training I doubted that what I was discovering could be right. It was not enough to impose willful change, or to assume that the New Testament writers meant something other than what I had grown up believing. All the key words, words which had simply become part of the language of 'cross-centered' Christianity, had to be rethought. For example, did the title 'Christ' have a more specific meaning than I realized? What prompted the use of the title? If Jesus was validated as the 'Christ' by God's resurrection power (Acts 2:36; Romans 1:4) how should the reader respond each time the title Christ is confronted? Wouldn't it imbue every passage where it is found with a resurrection predisposition?

I had to undergo similar processes with many words and phrases: *Lord, Witness, Gospel, Power of God, Apostle*, and others. They had to be transformed from either their generic or common usage as purely 'Christian' words, or words associated through tradition and practice as growing out of the sacrifice of Jesus, to words so infused with resurrection power that even the scripture passages surrounding them became caught up in the same 'halo'.

This process of rethinking was difficult and slow. It was also exciting. Little by little the New Testament became transformed and alive in my heart. I began to see how a resurrection predisposition was the only way to fully understand and make sense of the God-breathed document. That is the process we shall now undertake. Near the end of the book the subject of predisposition will be revisited, though with a different purpose—answers to the most important question, "What difference does the resurrection of Jesus make?" It is my prayer that by then we will have abandoned our current and unbalanced mindsets in favor of the very first attitudes which permeated the thinking of the first generations of Christians, and that we, like them, will have become witnesses of the resurrection of Jesus.

## CHAPTER TWO

# The Fundamental Question:
# Do You Believe In The Resurrection?

DO YOU BELIEVE in the resurrection of Jesus? Most Christians I know would be offended by this question. "Of course we believe it," they would say. "Without the resurrection there wouldn't be any Christianity." And they would be right. So with not a little hesitancy I suggest to you that, regardless of our indignation at the question, Christians seem to have difficulty understanding the importance or the power of the resurrection of Jesus! Throughout western Christendom emphasis is placed almost entirely on the suffering and death of Jesus, on the atonement, on the cross. Christians seem to be of the opinion that, while the resurrection of Jesus occurred—and praise God it did—our salvation is made complete solely in the death of Jesus on the cross. My rather provocative opinion is based upon statements like this, as suggested in an earlier chapter: "I'm so glad that Jesus died for me so that I could have forgiveness for sins and eternal life." I hear this almost every day—on Christian radio and television, from the pulpit, and from people who live exemplary lives of faith. When is the last time this phrase issued from your lips and your heart? But is the death of Jesus on the cross really all we need? Is our theology complete with this Good Friday emphasis? Was everything we need for salvation both initiated and completed when Jesus died? Are we even aware of the fact that the resurrection of Jesus plays but a little part in our religious and spiritual practices? In all my travels to churches of various denominations I have come to the conclusion, stated earlier, that our biggest problem is we don't realize we *have* a problem. We think the resurrection is getting fair play—it's only *other* churches, you know, the 'liberal' ones, that have the problem. As much as it breaks my heart to say it, and though some churches do a better job than most, I have yet to discover a church in Western Christendom where the death and resurrection of Jesus exist in equal emphasis.

I often ask Christians to look around and count the crosses in their sanctuaries. You'll be surprised how many places they appear: light fixtures, ends of pews, communion tables, banners, hymn book covers, pulpits, windows, bulletin covers, offering plates, the Christian flag, and most often on the chancel wall above the altar. There can be no mistaking that the symbol of the cross is synonymous with the Christian faith. In one conservative Protestant church of about 150 members I counted 496 crosses in the sanctuary: three for every member with forty-six left over for visitors!

After you have counted the crosses look for any visual symbol of the resurrection of Jesus. Wherever I speak, parishioners say, "But our crosses are empty. Isn't the empty cross a resurrection sign?" I grew up saying the same thing, thinking the empty cross was a sign of the risen Christ. The truth is that for his followers and friends, the empty cross was not a sign of a resurrected Jesus. Remember, Jesus was dead when taken from the cross. He was in the tomb Friday night, all day Saturday, and into the early hours of Sunday, and the cross was empty. The empty cross did not convince the disciples that Jesus had been raised from the dead, even though he had prepared them for such a miracle; they were still hiding for fear of the authorities and denying they had ever known him. The empty cross did no more than remind them that the dead body of Jesus had been removed from it. At best, and it was the Apostle Paul who said it, the empty cross is an 'in house' sign: for those who already are believers it can have resurrection meaning—we know the end of the story. But to the unbelieving world the cross is just another sign of what they consider to be our death-mindedness. Shocking, but true. I have heard this myself a number of times. The Apostle Paul knew it too. Listen to what he wrote:

> For the word of the cross is folly to those who are perishing, but to us who are being saved it is [a demonstration of] the power of God [that is, His resurrection power]. (I Corinthians 1: 18 ESV)

> ...we preach Christ crucified, a stumbling block to Jews and folly to Gentiles.... (I Corinthians 1: 23 ESV)

The next question is always the same: "If the empty cross is an in-house sign, what about the empty tomb as a sign of resurrection?" Unfortunately, the empty tomb doesn't suggest a risen Christ either. The first witnesses on Easter morning, when discovering the empty tomb, thought the body of Jesus had been stolen or moved to another place. And believe it or not, some so-called Biblical scholars actually suggest that the women went to the wrong tomb; if they had gone to the right tomb, these scholars say, they would have found his body. The empty cross and the empty tomb spoke only of the absence of a dead Jesus. Only the actual appearance of the resurrected Jesus was evidence powerful enough to dispel the disciples' gloom. This remarkable transformation, prompted by their encounter with the risen Lord, will be discussed in great detail later in the book. It is a sad truth that we exalt the symbol of an object responsible for their despair—the cross—and have yet to find or introduce any symbol which elicited their joy and drove them to be witnesses.

How is it then, people ask, that we arrived at the use of the cross as a symbol of the Christian faith at the expense of some other symbol that might have expressed the resurrection of Jesus? The answer is complex and, admittedly, has rarely been asked. To understand a culture, one looks at its works of art. This has always been true. It is commonly accepted that art mirrors the thought of its time. Church art for centuries has concentrated on the suffering and dying Jesus. Frescoes, mosaics and stained glass are filled with Passion themes. Artists were commissioned by the Church and told what themes were to be presented. Throughout the western world of Protestantism and Roman Catholicism I doubt more than a figurative handful of churches portray in any guise or symbolic form anything approaching Christ's resurrected presence. Whatever religious art we see mirrors the theology of its time. If the resurrection of Jesus was a more prominent theme in Western Christendom you can be sure it would be reflected in church art.

What, then, do the absence of resurrection art and the prominence of the crucifixion motif over the last thirteen hundred years tell us about the practice of the Christian faith? Notice I said thirteen hundred years, not two thousand!

There *was* a time when the resurrection of Jesus, or God's wonderful plan for deliverance from death to life, permeated artistic manifestations. It may come as a complete surprise to you, but it was almost 600 years after the resurrection and ascension of Jesus before church art began to depict Jesus *on* the cross. The first time Jesus is identified with a cross in art is around the year 500 AD, on the wood-carved doors of Santa Sabina Church in Rome. Here, however, he stands in front of the cross, resurrected, but for the first time in art we see that the cross was part of his past, his history. When Jesus was shown on the cross—an illustrated manuscript in the *Rabbula Gospel Manuscript* of 586 AD—it marked the beginning of a transition away from the centrality of the resurrection toward an emphasis on the sacrifice of Jesus. *(The Rabbula Gospel Manuscript is an illuminated Syriac Gospel Book whose origin is in the Monastery of St. John of Zagba, and is named for the scribe Rabbula, about whom little is known.)*

The crucifixion became the central theme of Christianity, and has remained the dominant image for the last 1300 years.

Even the *Church of the Resurrection* in Jerusalem, commissioned and named by the mother of Emperor Constantine in the early 4th century immediately following the legalization of Christianity, underwent a name change reflecting the shift of emphasis. Centuries later, it became known as, and continues to be referred to as the *Church of the Holy Sepulchre.* Do you see the historical trend?

It is also true the great music written for the Church over the centuries gives far less emphasis to the resurrection than to the crucifixion. Religious masterpieces focus almost exclusively on the Passion of Jesus. Even today most church choirs perform their special concerts on Maundy Thursday or Good Friday, simply because there are fewer cantatas, motets, oratorios or anthems with Easter themes. Not only the great musical works of art, but also our hymns testify to our death-fixation. A cursory examination of any hymnal would reveal a far greater number of hymns focusing on the cross, the Passion of Jesus, the crucifixion, than on the resurrection or the life we now live because of it.

Even the way we celebrate the seasons of the Church year betrays our unbalanced conception of the two great Christian themes of crucifixion and resurrection. Many churches celebrate the season of Lent, the forty days from Ash Wednesday to Palm Sunday. Much is made of this introspective season commemorating the days leading up to the suffering and death of Jesus. If any season of the Church year is filled with special services, lecture series' and guest speakers it is the season of Lent. Holy Week follows. We gather for Communion on Maundy Thursday to commemorate the Last Supper, set aside three hours Friday afternoon for prayer, and listen that night to the choir's musical presentation of the Passion of Jesus. Then, after more than six weeks of cross-mindedness, we assemble in great numbers for the powerful Easter Sunday service, complete with processional, trumpets and pulpit eloquence. On Easter Monday the minister, worn out from the frenzy of Lent and Holy Week, begins a forty-day vacation!

There *is* a celebration called Eastertide that comprises the forty days from Easter to Ascension, placed there by the early Church

Fathers as a perfect counter-balance to Lent. In Eastern Orthodox communities it is the most important season of the church year; even Christmas takes a back seat to Eastertide. However, most Protestant denominations have abandoned Eastertide, and I dare say many are not even aware the season ever existed. This was certainly true in the little basement Free Church I grew up in. I think the fact that so few churches ever make anything special of the time following Easter Sunday is another example of how we have diminished the importance of the resurrection. As most ministers would agree, the period following Easter comprises one of the lowest points of the Church year; some churches refer to the Sunday after Easter as 'Low Sunday'. The suffering and dying Jesus gets the forty days of Lent plus Holy Week, and the risen Christ gets one day! What kind of theological sense does that make?

To carry the argument to its justified point of absurdity, have you ever noticed how awkward people feel singing Easter hymns any Sunday other than Easter? Have you also noticed how often we sing hymns that recount the suffering, shed blood and death of Jesus when it isn't Good Friday without feeling a bit funny? Why is it that Easter seems limited to just Easter, but the crucifixion of Jesus seems absolutely appropriate any time of the year? Does this fact not suggest we give far more theological weight to Jesus' sacrifice than to his resurrection? Or is it that we have considerable difficulty *really* believing resurrection is possible, or at the very least struggle with comprehending it?

When you really think about it, our emphasis on death rather than resurrection is not so difficult to understand. After all, death is something we know; we've seen it in its myriad forms of expression. We've been there when it took our loved ones and friends. We know we'll experience it ourselves.

It's easier to relate to a Jesus who died, who experienced flesh in the same way we do—who suffered—who wept—who was abandoned even by those who professed to love him—who was so racked with pain that he felt no one could help him. The pain was excruciating.

Indeed, that word in our vocabulary has its roots in the Latin, which means 'from the cross'. After seeing Mel Gibson's film from early in this century, *The Passion of the Christ*, we have a sobering and moving picture of what 'excruciating' means. Yes, it's easier to identify with a Jesus who truly knows what life's trials are all about.

Resurrection? It's way beyond our reckoning; we've never seen one. It seems mythic, or something akin to fantasy. We *want* to believe it. Perhaps we *do* believe it. But it's so hard to wrap our minds around it—so hard to discuss it—so hard to depict it.

Death is easier. There are words out of personal experience to describe it. An expansive verbal and symbolic vocabulary has grown up around it. People respond emotionally, and death elicits powerful emotions. Emotional connections, even in their tragic manifestations, seem more natural to us, more acceptable, more comfortable. Emotions are doorways. We can walk through them and find some sense of relief, a bit of healing, or maybe even transformation on the other side. We've learned how to continue living even after death has invaded our circle

Resurrection isn't like that. It doesn't hit us where we live. We've not been on the far side of a resurrection (Jesus excepted). So believe in it, hope in it, trust in it, but don't put something as confusing, as difficult to describe or depict as resurrection in too prominent a place! That seems to explain why, in spite of what we profess to believe, death seems to reign supreme in our practices.

You might ask, "This so-called 'death fixation' you ascribe to the Church, does it suggest there is a problem with the Christian faith?" Not at all! The problem is not with the Christian Faith, but rather with our practice of it. I guess we need to define 'Faith' in order to understand what I'm getting at.

Faith, Scripture tells us, is the *substance of things hoped for*. What a strange statement. Hope is future. It has no substance—yet. And sometimes our hopes are not realized. How can there be something solid and real—something we can touch or hold—in an event or an idea that has yet to be?

Faith, the Scriptures continue, is the *evidence of things not seen;* tell that to a jury and say, "Just trust me". Death—our death, or the death of Jesus—takes no faith; it's part of the factual, historical record, and part of existence from the beginning. But Resurrection absolutely demands faith. Are we, then, truly people living out real faith when we relegate the very thing that demands faith to a secondary position in our lives and in our worship? We unwittingly suggest that everything we need for salvation—forgiveness for sins and eternal life—was initiated *and* completed when Jesus died. That takes us off the hook. It makes our difficulties with the resurrection of lesser consequence. In my opinion that is exactly what the Church Universal has done, even though we would be reluctant admit it. Admission or not, this is how we *practice* our faith, in spite of how we *profess* our faith. Even though we profess faith in the resurrection, it really doesn't appear to invade our spiritual practices on a regular basis.

Think about it! If people who knew absolutely nothing about Christianity were to visit just about any church on any random Sunday morning other than Easter, would they leave knowing beyond a shadow of a doubt that Christians worship a risen Lord? Good question! Chances are they would leave with the notion that the figure at the center of the Christian faith is a man who suffered, bled and died so that we might have everlasting life. The true gospel in all its richness and fullness would not have been proclaimed, for, unfortunately, this notion that the death of Jesus, by itself, provided eternal life is biblically inaccurate. Paul said it:

> *And if Christ has not been raised, then our preaching is in vain and your faith is in vain…. And if Christ has not been raised, your faith is futile, and you are still in your sins. (I Corinthians 15: 14 & 17 ESV)*

The event that stands above all others in my experience as a symbol of our death-fixation and benign neglect of the resurrection occurred on Palm Sunday, 1983, in Jerusalem. My wife and I were thrilled at the prospect of worshiping in the beautiful setting of the Garden Tomb just outside the Damascus Gate. Just a short distance away—we could see it—was Golgotha, the hill of the crucifixion. We arrived early and took our places with nearly five hundred other pilgrims from around the world. The service began. The organ prelude was solemn. I recognized the melodies being played as hymns of Jesus' Passion. I thought it was an effective way to begin, thinking that to move from the mood of Good Friday to the joy of the empty tomb and the risen Christ would make an indelible impression on the hearts of the worshipers gathered there. To my surprise, and to my horror, the service never moved past the Good Friday spirit. The minister, a man from England, stood directly in front of the empty tomb of the risen Christ and spoke only of the power of the cross, the atoning death of Jesus, the event that took place a hundred yards or so to his left, not once mentioning that Jesus broke the bonds of death, perhaps in this very place just a few steps behind him, leaving forever the empty shell of a thwarted tomb. No words, not one, of the resurrection! My wife had a difficult time keeping me from leaping out of my seat.

Is this denial or unintended dismissal of the importance of the resurrection what the New Testament teaches? Can we find support in Scripture for our unbalanced emphasis on the Passion and death of Jesus to the near exclusion of his resurrection? I think not. We must recapture the spirit of the first Christians, and quickly. In Acts 4:33 (ESV) it is written,

> *And with great power the apostles were giving their testimony to the resurrection of the Lord Jesus...*

The Church grew by thousands, it says. Perhaps churches don't grow or exercise power in their communities because they have forgotten how to preach resurrection. Again in Acts 17:18 (ESV) it says,

> *...he [Paul] was preaching Jesus and the resurrection."*

The entire book of Acts (as we will discuss in detail) knows very little of the preaching of the cross. While the death of Jesus is part of the story in Acts, the only references to it are in ridicule and derision: "This Jesus, whom you crucified, God has raised up." One can almost hear the exulting, taunting tone of those words. The book of Acts speaks of the power of life over death. The crucifixion, though part of the deliberate will and plan of God for our salvation (Acts 2:23), was considered the work of fallen men; the resurrection was the power of God. For them the choice was easy: focus on the act of a powerful God rather than the act of fallen men. Death, because of the resurrection, had literally lost its sting. Over forty times in the *Acts of the Apostles* it is written that their preaching focused on the power of the resurrection. Yes, the crucifixion was absolutely necessary. It was a loving act, a willing sacrifice by a sinless Savior on my behalf—he had to die for me; I had no other way to be freed from my fallen state and my sin. But the resurrection was the significant event that honored and accepted that sacrifice, redeemed its purpose, and established and validated its atoning significance. To understand the fusion between the crucifixion and resurrection of Jesus intended by the writers of the New Testament we will concentrate on the writings of the apostle Paul. It may come as a surprise that Paul, who some scholars have called *the author of the theology of the cross*, never separates the death of Jesus from his resurrection; we'll give ample Scriptural evidence to support that premise. Beyond that, the question will be raised, "Did Paul place the resurrection of Jesus in supremacy over the cross?"

Finally, if we come to agree that the resurrection of Jesus is absolutely essential to Christian faith and life, we must then address the questions, "What difference does the resurrection make?", and "How would my life be different without it?" In other words, is there a 'Resurrection Difference'? Our final chapter will address these questions in great detail. May the risen Lord guide us in our journey!

CHAPTER **Three**

# The Anticipated Messiah:
# What The Disciples Believed About Jesus

ANY STUDY OF the art of the Roman catacombs, however cursory, would reveal to us what was central to the faith of the early Christians. Covering their walls for nearly three centuries under the persecution of the Roman Empire were hundreds of images of deliverance and resurrection hope. Two centuries after the *Peace of the Church in 313 AD* Christian art changed. Adorning the walls and windows of the now-legalized Church were images of the sacrifice of Jesus; the resurrection had nearly vanished from Christian art. If art mirrors the thinking of its day—and this is a common understanding—we are left wondering what happened to those vibrant images of hope that encouraged a Church under attack, sustaining it even until it overwhelmed its Roman persecutors.

The story begins several centuries earlier in the opening decades of the first century during the lifetime of Jesus of Nazareth. Our quest is to discover what was in the minds and hearts of his twelve disciples as they walked together and shared their lives with him. We want to uncover the answers to five questions: (1) What kind of Messiah were they expecting? (2) What kind of Messiah did they get? (3) What did they believe about Jesus prior to his death? (4) What did they feel at the point of his suffering and death? (5) What did they come to believe upon confronting his resurrected presence?

## What kind of Messiah Were the Disciples Expecting?

The disciples, and all of Judaism, looked eagerly for the coming of Messiah. One would think these followers of Jesus knew their scriptures. They were familiar with all the prophecies regarding his appearance. They were consumed by questions: What role would this Messiah take upon himself? How would the world respond to him?

We have the advantage of hindsight, of seeing how it unfolded. We look at the Old Testament, the Hebrew Scriptures, and very clearly see prophetic words about the Son of God who was going to come to earth, die and be resurrected. We know that Jesus fulfilled every prophetic word that had been written in those holy scrolls of Israel. Our error is that we tend to think the Jewish world at the time of Jesus viewed these prophetic words with the same understanding we now in hindsight possess. We who live on this side of the resurrection now find it easy to see in the Old Testament prophecies the clarity of the eternal design: incarnation, miracles, suffering, death, and resurrection. We assume that when Jesus said he was going to die and be resurrected his followers were convinced by those words that he was the fulfillment of all the prophecies, just as we are. But the actual response of the disciples to the prophetic unfolding gives us pause; by their actions they seemed confused and uncertain. So a question arises: Did the disciples believe Jesus when he said continually that he would die and then be resurrected? I'm convinced they didn't. The New Testament confirms their confusion. The truth of the matter is that in the Jewish mindset at the time of Jesus there was little if any concept of a dying and rising Messiah. Furthermore, only a relative handful of religious leaders believed in any kind of resurrection at all—for anyone, not just Messiah.

Resurrection was a relatively new and somewhat foreign concept. The notion of a bodily resurrection in the Hebrew Scriptures is mentioned in only a few texts. The Sadducees, largest of the Jewish religious groups, had difficulty with such resurrection thinking and dismissed it.

> *There came to him some Sadducees, those who deny that there is a resurrection… (Luke 20: 27 ESV)*

> *Now when Paul perceived that one part were Sadducees and the other Pharisees, he cried out I the council, "Brothers, I am a Pharisee, a son of Pharisees. It is with respect to the hope and the resurrection of the dead that I am on trial." And when he had said this, a dissension arose between the Pharisees and the Sadducees, and the assembly was divided. For the Sadducees say that there is no resurrection, nor angel nor spirit, but the Pharisees acknowledge them all. (Acts 23: 6 – 8 ESV)*

The Pharisees, smaller in number, had come only recently to accept the idea of a bodily resurrection. However, in their view the resurrection of the body was for all people at the end of time. They based their belief in resurrection on a passage from the book of Daniel. Perhaps the Sadducees rejected the notion of resurrection because it did not come from the Torah, but rather from the later words of Daniel, who in their eyes was a minor prophet:

> *At that time shall arise Michael, the great prince who has charge of your people. And there shall be a time of trouble, such as never has been since there was a nation till that time. But at that time your people shall be delivered, everyone whose name shall be found written in the book. And many of those who sleep in the dust of the earth shall awake, some to everlasting life, and some to shame and everlasting contempt. And those who are wise shall shine like the brightness of the sky above; and those who*

*turn many to righteousness, like the stars forever and ever.*
*(Daniel 12: 1 – 3 ESV)*

As is plain to see from reading the Daniel passage, this resurrection was for all people. It was not associated with Messiah because he would have no need for it—he wouldn't die. So there was, in part of the religious community of the Jews, a sense of resurrection at the end of time, but nowhere a sense of a dying and rising Messiah in the middle of time.

## Messiah as 'Davidic King'

If we are to recreate the Jewish mindset at the time of Jesus we must examine three concepts of Savior or Deliverer that are developed in the Old Testament. The first of these is that of the *Davidic King* (Isaiah 9: 2 – 7 ESV):

> *The people who walked in darkness have seen a great light; those who dwelt in a land of deep darkness, on them has light shined. You have multiplied the nation; you have increased its joy; they rejoice before you as with joy at the harvest as they are glad when they divide the spoil. For the yoke of his burden, and the staff for his shoulder, the rod of his oppressor you have broken as on the day of Midian. For every boot of the tramping warrior in battle tumult and every garment rolled in blood will be burned as fuel for the fire. For to us a child is born, to us a son is given; and the government shall be upon his shoulder, and his name shall be called Wonderful Counselor, Mighty God, Everlasting Father, Prince of Peace. Of the increase of his government and of peace there will be no end, on the throne of David and over his kingdom, to establish it and to uphold it with justice and with righteousness from this time forth and forevermore. The zeal of the Lord of hosts will do this.*

The Jewish nation believed in and looked forward to the advent of this *Davidic King*. He would be a descendant from the line of David. He would set up his kingdom on earth. The evildoers would be thrown out. He would rule forever. The oppressors would be destroyed, the tools of war banished, and peace, justice and righteousness would prevail. There is no mention in the Isaiah passage of a *Davidic King* who would first have to die for his people, be resurrected, and *then* accomplish the purposes of his kingdom. This *Davidic King* was a powerful figure destined to reign and rule in his sovereignty *immediately*. The eleventh and twelfth chapters of Isaiah amplify this theme, suggesting that this *Davidic King* would be a righteous figure with the Spirit of the Lord resting upon him.

The followers of Jesus, like all Jews, must have hoped for the coming of this *Davidic King*. If they thought Jesus was the *prophesied One* it would be impossible for them to understand his talk of dying, because there was no understanding of the Scriptures which considered a *Davidic King* who would first have to die before establishing his kingdom.

## The Suffering Servant

Second is the concept of the *Suffering Servant*. Isaiah 53, in light of the life, death and resurrection of Jesus, has long been considered a prophetic passage regarding the *Suffering Servant* who would die for his people. Here are a few excerpts from that chapter:

> *He had no beauty, no majesty to draw our eyes…there was no grace to make us delight in him…he was despised, he shrank from the sight of men, tormented and humbled by suffering…we despised him, we held him of no account, a thing from which men turn away their eyes…yet on himself he bore our sufferings, our torments he endured, while we counted him smitten by God, struck down by disease and misery…but he was pierced for our transgressions,*

*tortured for our iniquities…the chastisement he bore is health for us and by his scourging we are healed…. The Lord laid upon him the guilt of us all…and who gave a thought to his fate, how he was cut off from the world of living men, stricken to the death for my people's transgression? (excerpts from Isaiah 53)*

We who live on this side of the resurrection can see Jesus prefigured in this passage: it is a detailed, multi-layered prophecy that Jesus fulfilled to the letter. However, in the Jewish mind, the *Suffering Servant* was thought by many to be a figure of the people or nation of Israel, not someone who came from God, not Messiah. It was the nation of Israel itself that would suffer and be vindicated, and would come into a sense of promise and hope in the end time.

*With the important qualifications derived from Trypho's discussion with Justin at Ephesus circa 137, and the possible application of the Suffering Servant motif to the Teacher of Righteousness, there is no evidence in contemporary Judaism for a suffering messiah of the Davidic line, taking its inspiration from the great Servant passage in Deutero-Isaiah. Indeed, these passages seem not to have been applied by the Jews to the messiah at all. Origen quotes an interesting discussion which he had with some Jews on the subject. He himself had referred Is. 52:13-53:8 to Jesus, but the Jews had claimed that the prophecies referred 'to the whole people as though of a single individual, since they were scattered in the Dispersion and smitten', though as a result of this scattering many proselytes were made. The Targum also diverts the element of humiliation, suffering and death from the person of the Servant-Messiah and transfers it to Israel or to the heathen nations.[1]*

Understanding the Hebrew Scriptures, few if any would have taken

Isaiah as a prophetic passage regarding Messiah, for Messiah wouldn't suffer and die; rather, he would come to be the victorious King.

# Son of Man

In addition to the figures of the *Davidic King* and the *Suffering Servant*, a third concept coming out of the Old Testament is that of the *Son of Man*. Interestingly enough, this is the way Jesus most often referred to himself, so it is important to pay particular attention to it. In many ways the concept of *Son of Man* parallels that of the *Davidic King*.

> *I saw in the night visions, and behold, with the clouds of heaven there came one like a son of man, and he came to the Ancient of Days and was presented before him. And to him was given dominion and glory and a kingdom, that all peoples, nations and languages should serve him; his dominion is an everlasting dominion, which shall not pass away, and his kingdom one that shall not be destroyed. (Daniel 7: 13-14 ESV)*

Again, there is no thought of a Son of Man who would come, die and be resurrected. He was one who was sovereign, glorious, and whose kingly power was invincible and indestructible. Son of Man was considered a Messianic title stressing manhood of a unique, one-of-a-kind order compared to other men. Son of Man was declared to be 'of heaven', knowing fully our human condition, but apart from sin.

Recall that Jesus himself used the Son of Man identification in response to questioning from those set against him:

> *Then some of the scribes and Pharisees answered him, saying, "Teacher, we wish to see a sign from you." But he answered them, 'An evil and adulterous generation seeks for a sign, but no sign will be given to it except the sign of the prophet Jonah. For just as Jonah was three days and*

> *three nights in the belly of the great fish, so will the Son of Man be three days and three nights in the heart of the earth. (Matthew 12: 38 – 40 ESV)*

Early in Jesus' ministry, as he and his disciples were gathered together, he asked them who people said he was. It was at this point that Jesus for the first time referred to himself as the Son of Man. At those words their ears must have perked up and their hearts must have pounded with excitement. He was the One Israel hoped for, the promised One of God, One about to establish his eternal kingdom—by using that reference he was admitting it.

> *Now when Jesus came into the district of Caesarea Philippi, he asked his disciples, "Who do people say that the Son of Man is?" And they said, "Some say John the Baptist, others say Elijah, and others Jeremiah or one of the prophets." He said to them, "But who do you say that I am?" Simon Peter replied, "You are the Christ, the Son of the living God." And Jesus answered him, "Blessed are you, Simon Bar-Jonah! For flesh and blood has not revealed this to you but my Father who is in heaven. (Matthew 16: 13 – 17 ESV)*

Peter had received a special revelation and he declared it boldly. But before Jesus' declaration had dissipated in the evening air he continued with the first words of his coming death:

> *From that time Jesus began to show his disciples that he must go to Jerusalem and suffer many things from the elders and chief priests and scribes, and be killed, and on the third day be raised. And Peter took him aside and began to rebuke him, saying, "Far be it from you, Lord! This shall never happen to you." But he turned and said to Peter, "Get behind me, Satan! You are a hindrance to me. For you are not setting your mind on the things of God,*

*but on the things of man." (Matthew 16: 21 – 23 ESV)*

In Peter's mind, if Jesus was put to death, if he died, he couldn't be the prophesied One Israel had been longing for. He couldn't be the Davidic King or the Son of Man who would establish his kingdom and rule. From this time until the crucifixion it is not difficult to understand why Peter seems to waver. The seeds of doubt and confusion had been planted and would be harvested in the courtyard of Caiaphas the High Priest. It was there, following the last Passover meal, where Peter denied vociferously that he had ever known Jesus. This treatment, Peter must have thought, this beating and flagellation proved that Jesus was not the 'hope of Israel'; Messiah would never allow such humiliation.

To complicate and confuse their lives even further Jesus challenged their faithfulness by suggesting that they would need to carry their own crosses as part of their commitment to him:

> *"If anyone would come after me, let him deny himself and take up his cross and follow me…" (Mark 8: 34 ESV)*

Those were not easy words to digest. The countryside around Jerusalem was often littered with hundreds of crosses bearing the bodies of convicted criminals. It was Rome's way of intimidating the people and stifling insurrection. For Jesus to hint at such a fate had to have been more than a little disconcerting.

Jesus kept confusing his followers with words that he, the Son of Man, would die and on the third day be raised. This was not the Son of Man they anticipated. They wanted to believe him. They wanted to believe that Jesus was the prophesied Redeemer of Israel, but the things he was saying to them made it very difficult. Make no mistake—the disciples were completely baffled and bewildered about his constant talk of dying and rising. This was not what they and Israel had hoped for. Follow their confusion in the following passages from Mark and Luke:

*And as they were coming down the mountain [following his transfiguration], he charged them to tell no one what they had seen, until the Son of Man had risen from the dead. So they kept the matter to themselves, questioning what this rising from the dead might mean. (Mark 9: 9 – 10 ESV)*

*…"The Son of Man is going to be delivered into the hands of men, and they will kill him. And when he is killed, after three days he will rise." But they did not understand the saying, and were afraid to ask him. (Mark 9: 31 – 32 ESV)*

*And taking the twelve, he said to them, "See, we are going up to Jerusalem, and everything that is written about the Son of man by the prophets will be accomplished. (Luke 18: 31 ESV)*

Imagine what was going through their minds at this point—he was going to the center of power to set up his kingdom, according to their understanding of the Scriptures. But then they must have felt a tremendous blow to their spirits when he continued with the following words:

*For he will be delivered over to the Gentiles and will be mocked and shamefully treated and spit upon. And after flogging him, they will kill him, and on the third day he will rise." But they understood none of these things. This saying was hidden from them, and they did not grasp what was said. (Luke 18: 32 – 34 ESV)*

*"Let these words sink into your ears: The Son of Man is about to be delivered into the hands of men." But they did not understand this saying, and it was concealed from them, so that they might not perceive it. And they were afraid to ask him about this saying. (Luke 9: 44 – 45 ESV)*

The disciples were confused; they didn't understand. He kept referring to himself as the *Son of Man*, which should have given them hope, but when he coupled that Messianic phrase with his coming death they didn't know what to think. This was not what they had expected of Messiah.

Then why did they continue following him? Why did they insist on sticking with this baffling person, leaving their families behind, leaving their fishing nets, leaving their livelihoods, living hand to mouth. If he wasn't the one they really were expecting, and they had every reason to doubt by virtue of what he was saying—which went against everything they understood from their Scriptures—why did they stay by him? One answer might be that they thought he was speaking in riddles or parables; he had been known to do that.

> *With many such parables he spoke the word to them, as they were able to hear it. He did not speak to them without a parable but privately to his own disciples he explained everything. (Mark 4: 33 – 34 ESV)*

They were always asking what those parables meant, so perhaps they thought his words about dying and rising were meant to be allegorical and in need of a simple interpretation.

The answer to our previous question may also have had something to do with that enticing word *hope*. Haven't you had some kind of hope; haven't you put some kind of trust in someone on whom you wanted to rely? Were you willing to go the extra mile with that person even though there were hints that it wasn't going to work out? Hope does that to people. How many times have you been let down? How many times in your life has your hope in people been betrayed? Yet you continued to hope, to trust, as that may have been the best, if not the only option.

Jesus' followers were hoping that he was the One, the prophesied One, who would set up his kingdom, throw out God's enemies, and rule. (Even Cleopas in his conversation with the 'stranger' on the

Emmaus Road following the crucifixion said, "We had hoped he was the Messiah…") They wanted to be there when it happened, but they were puzzled. For three years, in spite of what he said about dying, they continued to hope and follow him.

Then they headed toward Jerusalem. The time was at hand. Jesus knew the path that lay ahead for him: sorrow, betrayal, denial, flight, scourging, and crucifixion. But the disciples anticipated none of that. Instead they saw power, and their own seats at the right hand of power. Now, at last, he would vanquish the enemies of God and establish his kingdom. He would finally do what *Davidic King* and *Son of Man* were meant to do.

> As they heard these things, he proceeded to tell a parable, because he was near to Jerusalem, and because they supposed that the kingdom of God was to appear immediately. (Luke 19: 11 ESV)

In their minds they were not following Jesus to his days of suffering and death. We need only to listen in on their conversations as they approached the city of power: *"When he comes into his kingdom, which of us will be seated at his right hand?"* The prospects of power and glory had shoved all his incomprehensible talk of dying completely out of their minds.

The two sons of Zebedee, James and John, must have infuriated the other disciples by their jockeying for power and the favor of Jesus. This scenario from Mark is further evidence that his followers had no clue that suffering and death were forerunners to kingdom activity:

> And James and John, the sons of Zebedee, came up to him and said to him, "Teacher, we want you to do for us whatever we ask of you." And he said to them, "What do you want me to do for you?" And they said to him, "Grant us to sit, one at your right hand and one at your left, in your glory." Jesus said to them, "You do not know what you are

*asking. Are you able to drink the cup that I drink, or to be baptized with the baptism with which I am baptized?" And they said to him, "We are able." (Mark 10: 35 – 39 ESV)*

If they truly understood what Jesus meant by drinking from his cup or being baptized by his coming 'baptism' of suffering leading to death, they would never had said, "We can". It was challenging enough to try to wrap their minds around the notion that Messiah would die—at best they must have hoped he was talking figuratively, not literally. Making understanding even more complicated was his talk of rising from the dead, not at the end of the age as the Pharisees believed, but in the middle of time, which no one believed. So Jesus' death would most certainly mean their death as well. In a few more days history would record their response to the 'cup that he drank': contrary to their declarations of willingness to die with him, their response would be flight and fear.

Their confusion prompted by Jesus' perplexing words vanished as they saw the crowds gathering outside the golden city walls of Jerusalem. Their journey to power had reached its apex and the massive cheering crowd confirmed their expectations. My wife and I experienced a Palm Sunday procession in Jerusalem, and it was thrilling. We sat on the top of the Jerusalem wall above the gate that Jesus had entered nearly two thousand years earlier. We saw the crowds gathering at the top of the path that runs along side Gethsemane—crowds from across the world. Hymns from every culture sounded off the walls and echoed back to the hills from which they came. The multitudes waved palm branches. Down the Mount of Olives, across the Kidron valley and up the slight incline they came, entering directly beneath our feet and through the city gates. The throng's 'hosannas' were deafening.

That glorious hosanna-strewn procession as Jesus entered the city of power must have dispelled all doubts. Listen to the people, their prayers and their voices echoing off the golden walls of the city, across the Kidron valley into the hills, the hills that knew a different kind of prayer was soon to come. Look at the throngs, stretching as far as they could see; allegiance and devotion promised a great and long reign. And they, his chosen disciples, were his appointed cabinet. They must have thought: *'At last we've come to the promised day; our leader is going to set up his reign in this city. Our hope and perseverance is about to be rewarded: the kingdom of God is at hand.'*

A few short days later hope for the kingdom of God gave way to a somber Passover meal where Jesus talked again of betrayal, denial, flight, suffering and death. It had been easy to dismiss his confusing words while being swept along by the praising crowds, the miracles and the healings. This Passover meal was anything but a remembrance of deliverance. Each disciple must have engaged in deep soul searching as Jesus uttered the words that one seated with him would betray him. Each must have thought, *'Is it me?'*

After the last hymn they would sing together they crossed the valley into the Garden of Gethsemane. Had this been their nightly routine since entering Jerusalem? Had these times of praying been a blessing to them? Perhaps too much wine at Passover had made them drowsy. The only one praying was Jesus; the others slept. His agony was palpable. Anguish overwhelmed him. He was the Son of God; he could have abandoned the necessary 'once for all' sacrifice that lay ahead. He also knew it was not the end, but rather the beginning; there would be a resurrection three days hence. As the weight of all the sins of past, present, and future gathered into his body, Jesus must have cried out in a silent pain never heard before this moment and never to be heard again. Where were the disciples? He had roused them once only to see them sleeping again. Now, however, there were the soldiers, the darkness, and Judas. A kiss, normally a sign of affection and relationship, now became a slap in the face, the ultimate irony of abandonment.

One cannot help but wonder about Judas. How could a follower of Jesus betray him if he really believed him to be who he said he was and looked forward eagerly to the establishment of the kingdom? After witnessing Jesus' healing miracles how could one of his followers have given him over to the authorities? Was Judas the only one who really believed Jesus had to die first in order for his sovereignty to come to fruition? Did he act with the knowledge that he was part of God's secret plan? Or, far more likely, was Judas the only one of the twelve to act upon his disillusionment, thinking the about-to-be crucified Jesus had deceived them all with his declaration of Son-ship? If Judas had truly believed Jesus had to die only to be resurrected on the third day, no amount of silver could ever have persuaded him to abandon the One whose victorious leadership was soon to begin. While Judas' actions constituted the ultimate betrayal, the thinking of the other eleven couldn't have been much different from his.

Where was hope now? Certainly there could be none. He was not the prophesied One. They had been deceived. According to one of the Gospel accounts Peter challenged the soldiers with his sword. The other Gospels only record the fear and flight of the disciples. Jesus was led away in one direction; the disciples fled in the other.

The events that took place over the next days were rather revealing, confirming the disciples' abandonment of hope. That night, after Judas' betrayal, curious Peter waited outside the courtyard of the place where Jesus was being held prisoner to determine what was happening. The Gospel of John (18: 15) mentions that a second disciple accompanied Peter into the courtyard, but we never hear any more about him. We already know about Judas. That leaves nine. Where were they? No mention is made of them anywhere in the Gospels. So much for their declaration of solidarity with Jesus' suffering uttered just a few days earlier!

In the courtyard Peter denied three times that he knew the man Jesus. This same Peter, who just minutes early had taken up the final defense of Jesus with his sword, now cowered in the shadows. So much for hope, and so much for his confession that he had absolute faith this man was the prophesied One who would establish his kingdom and reign. Even Peter, probably the strongest follower, the boldest of the disciples, didn't have enough hope to sustain him on that night. Peter would have been defiant, almost arrogant in declaring his kinship with Jesus had he firmly believed the authority of God was about to be declared. He, after all, was the one who had said, *'You are the Christ, the Messiah, Son of the living God'*. But Thursday night he denied vehemently that he had ever known Jesus. If this was happening to the boldest of the disciples, imagine the depth of cowardice of the other ten.

Parenthetically, I find it ironic that Peter, who had known Jesus for three years, had seen him work miracles—calming the sea, changing water into wine, giving sight to the blind, healing to the lame, life to the dead—now, in the courtyard of the enemies of Jesus, on three occasions denied he ever knew him. On the other hand Pilate—the 'bridge' between Rome and the Jews, confronting Jesus for the first time—on three occasions during the trial, hounded by the enemies of Jesus, declared him completely innocent of the charges. That irony is a stark depiction of the depths to which the followers of Jesus had fallen because their Messianic anticipations had not been met. Pilate saw Jesus as a man who did not meet the criteria of guilt as prescribed by law. It appears Peter saw Jesus as a man who did not meet the criteria of Messiah as prescribed by the Scriptures. Pilate's declaration of Jesus' innocence as a man was countered and contrasted by Peter's cowardly declaration of Jesus' guilt for not being Messiah.

On Friday morning, after being scourged, Jesus was forced to carry his cross along the path to Golgotha, the *Via Dolorosa*, the winding *'street of sorrows'* weaving its way through Jerusalem. I have walked that path several times, stopping along the journey at the places where it is said Jesus stumbled and fell. On one occasion I had the humbling privilege to carry the cross in a procession led by Franciscan monks in Jerusalem. Though my journey was short and physically easy, I felt an enormous burden—the burden I had placed on Jesus—as I recalled the Scripture accounts of that Good Friday long ago.

He fell. Where were the disciples? Jesus had told them that in order to follow him they would have to be cross-carriers. They were nowhere to be found. The soldiers had to draft someone out of the crowd to carry the cross for him. Poor Simon of Cyrene, an unfortunate tourist to Jerusalem, in the wrong place at the wrong time. His bad fortune lasted only one day. Imagine the thoughts racing through the minds of the fleeing disciples. Their bad fortune had lasted three years, beginning when they left their livelihoods to follow a man they thought promised the Kingdom, only to find themselves victims of just another zealot, one of many who had plagued Israel with dashed promises.

That same day Jesus was hanged on a cross between two thieves. Matthew, Mark and Luke make no mention of any one of the remaining eleven disciples at the scene of the crucifixion, not even bold Peter. Only John's Gospel mentions that the *'one whom Jesus loved'*, John himself, was there. Their absence is incredible! Why weren't they present? I have asked myself: If I was one of the disciples, and if I really believed in this man Jesus, seeing what I had seen for three years, would I have been there? Even though my understanding of the Scriptures didn't allow for a dying *Messiah*, a dying *Davidic King*, a dying *Son of Man*, would I have been there? Would I have said, "He has me so convinced that he is the *Son of Man*, that he is the *Davidic King*, the *Messiah*, that maybe I misread my Hebrew Scriptures; maybe I misunderstood what he has been saying. I'll go with him. He says he is going to rise again. I'll wait and see." If you really believed Jesus' words about resurrection where would you have been on Good Friday? Would you have been bold enough to pick up the cross and carry it for him? Would you have been at Golgotha, hands folded across your chest waiting for the vindication of Jesus through God's resurrection power? Would you have been thinking: "You evil men think you're getting rid of this man, but I know what is going to happen three days from now. I can hardly wait to see the looks on your faces when he comes back to life. You're in for a great surprise. The joke's on you; we'll have the last laugh." The sad, revealing truth, however, is that none of them were there. The doubly sad and revealing truth is that my own confession, in spite of my protestations to the contrary, would have been no different than theirs. Jesus' teaching on his resurrection had been for naught. They plainly couldn't fathom the idea.

Jesus was dead. Completely dead. His heart stopped, his brain flat-lined, his organs stilled, meeting every criterion of human cessation of life; Jesus was stone cold dead. Three years of untold joy and anticipation bled dry and buried with him.

> Joseph took the body and wrapped it in a clean linen shroud and laid it in his own new tomb, which he had cut in the rock. And he rolled a great stone to the entrance of the tomb and went away. Mary Magdalene and the other Mary were there, sitting opposite the tomb. (Matthew 27: 59 – 61 ESV)

This passage puts the lie to one of the theories posited to refute Jesus' resurrection: that his followers forgot which tomb Jesus was buried in and went to the wrong tomb, an empty tomb on Sunday morning. The two Marys saw the place of burial; they saw Jesus' body put in the unused tomb of Joseph of Aramathea. They knew exactly where Jesus was buried.

One might have reason to wonder whether all Jesus' talk of rising from the dead on the third day was making an impression on the Jewish leaders, if not on the disciples. The disciples had run from Gethsemane, abandoned Jesus on the day of crucifixion, and removed themselves as far as possible from the place of burial. Jesus' enemies, on the other hand, made every effort to protect their decision to kill him by guarding the tomb. They at least made an attempt to thwart the possibility of Jesus' followers perpetrating a hoax:

> The next day, that is, after the day of Preparation, the chief priests and the Pharisees gathered before Pilate and said, "Sir, we remember how that impostor said, while he was still alive, 'After three days I will rise.' Therefore order the tomb to be made secure until the third day, lest his disciples go and steal him away and tell the people, 'He has risen from the dead,' and the last fraud will be worse than

*the first." Pilate said to them, "You have a guard of soldiers.*
*Go, make it as secure as you can." So they went and made*
*the tomb secure by sealing the stone and setting a guard.*
*(Matthew 27: 62 – 66 ESV)*

The tomb of Jesus was made secure. There was indeed a guard placed in front of it and an official Roman seal was set on the stone rolled over the entrance to the tomb. Every precaution was taken.

The question has been raised: what type of guard protected the site of the tomb? Was it a Jewish Temple Guard or a Roman Guard? Either type of guard would have insured that the eleven disheartened disciples would not have been successful in any attempt to steal the body. The seal was a Roman seal, carrying a severe penalty if broken, no matter which guard was employed.

Another question: how likely would it have been for a Jewish Temple Guard to be employed on Passover, the most sacred feast on the Jewish calendar? If it were a Jewish Temple Guard, it would have been a smaller group than a Roman Guard. They would have had fewer weapons than the Roman Guard, but still would have been armed. Even in this instance any attempt to steal the body would have met resistance and someone would have been injured. Scripture makes no mention of any of the eleven disciples—or for that matter any of the guard—having sustained injuries.

Good arguments can be made to support the proposition that it was a Roman Guard stationed in front of the tomb of Jesus. While the arguments are not necessary to our thesis, it is nonetheless critical to our understanding of just how unlikely it would have been for the disciples to steal the body. Briefly, such a guard would have employed sixteen soldiers, highly armed: plumed helmets making them appear larger than they were, with shields, spears and swords in each soldier's hands. They would have been stationed in four rows of four soldiers each, one row in front of the other. The four immediately in front of the tomb would be awake and alert; the other twelve could be sleeping. At regular intervals they would exchange positions, thus keeping a fresh guard in front of the tomb. If any of the four soldiers in the front line of defense were caught sleeping all sixteen troops would have been put to death. We can be sure that each of the four kept a watchful eye on the other three! Given this scenario who could honestly suggest a successful theft of the body by eleven thoroughly defeated and fearful disciples?

Yet the tomb was empty the morning of the third day! The Gospels say little about how the resurrection transpired, only that the stone was rolled away, Matthew says by an earthquake. Apart from the guard there were no actual witnesses to the event itself. However it happened, we can be confident it was no hoax, though every effort was made by the authorities to label it as such:

> ...some of the guard went into the city and told the chief priests all that had taken place. And when they had as-sembled with the elders and taken counsel, they gave a sufficient sum of money to the soldiers and said, "Tell people, 'His disciples came by night and stole him away while we were asleep.' And if this comes to the governor's ears, we will satisfy him and keep you out of trouble." So they took the money and did as they were directed. And this story has been spread among the Jews to this day. (Matthew 28: 11 – 15ESV)

It strikes me as rather curious that none of those guarding the tomb was reprimanded, not to mention executed for dereliction of duty. Under Roman law that was the only option in a failed mission, in a broken seal. Obviously there was no explanation for what had happened. The story told by the guard was accepted without question by the authorities. Does this suggest that in their heart of hearts they knew something miraculous had happened? If Jesus was truly resur-rected how would the perpetration of a lie suggesting the body was stolen hold up when the 'resurrected One' made an appearance? It was a desperate situation and they did what seemed the only thing to do. I wonder, though, if somewhere deep inside their muddled minds lurked the fear that they indeed had murdered Israel's anticipated Messiah? The best they could hope for was that the people would accept the story of a stolen body. The worst case scenario would be the return of the 'criminal' they had put to death.

## The 'Third Day': The Women Go to Anoint the Body

The events of Sunday, that 'third day' Jesus had predicted, add credence to the verity of the resurrection. The story unfolded in three phases: the women visited the tomb and saw Jesus; Cleopas and his friend encountered Jesus on their way back home to Emmaus; and Jesus appeared to his disciples in the upper room, huddled together in fear of discovery.

The disciples weren't alone in their disbelief. It was the 'first day of the week' when the women went to the tomb. The women did not go expecting the risen Jesus to reveal himself. They, along with the others, had not believed Jesus would rise from the dead. They had come to anoint the body, as there had not been enough time to do so before the Sabbath began. How they thought they were going to move a nearly two-ton stone up an incline in order to enter the tomb will forever remain a mystery, though Mark's Gospel suggests they asked among themselves how the stone would be moved.

> But on the first day of the week, at early dawn, they went to the tomb, taking the spices they had prepared. And they found the stone rolled away from the tomb, but when they went in they did not find the body of the Lord Jesus. (Luke 24: 1 – 3 ESV)

Their first thought was that the body of Jesus had been stolen or moved. When they stared headlong into the empty tomb their questions must have been, "Isn't it enough that they killed him? Why did they also have to do away with the body?" You would think their first reaction to the empty tomb would have been that Jesus had been raised just as he had predicted in their presence numerous times during the past three years. No, Scripture says they were perplexed. Doesn't this suggest that Jesus' words of resurrection had been completely dismissed by all his followers?

> While they were perplexed about this, behold, two men stood by them in dazzling apparel. And as they were frightened and bowed their faces to the ground, the men said to them, "Why do you seek the living among the dead? He is not here, but has risen. Remember how he told you, while he was still in Galilee, "that the Son of Man must be delivered into the hands of sinful men and be crucified and on the third day rise." (Luke 24: 4 – 7 ESV)

Then it dawned on them! His words of resurrection coalesced in their minds. Jesus was alive! They ran to where the disciples were gathered, most certainly hiding for fear of the authorities, and told them what they had seen.

> And they remembered his words, and returning from the tomb they told all these things to the eleven and to all the rest. Now it was Mary Magdalene and Joanna and Mary the mother of James and the other women with them who told these things to the apostles… (Luke 24: 8 – 10 ESV)

Pause here for a moment. The eleven were huddled together for fear of the authorities, yet another evidence they had not dared venture out to steal the body and perpetrate a hoax. They must have been wondering what would be next. Would they be discovered? Would they be led away to their own crucifixions? Would it cross their minds to repeat over and over again Jesus' predictions of his resurrection and wonder if maybe they should find a way to believe them? It was after all the third day he had talked about many times. Jesus had done everything else he had declared. There were still hours left in the third day; maybe there was still reason to hope. The women came to them and reported that they had seen Jesus. One eyewitness report by the women should have been enough to dispel doubt and consternation. Sadly, that was not their reaction:

> ...but these words seemed to them an idle tale and they did not believe them. (Luke 24: 11 ESV)

Would expectant and hopeful followers, convinced of Jesus' words, have called the first resurrection announcement nonsense? If the disciples had really understood and believed Jesus when he said he would die and rise on the third day wouldn't this first report have been enough to convince them? Their behavior seems to us incredible, as it doesn't suggest a shred of evidence to support the notion that they had taken Jesus at his word. The women's report fell on deaf ears. The disciples may have been thinking, 'Silly women and their fanciful tales! When will they ever change?'

Here we need to explain an historical fact regarding the testimony of women. In Israel during the time of Jesus a woman's testimony was not admissible in a court of law. Their testimony was not to be trusted: all the more reason for us to accept the resurrection of Jesus as a real event. If any Gospel writer wanted to invent a hoax about the resurrection of Jesus, he wouldn't have used women as the first witnesses and expect to be believed. Yet all four Gospels indicate that women were the first to see the risen Lord and report what they had seen.

It is also fair to suggest that Jesus, throughout his three ministry, had treated women as equals to men. In his entourage women had played a key role. As a matter of fact, women had been much more reliable than his male disciples. They were there through 'thick and thin'. Can we reasonably assume that the disciples' attitudes toward women might have been tempered somewhat by what they observed from Jesus? In spite of this possible scenario, the disciples did not believe the resurrection report of the women.

## The 'Third Day': The Emmaus Road Encounter

Sunday afternoon Jesus met two men, Cleopas and another, on the road to Emmaus, a dusty, barren road, somewhat hilly. There is currently no village in Israel by that name, though several sites claim they were the historical Emmaus. Considerable archeological research is being done to determine which is deserving of the honor. In 1974 I wanted to experience the road Cleopas and his friend traveled. Not knowing for certain how to proceed I decided to visit the location Franciscan monks have designated, as they have a long history in Israel. Indeed, the road was dusty and the Franciscan site of Emmaus not too far from Jerusalem, perhaps eight miles. Somewhere along this road, probably closer to Emmaus than to Jerusalem, Cleopas and his friend, disciples of Jesus though not of the *Twelve*, discouraged and defeated by the crucifixion of their friend, were heading home.

> That very day two of them were going to a village named Emmaus, about seven miles from Jerusalem, and they were talking with each other about all these things that had happened. While they were talking and discussing together, Jesus himself drew near and went with them. But their eyes were kept from recognizing him. And he said to them, "What is this conversation that you are holding with each other as you walk?" And they stood still, looking sad. Then one of them, named Cleopas, answered him, "Are you the only visitor to Jerusalem who does not know the things that have happened there in these days?" And he said to them, "What things?" And they said to him, "Concerning Jesus of Nazareth, a man who was a prophet mighty in deed and word before God and all the people, and how our chief priests and rulers delivered him up to be condemned to death, and crucified him. But we had hoped that he was the one to redeem Israel." (Luke 24: 13 – 21 ESV)

First of all it must be said that this 'stranger' was flesh and blood, not a ghost or a spirit; Cleopas and his friend were not frightened by his presence. Though they didn't recognize him, this was Jesus in his resurrected body—bones, muscle, tissue, arteries and veins, organs, skin—fully alive, fully functioning.

Second, their response to his first question indicates that all Jerusalem had been in an uproar over the punishment and crucifixion of one many had considered at the very least a prophet, if not the Messiah: *"Are you the only one visiting Jerusalem and unaware…?"* So this stranger appeared to them as an outsider, completely unaware of the terrible events of the last few days.

Third, it is apparent that Cleopas and his friend had stayed in Jerusalem past the day of crucifixion. Had they been in hiding like the other disciples? Had they waited for the 'third day' to see if Jesus would fulfill his own prophecy of rising? If so, would that indicate that they, unlike the others, had held on to a shred of belief and had been willing to 'wait and see'?

Finally, it appears they had run out of hope. The text says, *'We were hoping'*—no longer hoping. Other translations read: *'had hoped'*, past tense; or *'had been hoping'*, past perfect tense. They weren't suggesting, seeing it was still daylight of the 'third day', that there might still be a chance. No. It was over, finished, and they were going home, lucky to have escaped Jerusalem with their lives.

Then Jesus began to reveal the Scriptures to them. They still didn't recognize him.

> *And he said to them, "O foolish ones, and slow of heart to believe all that the prophets have spoken! Was it not necessary that the Christ should suffer these things and enter into his glory?" And beginning with Moses and all the Prophets, he interpreted to them in all the Scriptures the things concerning himself. (Luke 24: 25 – 27 ESV)*

This would be the first time that Jesus employed 'hindsight' as a teaching tool to see the Hebrew Scriptures from the vantage point of his fulfillment of all the prophecies. It would happen again for his other disciples and followers, who then, in turn, would reveal the Scriptures' fulfillment in Jesus to others. Every time we read in the sermons of the apostles the words *'according to the Scriptures'* they are re-interpreting the Hebrew Scriptures in light of the resurrection of Jesus.

> *So they drew near to the village to which they were going. He acted as if he were going farther, but they urged him strongly, saying, "Stay with us, for it is toward evening and the day is now far spent." So he went in to stay with them. When he was at table with them, he took the bread and blessed and broke it and gave it to them. And their eyes were opened, and they recognized him. And he vanished from their sight. (Luke 24: 28 – 31 ESV)*

What I find wonderful about this passage is the reverent way author Luke describes the simple sharing of bread. In Jesus' hands the bread becomes life itself, for in the eyes of Cleopas and his friend the bread became the window through which the image of Christ-Messiah was fully revealed. No wonder, then, that the language employed by Luke found its way into our Eucharistic liturgy: *"He took bread, gave thanks, broke it and began to give it to them".* One other thing—remember this moment of recognizing the risen One through the sharing of bread. We shall revisit it shortly.

Another remarkable turn of phrase says Jesus *'disappeared from their sight'.* He didn't excuse himself, get up, and go out the door. He disappeared! What kind of properties does this risen flesh and blood have—this body that can be touched, can eat, can carry on a conversation, can appear and disappear? Is that what awaits us in our own resurrection? Perhaps so, if we take the biblical concept of *first fruits* seriously. The risen Lord is only the 'first', suggesting that those who embrace him will follow in like manner. But this is a topic for theologians.

So all of a sudden, in the breaking of bread with this stranger, their eyes were opened. It became apparent they were with Jesus. He was alive! Then he disappeared; he vanished. If you were Cleopas or his friend what would you have done next? Finish the loaf? Ask for seconds? Or would you do what they did: run bursting with excitement to tell the others, all the way back the hilly, dusty road to Jerusalem.

> And they went back and told the rest, but they did not believe them. (Mark 16: 13 ESV)

The upper room gathering must have been rather large: the disciples, the women, and perhaps other followers who had been part of their clan, gathered in secret, hiding from the authorities. This marks the second time the disciples had been told of Jesus' appearance: first the women, now Cleopas. The report this second time was by men, not women. Again they disbelieved. Their continued disbelief is not the behavior of people who were waiting for Jesus' predictions to be fulfilled; rather, it is the response of thoroughly defeated, unbelieving men who had not accepted or understood the resurrection words of Jesus. If they really believed what Jesus had been telling them for a long time, one report of his resurrection would have been enough, even if the report *was* from the women. That they disbelieved two reports is hard to understand. Yet we must remember that nothing, absolutely nothing in their growing up with their Scriptures had prepared them for a dying Messiah who would then be resurrected in the middle of time.

## The 'Third Day': The Upper Room

Then came the evening of the *'third day'* in the upper room, and all of a sudden Jesus appeared. Just as he had 'disappeared' from the sight of Cleopas, so now he 'appeared' to his disciples. Did the physical appearance of Jesus himself cause them to immediately believe? Apparently not.

*As they were talking about these things, Jesus himself stood among them, and said to them, "Peace to you!" But they were startled and frightened and thought they saw a spirit. And he said to them, "Why are you troubled, and why do doubts arise in your hearts? See my hands and my feet, that it is I myself. Touch me, and see. For a spirit does not have flesh and bones as you see that I have." And when he had said this, he showed them his hands and his feet. And while they still disbelieved for joy and were marveling, he said to them, "Have you anything here to eat?" They gave him a piece of broiled fish, and he took it and ate before them. (Luke 24: 36 – 43 ESV)*

When Jesus ate the fish their eyes were finally opened. At last they were willing to believe that this was truly Jesus. He was indeed risen, just as he had said. At this recognition they must have exploded with joy. The text says: *While they still did not believe it because of joy and amazement…*This phrase might parallel a saying from our day—when, for example your favorite team scores a comeback in the final second after trailing miserably throughout the game—*I can't believe it!* You do believe it, but it seemed improbable and impossible. That must have been the emotion behind their behavior that night.

Two physical acts of Jesus had completely turned his followers into believers: the *'breaking of bread'* on the Emmaus road, and the *'eating of fish'* in the upper room. Perhaps as a result of those two transformational Resurrection Day events, *Bread* and *Fish* became early symbols of the risen Lord. On the walls of the catacombs in Rome, beginning by mid- second century AD, images of bread and fish are often seen linked together into one image. At first glance Jesus' miracles of *loaves and fishes* comes to mind. As a student of catacomb art, I have come to see this union not as a sign of the feedings of the four- and five-thousand, but rather as a 'resurrection sign', rejoicing in the *bread and fish* of Emmaus Road and the Upper Room on *Resurrection Sunday*. To go even further, approximately fifty-eight

Eucharist portraits or fragments appear on the catacomb walls and in sarcophagus fragments. In all fifty-eight bread and fish are on the table. The interpretation leads us to consider that the Eucharistic meals being celebrated in this art are meals with the risen Lord. Conversely, there are no Eucharistic portraits of a meal identified with the *'Last Supper'* or Maundy Thursday meal. The early Church, the Church under the persecution of the Roman Empire, found its hope almost exclusively in the resurrection of Jesus. They appear to have based their sacred meals on the post-resurrection meals Jesus celebrated with his followers. *(See Appendix I for evidences surrounding the existence of a Eucharist based upon the post-resurrection meals with Jesus).* Their artistic themes concentrate on the deliverance from death by God's intervention. Before legalization—the *'Peace of the Church'* under Emperor Constantine in 313 AD—no crosses or death themes appear in the vast catalog of catacomb art. Just as the resurrection of Jesus appears to be the magnificent turning point for the disciples, so it was the promise for the Church under the attack of the Roman Empire.

We have used Luke's Gospel account for the events of *Resurrection Sunday*. While all four Gospels agree in the most important aspects— women as the first witnesses of the resurrection of Jesus, the disciples discounting of the women's report, and his appearance to the disciples—there are some differences. Scholars recognize the differences and argue that they add credibility to the message of the resurrection. They say that if all the accounts were similar in every detail it would suggest some kind of collusion or conspiracy to get their stories straight to guarantee the success of the hoax. Briefly, let us look at some of those differences.

Matthew's Gospel, chapter 28, says the women went to the tomb, saw an angel, and then saw Jesus. The disciples, on their way back to Galilee, saw Jesus. Some remained doubtful.

Mark's Gospel, chapter 16, says the women saw a youth in white robes who told them Jesus had been raised from the dead. They ran away in terror and said nothing to anyone out of fear (vss. 6 – 8). Jesus then appeared to Mary Magdalene who then ran and told the disciples, who didn't believe her report (vss. 9 – 11). Finally, Jesus appeared to two others, unnamed (Cleopas and his friend?), who ran and told the disciples, who didn't believe their report either (vs. 12).

John's Gospel, chapter 20, says Mary Magdalene went to the tomb, saw the stone rolled away, and thought the body had been removed. She ran and told Peter and one other disciple who raced to the tomb, found it empty, and believed (vss. 8 – 9 ESV). John says:

> …for as yet they did not understand the Scripture, that he must rise from the dead.

Mary Magdalene stayed at the tomb, saw two angels, then saw Jesus, and ran to the disciples, saying: *"I have seen the Lord."*

Looking back, does it appear that these people really had held any hope, given his talk of suffering and the fact of the crucifixion, that Jesus was their anticipated Messiah? Does it appear that they really believed and were waiting until he showed himself again? They didn't believe because their understanding of the Scriptures didn't prepare them to believe. They were baffled. They were puzzled. They didn't understand his talk of dying and rising.

The point is this: psychologically, the events between the Last Supper Passover Meal and Jesus' appearance Sunday night had left the disciples devastated. Their faith had been destroyed; they were defeated. Some biblical scholars say they had already left Jerusalem and were on their way back to the Sea of Galilee and their fishing nets (as found in Matthew's Gospel account). If Peter, the strongest among them, had denied that he knew Jesus, would any of the other ten ever risk admitting that they had had anything to do with the crucified One?

We know what the death of Jesus had done to these men. What do you suppose happened psychologically when he appeared to them in his resurrected state? Is it even possible to talk about the two contrasting emotions in the same breath? Can you possibly imagine that after finally being convinced of his resurrection they would have responded by saying something like this: *"Hallelujah, thank God that Jesus died for us. Now we must begin spreading the good news of his death throughout the entire world"*? Does it make any sense at all that they would preach the death of Jesus? That was an event they wanted to forget, not because of Jesus, but because of themselves and the way they had responded to his death. Their behavior was an embarrassment to them. In spite of the wonderful healing action of the risen Christ, I'm certain that in their quiet moments the disciples remembered with much agonizing their treatment of Jesus in his days of suffering, trial and death.

It is much easier to think they would respond by saying, *"He is alive, and because he is alive and I have seen him I can be alive again."* To consider any other response simply flies in the face of human nature.

If there had been no resurrection the disciples would have been pathetic, humiliated, embarrassed and fearful individuals. They would have been the laughing stock of their fishing villages. After all, hadn't they abandoned their families and their livelihoods? Hadn't they been foolish enough to follow another in a long line of zealots promising the kingdom? Look at them now, trying to bear up under the 'I told you so's' and other ridiculing epithets of the villagers. Furthermore, could they ever have looked each other in the eye, embarrassed as they were by their treatment of Jesus? Even if he wasn't the Messiah, he had been their friend and deserved better than they had given him. Fear of discovery would have made them quake at the sight of strangers in their village, thinking perhaps they had been tracked by the authorities, only now to be led to their own executions. In this scenario would the name of Jesus ever have escaped their lips in company other than their own? Would a single word of the New Testament have been written? Can we really think Christianity would exist? Would such a movement have begun with disheartened and frightened men like these? Such is the legacy of a dead Jesus without the resurrection.

The command of the risen Jesus on Easter night was to take his message to the world. All four Gospels agree: *'I want you to be witnesses to what you have seen and heard.'* That might mean several things. It might mean the entire three-year ministry of Jesus, his miracle working, his sacrifice and his resurrection. On the basis of his resurrection and through the power of it that had been revealed to them it could also mean that he was equipping them with the authority to witness to that resurrection power first and foremost. In no way can it be interpreted as a command to bear witness to his suffering and death as the most important facts of his ministry or theirs. They would never have opened their mouths again short of the revelation of the risen Christ. So it is this *resurrection power* which had to have been the motivating force in the minds and hearts of the disciples. It could be nothing less. After forty days of eating and drinking with their risen Lord, forty days of healing and preparation, the disciples began preaching. The *Acts of the Apostles* tells us that their primary message was one of resurrection witness. We shall describe that message in detail in the next chapter.

## Is Jesus' Resurrection a Myth?

Some theologians say that Jesus did not actually physically rise from the dead. Resurrection faith, they say, grew up over a period of time in the hearts of his followers: the only thing we can validate is that eventually resurrection faith came into being; we cannot validate an actual resurrection of Jesus. While it is true no one witnessed the actual moment of resurrection itself (except perhaps the guard at the tomb who never reported seeing it happen), I find their position difficult to accept. Even discounting the Scriptural accounts of his post-resurrection appearances, the psychology of the situation forbids consideration of a resurrection faith that grew up over a period of time. There is no way, in my mind, that these people would have gone back to their fishing nets and conspired to create a cult, putting together a fanciful story of the resurrection of Jesus even though most people thought the notion of a resurrection was preposterous.

Even those who accepted the notion of a resurrection saw it as an event for all believers at the end of the age, certainly not for Messiah in the middle of time. To think that such men, in the emotional state described in the New Testament, could even consider foisting such a concoction on the world is ludicrous. Does it make sense that after six weeks they would go back to Jerusalem, the home of their enemies, and try to convince people that Jesus was really alive, if he wasn't? They did exactly that, which is further evidence that Jesus had truly been raised from the dead! If the authorities wanted to get rid of that notion all they had to do was produce the body. Did they? It would have been an easy thing to do, if indeed there was a body!

Are we to believe that eleven disciples who had been puzzled for the last year, who had been disillusioned on Maundy Thursday, who fled Gethsemane in fear, who denied knowing Jesus, who didn't go anywhere near the place of crucifixion on Friday, put their spirits back together and headed for the tomb? Are we to believe they sneaked through sixteen crack Roman troops or a very strong Jewish temple guard, rolled a two-ton stone up an incline without making a noise, entered the tomb, took their time unwrapping the body, even folding the facial napkin neatly, and strolled with the dead body of Jesus out into the night without the slightest inkling on the part of the guards? Can we visualize them the next day running through the streets of Jerusalem shouting, *"He's alive! He's alive!"* It is absurd to think that could have happened. We have already described the authorities' attempt at a massive cover-up of the disappearance of Jesus' body (Matthew 28: 11–15). The fact is they couldn't produce the stone-cold corpse of the criminal they had crucified days earlier.

The guard went to the authorities immediately, not years later, as those dissenting theologians' argument would suggest. To say that res-urrection faith grew up after a time ignores the testimony of Scripture. If it had taken twenty, thirty, or forty years for this resurrection faith to develop the contrarians might have a point. Myths sometimes do arise in history, but they evolve over long periods of time. The myth begins as a simple tale and grows ever more elaborate over the years.

But this resurrection preaching began immediately, within weeks, and the fact of its immediacy, when the Jews or the Romans could have produced the body and shot the fledgling faith all to pieces makes it very difficult to believe in anything other than an actual, physical resurrection.

Going further, the women didn't run from the garden. If Jesus had been a ghost they would have. The person they met appeared to them as a human being; they recognized him as such; they didn't flee. He was flesh and blood.

The twosome on the Emmaus Road didn't run from the stranger. He was no spirit. Eventually they came to recognize him as the person Jesus they had known. Sunday night Jesus himself said he was flesh and blood, not a ghost. He was hungry, he ate, he still bore traces of his wounds. The resurrected Jesus was seen by enough people so as to dispel the notion that a select group could have fabricated the story. The apostle Paul wrote:

> ...and that he appeared to Cephas, then to the twelve. Then he appeared to more than five hundred brothers at one time, most of whom are still alive, though some have fallen asleep. Then he appeared to James, then to all the apostles. Last of all, as to one untimely born, he appeared also to me. (I Corinthians 15: 5-8 ESV)

What I have suggested in this chapter is that Jesus' disciples absolutely did not understand the prophesied One had to die before establishing his kingdom. Nor were they prepared to accept the resurrection of an individual before the end of time, if indeed they accepted the notion of resurrection at all. When Jesus was led away to die they abandoned all hope. With this scenario in mind, how would it have been possible for the eleven disciples to calm themselves, overcome the traumatic events of the previous three days, alter their entire concept of the Scriptures and rationally prepare an argument for Jesus' resurrection that would stand up to the fact of the crucifixion and the authorities' inevitably producing a stone-cold body, and all this between Friday noon and Saturday night? It simply is not possible to believe something like this could have happened. As we have said, the psychology of the situation doesn't allow such preposterous thinking.

Resurrection preaching began, however, within a matter of a few weeks by a group of men who, in order to preach it, required an immediate radicalization of heart, mind, emotion and attitude. And to whom was the preaching directed? How could they have moved from cowardice a few days earlier to extreme boldness as they proclaimed the risen Messiah in the midst of the enemies of Jesus, a throng numbering in the thousands. They risked being beaten, imprisoned, stoned, and even put to death. Something of cosmic, earth-shaking proportions had to have happened. Only the actual appearance of Jesus' risen bodily presence could have affected so explosive a transformation!

We must admit and recognize that psychologically the disciples were going to emphasize what they had seen of the risen Jesus much more than they were going to emphasize what happened to Jesus before his resurrection. If human behavior is anything that we can understand, we have to say that the resurrection was going to be at the center of their thinking and, thereby, at the center of their preaching. Resurrection provided the rejuvenation of their dead spirits. Resurrection did away with their despair. The suffering and dying Jesus was at the heart of their denial and humiliation. The death of Jesus was for them a miserable ending to a wonderful period of promise. Only the resurrection of Jesus could put an end to their quest for anonymity. Only the resurrection of Jesus could put the sparkle back in their eyes, the lightness in their step, and the boldness in their witness. The resurrection of Jesus was the power source in their lives. Add to that the fact that Jesus commanded them to preach his resurrection and there emerges a very strong New Testament position: *the resurrection of Jesus is the key, the turning point of history*. That is where the disciples began. In time they came to understand the wonderful and marvelous purpose of Jesus' death, but without the resurrection there would have been no sense in even asking the question concerning the meaning of the cross. The same should hold true for us as well: start with the resurrection of Jesus and then reach back and embrace his atoning death.

One final stake in the preposterous notion that the resurrection of Jesus is a myth: would eleven men die for the sake of a lie? History records the tradition of the martyrdoms of eleven of the twelve apostles:

- Peter was crucified upside down by Emperor Nero in Rome. He felt unworthy to be crucified in the same position as his Lord Jesus Christ.
- Paul was beheaded in Rome by Emperor Nero.
- Andrew was crucified in Greece.
- Thomas was pierced with swords in India.
- Philip was put to death in Carthage, North Africa.
- Matthew was stabbed to death in Ethiopia.
- There are various accounts of the martyrdom of Bartholomew.
- James (Alpheus) was stoned and clubbed to death.
- Simon refused pagan sacrifice and was killed in Persia.
- Matthias was burned to death in Syria.
- James (Zebedee) was executed by Herod c. 44 A.D.
- John, the only one of the apostles who died of natural causes, was exiled to the Isle of Patmos where he wrote *The Revelation*.

No two of these men traveled together with the message of the risen Christ. And take note of the distances they had traveled with their message in so short a time. If, under severe torture leading to death, any one of them had proclaimed the resurrection of Jesus a myth or a hoax, no one else would have known. Or, they could have saved their life by declaring the resurrection a lie, even though they knew it was the truth. Either way we look at it, eleven men suffered and died and not one cracked under the pain and torture. What are the odds of this happening for the sake of a hoax? Is this not strong evidence in support of the actuality of the resurrection of Jesus?

If the crucifixion of Jesus had turned them into cowards (and it had), it was the resurrection of Jesus that made them bold, even unto death. The disciples were transformed by the resurrection. It became for them the fulcrum point, the reorienting gyro of their lives, and the turning point of history.

We must also turn ourselves around and start with the risen Christ. Only then will all else make sense. The fulcrum point of history is Sunday reaching back to embrace Friday, not the reverse. We must step forward two days from the position maintained by the Church for the last thirteen hundred years and turn loose that same resurrection power that once transformed the disciples and through them the world.

*Stand in the light of the resurrected Christ*
*and from that vantage point*
*reach back and embrace His sacrifice*

CHAPTER **Four**

# Resurrection Words And Phrases
# In The Acts Of The Apostles

I BEGIN THIS chapter with a personal story. To my mind it demonstrates the extreme difference that exists between the message of the contemporary Church and the witness of the *Acts of the Apostles*.

A few summers ago my wife and I went church hopping. On eight consecutive Sundays we visited eight different churches representing four Protestant evangelical denominations. In only one of the churches did anyone know us. We were there to worship. After many years of 'resurrection thinking' I have developed a finely tuned ear for 'resurrection nuance', as you might imagine. If any sense or hint of resurrection enters into the worship framework in any facet of the service I'll hear it because I'm listening for it.

What I experienced that summer may shock you, but I have come to realize that, sadly, it is typical throughout Christendom. In seven out of the eight churches, nowhere in the worship service, was there the slightest suggestion that Jesus was risen, alive, resurrected, raised from the dead, or any other way that event could be referenced: not in the congregational singing, not in the special music, not in the prayers, not in the testimonies of the people, not in the Scriptures that were read, not in the sermons that were preached. Nowhere! However, it was very evident that Jesus had died for us; that came through forcefully in every one of the seven churches.

I thought of speaking with the Pastors, but didn't. If I had, the conversations might have gone something like this: I would have asked whether the Pastor and the congregation believed in the resurrection of Jesus. The Pastor would more than likely have been offended by the question. I'm sure he would have said the resurrection of Jesus was absolutely necessary to the Christian faith; without it we have no hope. I would then have responded that I didn't hear any mention of it anywhere in the service. To this I think his response may have taken one of two paths. The first reaction would be one of surprise: "Are you sure?" You see (and this is a sad comment), we really don't know we're neglecting the resurrection; it isn't an intentional omission. We sincerely believe it is part of what we do, even when it isn't, and we're shocked when someone points out its absence. The second response to my stating the absence of the resurrection might have been, "That's because it isn't Easter". To which I would have responded, "I heard a lot about the cross today, and it isn't Good Friday".

Why is it that we can focus on Jesus' sacrifice any Sunday of the year, while resurrection preaching seems limited to Easter and funerals? The title of this book says it all: *The Easter Jesus and the Good Friday Church*. Indeed, almost all the Christians I know believe Jesus was raised from the dead, but our practices, both as individuals and as a corporate community of worshipers, do not reflect our 'resurrection certainty'. So, then, our faith is not suspect, but the practice of our faith most certainly is!

It wasn't always like this. Jesus commanded his followers, his disciples to take his message to the uttermost parts of the earth. They heeded his challenge. The *Acts of the Apostles*, placed immediately after the four Gospels in the Greek Scriptures, tells the story of the spread of the message of Christ to the far reaches of the Roman Empire.

Before discovering the message itself, we need to give a brief overview of the book. Luke, the author of the Gospel by that name, was also the author of the *Acts of the Apostles*. He was a fellow traveler with the Apostle Paul, accompanying him on much of his journey throughout the Greco-Roman world. His account of the spread of the Gospel begins with Pentecost in Jerusalem, and follows the explosion of the message outward from Jerusalem to Judea, Samaria and eventually to the uttermost parts of the earth. The message begins in the Jewish world with God's chosen people, and quickly spreads to the Gentile world. Luke's account covers somewhere between twenty-five and thirty years. By the time the *Acts of the Apostles* ends the world of believers in the risen Christ has grown from a few hundred to tens of thousands. Luke's account ends with the Apostle Paul imprisoned in Rome.

We can say of the entire New Testament that none of it would have been written without God's power intervening in the death of his son, restoring him to life. Christianity would not exist without that fact—it is indisputable. As was stated earlier, unless Jesus had been raised from the dead the disciples would have spent the rest of their lives trying to forget that false prophet Jesus, who promised the kingdom and ended up dead like every other zealot that came to mind. They would have gone to their graves denying, like Peter, that they had had anything to do with the man.

To suggest the *Acts of the Apostles* is first and foremost a witness to the power of the resurrection hardly begins to tell the story. It will be my intent to briefly outline a number of ways in which the resurrection of Jesus is made the central theme.

The book begins by recounting the resurrection appearance of Jesus and his command to 'witness':

> He presented himself alive to them after his suffering by many proofs, appearing to them during forty days and speaking about the kingdom of God. And while staying with them he ordered them not to depart from Jerusalem, but to wait for the promise of the Father, which, he said, "you heard from me; for John baptized with water, but you will be baptized with the Holy spirit not many days from now"... "But you will receive power when the Holy

> *Spirit has come upon you, and you will be my witnesses*
> *in Jerusalem and in all Judea and Samaria, and to the end*
> *of the earth." (Acts 1: 3–4, 8 ESV)*

Matthew, Luke, John and the long version of Mark all end with the fact of Jesus' resurrection and, except for John, the commission to deliver the 'good news' they had witnessed to the whole of creation. The purpose of the *Acts of the Apostles* was to recount how, in a period of less than thirty years, a renewed band of eleven disciples on sandaled feet and in sailboats grew into an incredible community of believers throughout the entire Greco-Roman world.

Author Luke recounts the appearances of the risen Christ to his remaining disciples by referring to them as 'many convincing proofs' (verse 3: *en pollois tekmeriois*). Some translations use the words 'infallible', 'many proofs', 'many demonstrations', or 'ample proof'.

> *The word 'tekmerion' (infallible proof) does not occur*
> *elsewhere in the New Testament. The question is, why is it*
> *then used in this passage? When Aristotle used this word*
> *in a discussion regarding the nature of logic, it was distin-*
> *guished from a mere 'semeion' ('sign' or' indication') in*
> *that it was a 'demonstrable proof'. According to Aristotle,*
> *a 'semeion' could be the basis for a probable argument*
> *to prove a conclusion, but a 'tekmerion' was a necessary*
> *sign that could be made into a demonstrative syllogism*
> *which could not be refuted.* [1]

> *...Since Luke often uses the term 'Semeion '...he must have*
> *deliberately chosen this rare word [tekmerion] in order to*
> *emphasize that the apostles came to knowledge of the*
> *resurrection through inescapable empirical evidence.* [2]

Obviously, unless Jesus was resurrected their ministry would have been built on a shaky foundation, if it were built at all. In other words,

Luke goes out of his way by using this word *tekmerion*, to say that the resurrection of Jesus is irrefutable, infallible; you can build your entire structure of faith on the solid foundation of the risen Christ. This foundation is as unshakable as any scientific law. What a way to establish the launching pad for the witness of the Gospel!

If we believe Luke's report, then it becomes difficult to assume we are dealing with a spiritual rather than a bodily resurrection, or that Jesus rose figuratively in the faith of his followers, as some would have us believe. The entire book of Acts must be viewed in this light.

What message did they preach that had such a powerful impact? Was it the message of the cross? In no way is it possible to suggest from the book of Acts that the cross of Jesus was the focus of their preaching. That Jesus died is a fact they acknowledge willingly, not because they wished to emphasize the redemptive significance of his death, but rather because it showed the absolute futility of men's desire to do away with him.

Allow me to interject at this point a defense of Jesus' willing death on the cross. Jesus *had* to die. We would be lost without his loving sacrifice. It is impossible to overstate the absolute necessity of the atoning sacrifice accomplished in the death of Jesus. Unless sin—my sin, our sin, the sin of all humanity past, present and future—was taken to the cross and the grave in the submissive, sacrificial act of Jesus, we would have no hope of forgiveness. However true that is, it is not the message of the followers of Jesus in the *Acts of the Apostles*. This book is a *history*, not a *theology*. The meaning of the sacrifice at Golgotha will receive full attention in the Epistles, primarily those of the Apostle Paul. But here the propellant for the first witness is not the act evil men perpetrated against Jesus; it is, rather, the powerful and death-defeating act of God in raising his son from the dead. It is the resurrection, and that alone, that is the message of the apostles.

In the *Acts of the Apostles* passages referring to the death of Jesus use the words 'murder', 'kill', 'crucify', 'hang on a tree (gibbet)', 'put to death'; the tone of these words simply describes the violent act of his enemies:

[Peter's second sermon] *"The God of Abraham, the God of Isaac and the God of Jacob, the God of our fathers, glorified his servant Jesus, whom you delivered over and denied in the presence of Pilate, when he had decided to release him. But you denied the Holy and Righteous One, and asked for a murderer to be granted to you, and* **you killed the Author of life, whom God raised from the dead** [emphasis mine]. *To this we are witnesses." (Acts 3: 13-15 ESV)*

*The God of our fathers raised Jesus,* **whom you killed by hanging him on a tree. God exalted him at his right hand** [emphasis mine] *as Leader and Savior, to give repentance to Israel and forgiveness of sins. And we are witnesses to these things…" (Acts 5: 30-32 ESV)*

[Peter again] *And we are witnesses of everything he did both in the country of the Jews and in Jerusalem.* **They put him to death by hanging him on a tree, but God raised him on the third day** [emphasis mine] *and made him to appear, not to all the people but to us who had been chosen by God as witnesses, who ate and drank with him after he rose from the dead. (Acts 10: 39–41 ESV)*

[Paul in the synagogue at Antioch] *And though they found in him no guilt worthy of death,* **they asked Pilate to have him executed** [emphasis mine]. *And when they had carried out all that was written of him, they took him down from the tree and laid him in a tomb.* **But God raised him from the dead** [emphasis mine], *and for many days he appeared to those who had come up with him from Galilee to Jerusalem, who are now his witnesses to the people. (Acts 13: 28–31 ESV)*

On approximately fourteen occasions in the *Acts of the Apostles* words describing the death of Jesus are used. In each case the killing of Jesus is portrayed as an act of evil men, as has already been stated: nothing more. All are followed by the words of heavenly intervention: 'But God raised him'. 'You killed him, *but* God raised him'. The use of the word *but* always places the phrase that follows it in a position of opposition to what was stated in the phrase preceding it. Usually the oppositional phrase is in authority or supremacy over the phrase that came before. The careful and I think intentional use of the word *but* in most of these passages reveals the writer's sense of the superior nature of the resurrection power of God. Said another way, if Luke had written 'you killed him *and* God raised him', both acts would have been seen as equal; but they are not. Luke always places God's act of raising his son in the superior position.

I. Howard Marshall, in his commentary on *The Acts of the Apostles*, writes:

> ...*The impression gained is rather that it was by virtue of being raised from the dead and exalted by the Father that Jesus received the authority to bestow salvation.... It is thus the resurrection and exaltation of Jesus which stands at the center of the preaching of Acts.*[3]

Knowing the extent to which Luke and all the other New Testament writers went to substantiate and emphasize Jesus' resurrection it becomes difficult to understand why the Church for the past thirteen hundred years has insisted on placing its emphasis on the instrument of death rather than on the One who submitted to it in order to conquer it.

## Criteria for Judas' Replacement

After Jesus' ascension the eleven disciples met with a larger congregation of believers to find a replacement for Judas Iscariot:

> *So one of the men who have accompanied us during all*
> *the time that the Lord Jesus went in and out among us,*
> *beginning from the baptism of John until the day when he*
> *was taken up from us—one of these men must become*
> *with us a witness to his resurrection. (Acts 1: 21-22 ESV)*

There were two criteria to be used in making this choice. First, the replacement had to have been with Jesus through his entire three-year ministry. He had to have witnessed Jesus' baptism, his miracle working, his teaching, his final Passover meal, his suffering and his death. The replacement had to have seen the risen Christ and fellowshipped with him until his ascension. Second, this new apostle had to be bold enough to become a witness to the world of the resurrection of Jesus the Christ.

It is extremely important to understand that of all the activities of Jesus' life, including his suffering and death, the one event singled out for apostolic calling and preaching was resurrection witness—exclusively: For one of these must become a witness with us of his resurrection.

The disciples, now called 'apostles', began to refer to themselves as 'witnesses to the resurrection'. Only having seen or witnessed the presence of the risen Jesus qualified one to become an 'apostle'. Apparently, apostolic authority was based upon a certifiable confrontation and companionship with the risen Christ. The fledgling Christian world wouldn't settle for anything less. Such a person, one who had actually seen the risen Christ and shared meals with him, could be trusted; such a person's words would be heeded and taken as truth.

Can we learn from the writing of Luke whether the apostles did what the criteria demanded? Yes. As the apostles moved from Jerusalem throughout the Greco-Roman world, to Jew and Gentile, poor and rich, ignorant and wise, the narrator of Acts again and again reports that:

[Peter speaking on the Day of Pentecost] *"This Jesus God*

*raised up, and of that we all are witnesses." (Acts 2: 32 ESV)*

[Peter and John before the Sanhedrin] *And as they were speaking to the people, the priests and the captain of the temple and the Sadducees came upon them, greatly annoyed because they were teaching the people and proclaiming in Jesus the resurrection from the dead. (Act 4: 1–2 ESV)*

*And with great power the apostles were giving their testimony to the resurrection of the Lord Jesus, and great grace was upon them all. (Acts 4: 33 ESV)*

[The apostles before the Sanhedrin] *"The God of our fathers raised Jesus, whom you killed by hanging him on a tree. God exalted him at his right hand as Leader and Savior, to give repentance to Israel and forgiveness of sins. And we are witnesses to these things…" (Acts 5: 30-32 ESV)*

This resurrection witness began to gather great numbers of converts. The authorities couldn't have been too pleased about that. It must be remembered that the very idea of resurrection was repulsive to the Sadducees, the largest religious group. And while the Pharisees accepted the idea of the resurrection at the end of time, they were not at all receptive to the preaching of Jesus' resurrection in the middle of time. Furthermore, it was a repugnant idea that Messiah would die; their understanding of the Hebrew Scriptures had not prepared them for such an odorous idea.

Even the apostle Paul, confessing that because of Jesus' resurrection all humanity had been given resurrection hope, found himself on trial because of his resurrection witness:

*Now when Paul perceived that one part were Sadducees and the other Pharisees, he cried out in the council, "Brothers, I am a Pharisee, a son of Pharisees. It is with*

*respect to the hope and the resurrection of the dead that
I am on trial." (Acts 23: 6 ESV)*

[Paul's speech before the Roman governor Felix] *"It is with
respect to the resurrection of the dead that I am on trial
before you this day." (Acts 24: 21 ESV)*

Consider two questions. First, if there was little or no concept of
resurrection in general, and no concept that Messiah (who, according
to their understanding of their Scriptures, wouldn't die) would need
one, would the apostles (products of the same teaching prior to their
association with Jesus) have created such a notion? Second, and even
more to our point, would Paul and the apostles have been on trial if
they were preaching the death of Jesus?

The answer to both questions is an emphatic 'no'. Particularly
regarding the second question—if the apostles had been preaching
Jesus' death the Jewish authorities would have left them alone. Such
foolishness, preaching about the kingdom of a dead man, would have
constituted no threat to them. Many zealots had garnered followers.
All of them had been put to death along with many of their adher-
ents. Whatever preaching continued after the death of a zealot soon
died out. Such preaching by the apostles of Jesus, if he had only died,
would soon have come to naught. They could be ignored at no cost to
the Jewish leaders or to Rome itself for that matter. It was resurrection
preaching that got the apostles and Paul into trouble.

The only basis for their hope was the precedent set in the resurrection of Jesus. The authorities were driven to stamp out this so-called
'heretical' resurrection witness. This is important: their ensuing persecution of the witnesses constitutes a sure sign of the success of that
witness. If their preaching had been ineffective, falling on deaf ears,
there would have been no urgency to stamp out their movement.

Likewise, consider the steadfastness of Stephen in the face of his
stoning, and Paul in his continual trials and persecution: their perseverance provides convincing evidence not only of the strength of

their resurrection witness but also of the truth it represented. Surely, no one would have persisted under such arduous and horrible attacks for the sake of a lie!

## Resurrection Words and Titles

Luke's narrative of the consistently proclaimed 'gospel' of resurrection reveals a second layer of interest. A number of critical words keep surfacing, words that continue to be part of Christian vocabulary, so to speak. In our day these particular words are ubiquitous in Christian conversations, sermons, prayers, and testimonies. However, they have taken on a 'generic' definition; the result is that we have lost their initial specificity. They have been watered down, and in that process have lost not only their original intent, but also their power. Were we to reclaim what I believe to be their specific and original definitions our reading of the *Acts of the Apostles* and the *Epistles* would change radically, revealing the power and centrality of the resurrection intended by the writers of those treatises. In my opinion five such words and titles are in need of being considered in their original resurrection context: *Apostle, Witness, Gospel, Lord, and Christ.*

## 'Apostle' and 'Witness' as Resurrection Words

The title *Apostle* is the first to surface (Acts 1: 21 – 22). Closely linked with it in the same passage is the word *Witness*. Therefore, to begin, it serves us well to consider them together. Recall the criteria for choosing a replacement for Judas: one who had been with Jesus from John's baptism through his ministry, suffering, death, resurrection, and ascension; singled out for future witness was the resurrection. Only such a person could be an apostle.

The words *witness* and *apostle*, then, are tied inextricably to the resurrection of Jesus and become in themselves resurrection words. An apostle is one who witnesses to the resurrection of Jesus. There can be no disputing this fact. The word *witness* throughout the *Acts of the Apostles* is used both as a noun (the one who is the witness), and a verb (what the witness does). About half the time the text says something to the effect, *'they went about witnessing'*, without identifying the nature of the witness. The other half, however, reveals a striking discovery. Whenever the witness is described it is always, exclusively focused on the resurrection of Jesus. The word *witness* is never—repeat, never—associated with the death of Jesus. Nowhere in the *Acts of the Apostles* is any witness given to the cross other than to ridicule it as a futile effort of sinful, corrupt men that gave way to the power of God manifested in the raising of his son. As we have stated previously, the Apostles were doing exactly what the criteria for apostleship and witness demanded, one hundred per cent of the time.

W.H.C. Frend, in his exhaustive study of martyrdom and persecution in the early Church, explains the nature of a witness during the New Testament period. He writes that the Greek word for *witness* is *martyr* and must be described in the general and legal sense as one who testifies to the resurrection of Jesus. At the point of the Gospels and the book of Acts there is not yet a penalty for this 'witness'. According to Frend, Stephen was called a martyr (witness) not specifically because he died but rather because he confessed the resurrection of Jesus. His martyrdom was merely proof of the power and sincerity of his witness.

If we were honestly to assess our witness in our own day could the same be said of us? How often does our witness focus on the sacrificial death of Jesus? And how often does that witness move forward to include his resurrection? In my own personal witness experience as well as my observation of the Church universal, I believe we have failed quite miserably to embrace the resurrection of Jesus. What we usually hear is, *"Jesus died for me so that I could have forgiveness for sins and eternal life."* In this instance we are suggesting that when Jesus died all we need was provided. The resurrection is left out of the equation. In response to this omission, as well as giving a defense for the omission, Christians have said that resurrection is being implied!

Now I ask you, "How does death imply that resurrection follows?" How can we 'assume' the resurrection when it only happened once? Such conversation can take place with meaning between Christians—we've been schooled in the Scriptures to believe that resurrection will follow death for believers. But such vocalizations only serve to reinforce our perceived 'death-mindedness' to the unbelieving world around us. Like it or not, I've heard numerous accusations of our 'death-mindedness' outside our Christian circle. *Witness* in the *Acts of the Apostles* is exclusively resurrection centered. So then I ask, "Can we legitimately be called witnesses when we limit our emphasis to the Good Friday event?" The author of Acts would respond with an emphatic 'no'!

Can we be called *apostles*? Technically, no. We were not there with Jesus, as one criterion for *Apostleship* demanded. However, we can legitimately be called *witnesses* in the New Testament sense of the word when our *witness* focuses on the resurrection of Jesus—only then.

Why were the cross and the death of Jesus not part of the apostles' witness? Was it because everyone was already aware of those events? After all, didn't Cleopas and his friend on the Emmaus road ask the 'stranger' if he was the only one in Jerusalem who didn't know what had happened to Jesus? This is not the answer. *Witness* and *Apostle* are being used in a different way. They point to the significant act of God's raising his son from the dead, which turned the tables on the desire of men to do away with Jesus by crucifying him. Furthermore, Jesus' death had caused the disciples to be scattered, to lose hope, to lose faith, to doubt, to run off to their fishing nets, to be humiliated. In their minds the death of Jesus was anything but a stimulating, significant event. We have said they were bewildered by Jesus' talk of his dying, as Judaism didn't interpret the scriptures regarding *Messiah* or *Son of Man* or *Davidic King* in that way. The crucified Jesus had not turned their lives around. Only the resurrected Lord did that. The power of apostolic witness in the *Acts of the Apostles* is directly and exclusively linked with the power of the resurrection—nothing else, and nothing less!

Today we have turned the tables. The significant event in our witness for the last thirteen hundred years has been the Good Friday act. While not denying the Easter event we have relegated it to second place. All we seem to need, if our hymns, art, clichés, prayers, symbols and sermons are any indication, was both sealed and delivered through the shed blood of Jesus on the cross. We know in our heart of hearts that's not the whole, complete truth of the Scriptures, but we persist in our partial truth nonetheless. Unfortunately, because the resurrection of Jesus plays little part in the various ways by which we manifest our faith, we are not *bona fide* New Testament witnesses.

Here is our challenge: every time we read the words *witness* and *apostle* we must stop and add a parenthetic phrase which amplifies the resurrection intent of the writer of the *Acts of the Apostles*. For example:

> *Apostle: One who has seen the risen Christ, and testifies to his resurrection.*
> *Witness (noun): One who has seen the risen Christ.*
> *Witness (verb): Speaking of the resurrection of Jesus.*

Write these parenthetic statements on the inside cover of your Bible. Every time you see either of these words, force yourself to insert the statement; this will insure that you are creating the resurrection context I believe the writer of the words intended.

## Resurrection Words and Titles: Lord and Christ

Another indication of the strong resurrection emphasis in the *Acts of the Apostles* is the particular and focused use of the word *Lord* (in Greek, *Kurios*). Throughout the Gospels *Lord* was used in two ways, one as a title of respect and the other as a sign of sovereignty, one supreme in authority. While biblical scholars are not completely clear on this, most consider the dividing point between the two uses to be the resurrection of Jesus. Prior to that event the word *Lord* seems to incline toward 'sir' or 'gentleman'—polite titles. The resurrection of Jesus changed that. Jesus had now proved he was the person he said he was, the one his followers had hoped for but evidently were reluctant to believe in. God's resurrection power validated the *Lord*-ship, the authority and sovereignty of Jesus.

Even more particular to the resurrection is the word *Christ* (in Greek, *Christos*; in Hebrew, *Messiah*). Believe it or not, some people think the word *Christ* is Jesus' last name, as if he is a member of the 'Christ' family: Joseph Christ, Mary Christ, and all the siblings Christ! It sounds ludicrous, almost blasphemous to say it, but you would be amazed how many are confused by this word. *Christ* is not a name; it is a title, meaning the *Anointed One*. In the first post-resurrection sermon, Peter said:

> "This Jesus God raised up, and of that we all are witnesses…. Let all the house of Israel therefore know for certain that God has made him both Lord and Christ, this Jesus whom you crucified." (Acts 2: 32, 36 ESV)

Does this suggest that Jesus was not *Lord* and *Messiah/Christ* before his resurrection? No. Jesus was always *Lord, Messiah/Christ*, from the time before time, when he was one with the Father; the resurrection validated Jesus as *Lord, Messiah/Christ*. While we may have doubted before, now we are certain. Jesus has been proved to be who he said he was through the resurrection power of God. In our minds Jesus became *The Lord*, he established his *Lord*-ship over sin and death by virtue of his resurrection. If we are to believe the *Acts of the Apostles* we must realize that Jesus was not *Lord* in this sense in the disciples' hearts prior to his resurrection. He was not *Lord* in this sense in the disciples' hearts when he was nailed to the cross. The power we ascribe to him was not actuated in their hearts before God raised him from the dead. When we confess *Jesus is Lord*, we are in reality confessing the risen Christ, whether or not we have known it. In our minds and hearts Jesus the man became the *Lord Jesus Christ* when he became the first-born from the dead. The phrase itself is symbolic in that Jesus, his earthly name, is flanked by his resurrection titles: *Lord*, a mark of his sovereignty, and *Christ*, the Anointed One, the fulfillment of the Old Testament Messianic prophecies. The title *Christ* is powerful and it belongs to Jesus alone. We are not accurate, nor are we biblical when we use the phrase *Lord Jesus Christ* in the context of his suffering and death, his shed blood, while ignoring the significant act that gave him the authority of that title—that is, the resurrection. It was the risen Christ who was able to say at the end of the gospel of Matthew:

> *"All authority in heaven and on earth has been given to me. Go therefore..." (Matthew 28: 18 ESV).*

Permeating the entire *Acts of the Apostles* is the use of the title *Lord* that is closely linked to the resurrection of Jesus and symbolized his conquest over death. Luke chose not to use the term merely as a polite title for he wanted to provide a vivid contrast between the *Lord Christ* and the crucified Jesus. We must once again realize and catch hold of that same contrast.

As with *witness* and *apostle*, a parenthetic statement should accompany every appearance of the words *Lord* and *Christ* to reinforce the biblical meanings of those titles. In my mind they were used as intentional resurrection titles by the authors of the New Testament and would have been understood as such by all who heard them. Reading them in this context brings into being a heightened awareness of the scriptures. Here are the parenthetic descriptions to be used:

> *Lord: Validated as **the** Lord, the sovereign One, through the resurrection power of God.*

> *Christ (Messiah): Validated as the Anointed One, the anticipated Messiah, through the resurrection power of God.*

# Resurrection Words and Titles:
# Gospel, Good News, Proclaim, Proclamation

The apostles—that is, those who had seen the risen Lord—began to witness to their ever-expanding world. Author Luke leaves no doubt as to the nature of their witness:

> And every day, in the temple and from house to house, they did not cease teaching and preaching Jesus as the Christ **[that is, the Anointed One, the anticipated Messiah, through the resurrection power of God]**. *(Acts 5: 42 ESV)*

> "And we bring you the good news that what God promised to the fathers, this he has fulfilled to us their children by raising Jesus..." *(Acts 13: 32 ESV)*

From these and other passages we see the various words used to describe the content of their testimony: words like *Gospel, Good News, Proclaim, Proclamation*. Our purpose is to examine exactly what they considered to be the *gospel* or the *good news*.

It is important to remember that it was the risen Christ himself who commanded his followers to witness to the good news of what they had seen and heard: that is, his three year ministry, his teaching, his miracle-working, his sacrifice and death, *and* his resurrection. To include everything up to and including the penultimate event in their preaching, while leaving out the ultimate event, would have been to preclude any hope of *good news* and leave Jesus' command unfulfilled. The message of Good Friday was anything but good news to the followers of Jesus. Without the resurrection Good Friday could never be considered 'good'. It is only 'good' when we look back at it through the portal of the resurrection.

No such mistake is made in the *Acts of the Apostles*. Aware that it was the Person of the living, resurrected Lord who gave the command, the followers began their preaching emphasizing the *final* event, the one that validated and rendered as significant everything which had preceded it. Obedience to Jesus' command was complete, consistent and thorough.

In our day we think we preach the *gospel* when we declare the sacrificial act of Jesus. Over the years I have asked many people to give me their definition of the word *gospel*. In every case the first response is that the *Gospel* is the *Good News*. "What is the *Good News*", I ask. The answer is always the same: "The *Good News* that Jesus died for us". Sadly, and this is not an exaggeration, I have never heard anyone include the resurrection in their description. It isn't because they don't believe in the resurrection of Jesus. It's simply because for decades, even centuries, we've been conditioned to accept its absence. We have become so firmly rooted in the sacrifice of Jesus that it has become, by default, our entire landscape of practice and confession. If we were to sit down and have a discussion about faith I'm certain most Christians would confess that the *Gospel* is not complete in Jesus' death alone. True, the *Gospel* message begins with the broken body and shed blood of Jesus. Unfortunately our message usually stops there. On occasion— if we have enough time, or if it is Easter Sunday or a funeral service—we may slide forward into a few words about the resurrection. Most of the time we don't move past Good Friday, being content to *assume* that, after all, everyone knows Jesus was raised from the dead. That is incredibly faulty reasoning. We cannot 'assume' resurrection; it doesn't happen when a person dies. It only happened for one person in all of history. Resurrection is not the natural consequence of dying; only God will make it so. This assumption, thinking erroneously that people automatically think *resurrection* when we say *crucifixion,* is robbing Christianity of its power. If we make any mistake at all, let it be that we speak exclusively of the resurrection of Jesus, assuming thereby that a death had to have preceded it! Better yet, don't omit either from our confession and discourse. Talk about both—the death *and* resurrection of Jesus—every time.

This is important*: nowhere in the Acts of the Apostles are the words 'Gospel' or 'Good News' associated with the suffering or dying Jesus, or with his shed blood.* These words appear about thirteen times in this book. Five of the thirteen are used in a general tone; that is, there is no identification of what the *gospel* is, as we find in the following passage:

> *Now when they had testified and spoken the word of the Lord, they [Peter and John] returned to Jerusalem, preaching the gospel to many villages of the Samaritans. (Acts 8: 25 ESV)*

However, by employing one of our parenthetic statements we can determine quite clearly that the *gospel* was associated with the resurrected Jesus:

> *Now when they had testified and spoken the word of the Lord* **[that is, the word regarding the One who was validated as the Lord, the sovereign One, through the resurrection power of God]** *they returned to Jerusalem, preaching the gospel* **[the good news of the resurrection of Jesus]** *to many villages of the Samaritans.*

For the apostles the death of Jesus was anything but good news. It was the source of their flight, denial and fear. Without the resurrection could you ever imagine their identifying themselves with him, much less their insistence on creating a movement in his Name? Emphasis on the risen Christ throughout the book makes it possible to suggest that the mindset behind the words, and perhaps the rise of the words themselves, can be attributed to the joy associated with the resurrected and living Christ. The *good news*, the *Gospel*, the *proclamation* was the explosive reappearance of the risen Lord—not the crucified Jesus, but God's response to his son's crucifixion. The early Church's view and our view of these words seem to be in need of reconciliation.

The way to attain this reconciliation is to insert another of our parenthetic statements:

> *Gospel, Good news, Proclamation: The Good news of the*
> *resurrection of Jesus.*

Several other passages relate the good news to the *Lordship* of Jesus—in other words, to the One whose Messianic validation and authority were established through the resurrection. Try adding the parenthetic statements to these two verses:

> *And the eunuch said to Philip, "About whom, I ask you,*
> *does the prophet say this* **[Isaiah 53: 7-8, He was led like**
> **a sheep to the slaughter, and as a lamb before the shearer**
> **is silent, so he did not open his mouth. In his humiliation**
> **he was deprived of justice]**, *about himself or about some-*
> *one else?" Then Philip opened his mouth, and beginning*
> *with this Scripture he told him the good news about Jesus*
> **[that is, the good news of the resurrection of Jesus]**. *(Acts*
> *8: 34 ESV)*

> *But there were some of them, men of Cyprus and Cyrene,*
> *who on coming to Antioch spoke to the Hellenists also,*
> *preaching* **[the good news of the resurrection of]** *the Lord*
> *Jesus* **[that is, the one validated as the Lord, the sover-**
> **eign One, through the resurrection power of God]**. *And*
> *the hand of the Lord was with them, and a great number*
> *who believed turned to the Lord* **[validated as the Lord...]**.
> *(Acts 11: 20–21 ESV)*

In chapter 20 Paul relates the command given to him by the risen Christ on the Damascus road:

> *But I do not account my life of any value nor as precious to*
> *myself, if only I may finish my course and the ministry that*
> *I received from the Lord Jesus* **[validated as *the* Lord, the**
> **sovereign One, through the resurrection power of God]**,
> *to testify to the gospel* **[the good news of the resurrection**

**of Jesus]** *of the grace of God. (Acts 20: 24 ESV)*

Other references are of a general nature, simply stating that the good news was preached in an ever-widening circle throughout the Greco-Roman world. Adding the parenthetic statement we have ascribed to *Gospel* or *good news* solidifies the context of the resurrection.

*When an attempt was made by both Gentiles and Jews, with their rulers, to mistreat them* **[the Apostles]** *and to stone them, they learned of it and fled to Lystra and Derbe, cities of Lycaonia, and to the surrounding country, and there they continued to preach the gospel* **[the good news of the resurrection of Jesus]**. *(Acts 14: 5-7 ESV)*

*"Men, why are you doing these things? We also are men, of like nature with you, and we bring you good news* **[the good news of the resurrection of Jesus]**, *that you should turn from these vain things to a living God..." (Acts 14: 15 ESV)*

*When they had preached the gospel* **[the good news of the resurrection of Jesus]** *to that city and had made many disciples, they returned to Lystra and to Iconium and to Antioch... (Acts14: 21 ESV)*

*And after there had been much debate, Peter stood up and said to them, "Brothers, you know that in the early days God made a choice among you, that by my mouth the Gentiles should hear the word of the gospel* **[the good news of the resurrection of Jesus]** *and believe. (Acts 15: 7 ESV)*

*And when Paul had seen the vision, immediately we sought to go on into Macedonia, concluding that God had called us to preach the gospel to them* **[the good news of the resurrection of Jesus]**. *(Acts 16: 10 ESV)*

## The Forgiveness of Sins in the Acts of the Apostles

One of the most interesting concepts stemming from the book of Acts, certainly the most challenging, is the attitude it assumes regarding the forgiveness of sins and salvation. It has often been said that Luke, in the writing of the *Acts of the Apostles*, was recording the history of the early Church, not its *Soteriology*, that is, its theological doctrine of salvation as established by Christ. That is true. However, while no systematic, organized doctrine appears here, there is not an absence of references concerning salvation and the forgiveness of sins. In a nutshell, what can be said is that in this documentation by Luke there is not the slightest linkage between the Good Friday event—the cross, the broken body and shed blood—and the origin or font of salvation. It will be left to the Epistle writers, the Apostle Paul most specifically, to answer the theological questions surrounding the sacrifice of Jesus. What we can take away from Luke's history of the spread of the Gospel is not the final word about the significance of the crucifixion, but as the event in need of an answer—that is, God's resurrecting power that became the rallying cry of the growing community of believers.

In the very first recorded post-resurrection sermon these words appear:

> *"Let all the house of Israel therefore know for certain that God has made him both Lord and Christ* **[that is, validated as the sovereign Lord and Christ, the anointed One, through the resurrection power of God]**, *this Jesus whom you crucified." Now when they heard this they were cut to the heart, and said to Peter and the rest of the apostles, "Brothers, what shall we do?" And Peter said to them, "Repent and be baptized every one of you in the name of Jesus Christ* **[validated as Christ the anointed One, through the resurrection power of God]** *for the forgiveness of your sins"… (Acts 2: 36-38 ESV)*

Notice that Peter uses the name Jesus, his earthly name, followed by the titles the resurrection bestowed upon him as validation of his claims. God, it appears, through the resurrection of Jesus, has established his son's authority on earth to be both Lord and Christ, or Messiah. If we take this passage at face value it seems as if Jesus did not possess that authority before his resurrection. Let's not make that mistake. Jesus was always Lord and Christ, as we have said earlier, from the foundation of the earth. His resurrection serves as proof he was who he said he was.

Then, at the conclusion of the stated passage, it says that forgiveness for sins can be found in the name of the risen One. In this passage no significance is attached to Jesus' dying; it is only mentioned as a violent act of men. We are not suggesting that this constitutes a full blown theology of salvation, but it *is* interesting that the first words recorded in the *Acts of the Apostles* regarding forgiveness of sins have only to do with the resurrected One and nothing to do with his sacrifice or death. It might be asked whether Acts stands alone in these attitudes, or whether other books substantiate what is said here. Romans 10: 9 (ESV), one of many references we could choose, seems to parallel the thought being discussed:

> *…if you confess with your mouth that Jesus is Lord* [**validated as the sovereign Lord through the resurrection power of God**] *and believe in your heart that God raised him from the dead, you will be saved.*

God validated Jesus as Lord through the resurrection, and Paul says that our confession of this risen One, and our belief that it was God whose power brought him back to life—*confession and belief, both together*—give us salvation. The confessions so often heard today: 'Jesus died that we might live' or, 'The blood of Jesus has given us eternal life'—avoiding the significant role the resurrection played—seem a far cry from the spirit of the *Acts of the Apostles*, not to mention the Epistles.

Even in the story of the jailer salvation comes through the risen One:

> *When the jailer woke and saw that the prison doors were open, he drew his sword and was about to kill himself, supposing that the prisoners had escaped. But Paul cried with a loud voice, "Do not harm yourself, for we are all here." And the jailer called for lights and rushed in, and trembling with fear he fell down before Paul and Silas. Then he brought them out and said, "Sirs, what must I do to be saved?" And they said, "Believe in the Lord Jesus* **[validated as the sovereign Lord through the resurrection power of God]**, *and you will be saved…" (Acts 16: 27–31 ESV)*

The risen One saves us, the risen One who was crucified. According to the examples in the *Acts of the Apostles* our testimony should read, "I confess that Jesus is my Lord and Savior through his obedient sacrifice and the mighty resurrection power of God!" When in your entire life have you ever heard that?

There is only one reference in the book of Acts to the idea of a suffering Messiah in the plan of God. Notice in this passage that it doesn't say 'Jesus would suffer'; it says 'Christ would suffer'. In other words it was foretold that the One who would be raised from the dead—Christ, validated as *Christ* through the resurrection power of God—was ordained to first endure suffering:

> *But what God foretold by the mouth of all the prophets, that his Christ* **[validated as Christ the anointed One through the resurrection power of God]** *would suffer, he thus fulfilled. Repent therefore, and turn again* **[to God]**, *that your sins may be blotted out… (Acts 3: 18-19 ESV)*

In an earlier chapter we said that Jesus' followers had no understanding of a Messiah who would suffer and die. In their understanding of the scriptures they saw a *Messiah, Davidic King,* or *Son of Man* who would come, throw out the evildoers, and establish his Kingdom. They had, in effect, misinterpreted the Scriptures and thereby failed to understand the prophecies. Now, in light of the resurrection, the Old Testament prophecies came alive. They gained a focus that was new to Jewish thought. God had fulfilled what he had foretold in the utterances of all the prophets—that his Messiah should suffer. Here, as we have suggested, is the only glimmer of understanding in Acts that *suffering* was also part of the plan of God, not just an act of evil men apart from God's plan. Yes, Christ/Messiah would suffer; but the passage says it is God who wipes out sin. It is God's power brought to bear in the resurrection.

In the response to confusion over the first miracle in the post-resurrection Christian community these words were proclaimed:

> "...let it be known to all of you and to all the people of Israel that by the name of Jesus Christ **[validated as Christ the anointed One through the resurrection power of God]** of Nazareth, whom you crucified, whom God raised from the dead—by him this man is standing before you well. This Jesus is the stone that was rejected by you, the builders, which has become the cornerstone. And there is salvation in no one else, for there is no other name under heaven given among men by which we must be saved."
> (Acts 4: 10-12 ESV)

Jesus, the stone rejected through the crucifixion, has become Christ, the capstone, the cornerstone, through the resurrection power of God. *Christ* is a resurrection title, and it is in the name of this risen Christ that we have salvation.

The pivot point of Christianity is the resurrection power of God invested in his son on *Resurrection Day*. What the *Acts of the Apostles* seems to be saying is that the history of the world would be the same with or without the death of Jesus, if that was all there was. It is the resurrection that divides the ages and ushers in the possibility of eternal life. Acts is consistent on this point: men defiled Jesus; God exalted or raised him:

> *"The God of our fathers raised Jesus, whom you killed by hanging him on a tree. God exalted him at this right hand as Leader and Savior, to give repentance to Israel and forgiveness of sins. And we are witnesses* **[those who have seen the risen Christ and testify about him]** *to these things..." (Acts 5: 30–32ESV)*

In this exaltation Jesus has become our leader and Savior. Again we have to confess that it is the resurrected Jesus who has the authority to bestow repentance and forgiveness of sins.

## The Wise Counsel of Gamaliel

The aforementioned passage goes on to say that these words hit some raw nerve endings in the Jewish council.

> *When they heard this, they were enraged and wanted to kill them. But a Pharisee in the council named Gamaliel, a teacher of the law held in honor by all the people, stood up and gave orders to put the men outside for a little while. And he said to them, "Men of Israel, take care what you are about to do with these men. For before these days Theudas rose up, claiming to be somebody, and a number of men, about four hundred, joined him. He was killed, and all who followed him were dispersed and came to nothing. After him Judas the Galilean rose up in the days of the census and drew away some of the people after him. he too perished, and all who followed him were scattered. So in the present case I tell you, keep away from these men and let them alone, for if this plan or this undertaking is of man, it will fail; but if it is of God, you will*

*not be able to overthrow them. You might even be found opposing God!" (Acts 5: 33–39 ESV)*

Gamaliel was a very wise man. He was also right. Other false prophets and zealots had gathered around themselves large crowds of followers and supporters only to fall to the authorities and see their movements fade away. I think Gamaliel sensed something different about this movement. Not that many weeks had passed since Peter stood in Jerusalem and faced thousands of people, many of whom were the enemies of Jesus who had been responsible for his crucifixion. Cowardly Peter, now emboldened by the resurrection of Jesus, preached one of the most powerful sermons in all of history. The Scripture tells us three thousand from that angry crowd became believers that day. One of the factors may have been that the authorities had tried to produce the body of Jesus but couldn't. They tried a cover-up, but evidently that had also failed. Now, seeing the miraculous transformation of Peter, could it be that they put it all together and finally saw that it was not a hoax? And might Gamaliel, a highly influential and respected member of the Sanhedrin, have been one in the crowd? Whatever the reason, Gamaliel's words of wisdom proferred sound advice then, and offer sound advice today: if Jesus' resurrection is true, and if it is the focus of our testimony, nothing will be able to stop it. The power of resurrection witness stood at the epicenter of the explosion of Christianity that transformed the world. It can become the same power source today.

Gamaliel's speech persuaded them:

> *...and when they had called in the apostles, they beat them and charged them not to speak in the name of Jesus, and let them go. (Acts 5: 40 ESV)*

Before the resurrection of Jesus his disciples would have cowered at the thought of physical punishment. Before the resurrection they would have heeded the threat of further beatings and retreated into silence. Not now:

*Then they left the presence of the council, rejoicing that they were counted worthy to suffer dishonor for the name* **[referring to the titles 'Lord' and 'Christ', both resurrection titles]**. *And every day, in the temple and from house to house, they did not cease teaching and preaching* **[the gospel concerning the resurrection]** *Jesus as the Christ* **[validated as Christ the anointed One through the resurrection power of God]**. *(Acts 5: 41–42 ESV)*

We said earlier in the chapter: the resurrection power of God stands in stark contrast and in a position of superiority over man's cruel act of crucifixion. The interjection of the word 'but' (you killed him, *but* God raised him) created the antithesis between the two. Again in these following passages we see the positive power of God overwhelming the negative deed of men:

[Peter at Cornelius' house in the presence of a large gathering] ***"They put him to death by hanging him on a tree, BUT God raised him on the third day* [emphasis mine]** *and made him to appear, not to all the people but to us who had been chosen by God as witnesses, who ate and drank with him after he rose from the dead. And he commanded us to preach to the people and to testify that he is the one appointed by God to be judge of the living and the dead. To him all the prophets bear witness that everyone who believes in him receives forgiveness of sins through his name." (Acts 10: 39–43 ESV)*

[Paul at Pisidian Antioch] ***"BUT he whom God raised up did not see corruption* [emphasis mine]**. *Let it be known to you therefore, brothers, that through this man forgiveness of sins is proclaimed to you and by him everyone who believes is freed from everything from which you could not be freed by the law of Moses." (Acts 13: 37–39 ESV)*

God has designated Jesus, the validated Christ, as the authority who acquits sin. He has done this through the exercise of his power in the resurrection of his son. Faith in the One God raised grants forgiveness. I can't help thinking that the Christian reader who is so used to hearing salvation is ours through the sacrifice and death of Jesus is feeling a bit distressed over the avoidance of such a testimony. As we have seen thus far, the *Acts of the Apostles* gives us little choice—the resurrection is God's answer to the crucifixion and validates the 'sin offering' of his son.

## Using Resurrections Words and Phrases

Before bringing this chapter to a close I suggest we apply our newly gained 'resurrection words and titles' to one more passage of Scripture: Romans 1: 1 – 4, 16. In this *Epistle to the Romans*, the Apostle Paul develops the major and defining theological basis for the atoning sacrifice of Jesus. Sixteen chapters build the foundation for understanding why the Son of God had to die. In some quarters Paul has been called the author of the 'theology of the cross.' I've deliberately chosen this epistle to demonstrate Paul's strong resurrection centeredness *because* of its emphasis on the meaning of the sacrifice.

You might wonder why the passage we're using is the opening verses that constitute the 'greeting'. Usually when readers begin any of the Epistles the temptation is to move quickly past the greeting to get to the 'heart' of the letter. We want to skip over the 'to whom it may concern', or 'dear sir or madam', or 'dear occupant', considering them perfunctory or void of any serious consequence. That is also what I used to think. No more.

In the 'greeting' the Epistle writer gives us a concise description of his position, his stance, or his context. He is telling us that no matter what subject he will develop in his letter, we should pay close attention to the greeting, the posture and platform from which he will address the issue. The remarkable discovery is that in every case the author of each Epistle approaches his concerns from a solid resurrection platform. He is telling us that everything he will write needs to be seen in the light of the resurrection of Jesus. The only way we can know that is to apply the 'resurrection words and titles' outlined earlier in the chapter. As I have done and have suggested for your practice, every time we come to one of the words or titles we will stop and put in the parenthetic statement which I believe reveals the resurrection intention of that word or title. Here is Romans 1: 1–4, and 16:

> *Paul, a servant of Christ Jesus* [stop: **Christ, that is, validated as Christ the anointed One through the resurrection power of God**], *called to be an apostle* [stop: **one who has seen the risen Christ and testifies about him**], *set apart for the gospel of God* [stop: **the 'good news' of the resurrection**]*—which he promised beforehand through his prophets in the holy Scriptures, concerning his Son, who was descended from David according to the flesh and was declared to be the Son of God in power according to the Spirit of holiness* **by his resurrection from the dead** [**emphasis mine**]*, Jesus Christ* [stop: **validated as Christ the anointed One through the resurrection power of God**] *our Lord* [stop: **validated as the sovereign Lord through the resurrection power of God**]... *(Romans 1: 1–4 ESV)*

So much for a 'to whom it may concern' greeting! What an overwhelming emphasis on resurrection, and that is just the first four verses of Romans! Let's continue with verse 16:

> *For I am not ashamed of the gospel* [stop: **the 'good news' of the resurrection**]*, for it is the power of God for salvation to everyone who believes... (Romans 1: 16 ESV)*

Who can dispute the fact that Paul is approaching his treatise on the meaning of Jesus' sacrifice from his very solid stand on the power of the resurrection? Everything he says in the letter to the Romans ab-solutely must be seen through the prism of Paul's 'resurrection eyes'. To consider all he says about the atoning sacrifice separate from the resurrection does Paul a great and tragic disservice and distorts our understanding of the fullness of the Gospel.

This is an example of how inserting the 'resurrection words and titles' can transform our reading and understanding of the *Acts of the Apostles* and all the *Epistles*. We hold in our hands the evidence of the certainty of the resurrection that propelled all the writers of the Greek Scriptures—the New Testament—and shined a beacon on what had given them the greatest of hope.

The early Church as portrayed in the *Acts of the Apostles* stood on the platform of *Resurrection Sunday* and saw that it was the risen Christ who bestowed salvation. It's very clear. We have seen it in nu-merous passages throughout Luke's account, and we didn't quote all of them.

How could we have missed it? The early Church was rooted in the resurrection of Jesus; the Church for more than one and a half millennia has planted itself in the crucifixion of Jesus: Friday for the contemporary Church, Sunday for the early Church. What a differ-ence two days makes! It is challenging for us to get to the resurrection through the eyes of the cross. We have attempted to demonstrate how our emphasis on Jesus' crucifixion sacrifice makes his resurrection recede from our consciousness. For the disciples on Good Friday the cross also was the end of the story, but for a different reason; no one had ever survived a crucifixion. Even after Jesus had told his follow-ers there would be a 'third day resurrection' they continued to be blinded by his crucifixion. They had a difficult time getting past his death. How much energy and confrontation did it take to convince the disciples, consumed by the remembrance of Friday that Sunday had given birth to a resurrected Jesus? It took fully three reports, the final the actual physical presence of Christ himself, a luxury not avail-able to us.

To transplant the contemporary Church from Friday to Sunday

will not and should not require that the Friday event be abandoned. That would be just as tragic as our inability to embrace Sunday. Jesus *had* to die. There was no other way our sins could be accounted for. *The problem is not our embrace of the Friday event; it is our benign disengagement with the Sunday event.* Jesus' sacrifice must not be diminished. It is his resurrection that needs to be greatly enhanced. We will elaborate on this in a later chapter, but for now we must come to realize this truth: Friday without Sunday has no power or authority to accomplish anything. More to the point, Sunday is the only way to make sense of Friday. The sacrifice only takes on meaning, power and authority through God's validation and acceptance of the sacrifice manifested through his resurrection power on Sunday. The Sunday event makes possible the embrace of Friday. Believing this, the proper, biblical way to approach the cross of Jesus is to go by way of the resurrection every time. The crucifixion has authority for salvation only because of the resurrection. We absolutely must root ourselves first and uppermost in the resurrection. This is the simple, clear message of the *Acts of the Apostles*.

The explosion of faith in the risen Christ transformed the Greco-Roman world. In a few short years the Gospel of the risen Lord spread throughout the empire resulting in tens of thousands of believers. And to think that all of this was accomplished by a few men in sandaled feet and sailboats! If the *Acts of the Apostles* shows the great results of preaching resurrection with limited resources, imagine what could happen in our day with our vast technological resources coupled with ease of transport, if we were to preach the same message of hope in the resurrection.

What are we to make of all this? Is our emphasis on Jesus' sacrifice totally out of step with the early Church, or with the New Testament for that matter? If the only New Testament book we had, apart from the Gospels, was the *Acts of the Apostles* our answer would have to be *yes*. The witness of the early Church grew out of the resurrection of Jesus and concentrated on it almost single-mindedly. From the very first steps ventured out from the upper room to the proclamation at the center of the Roman Empire almost thirty years later, words of witness and the plan for salvation were fused with the resurrection of Jesus. That it was a successful message is an understatement. We are told that thousands believed in a single day! As we have said, Acts, chapter two, tells us that following the first post-resurrection sermon preached by Peter, three thousand converts were baptized. Resurrection preaching is incredibly explosive.

While this fact is wonderfully exciting it is nonetheless an incomplete picture. There are other books, and they ask the question, *"What was accomplished by the death of Jesus? He had to have died for a reason."*

As we continue it will become clear that both the death and resurrection of Jesus are important in the plan of salvation. We will see an unusual and unique relationship between those two events. Suffice it to say, at this juncture, that the event of the crucifixion will never outweigh the event of the resurrection anywhere in the New Testament corpus. The resurrection stood supreme in the witness of the early Church. Where is that supremacy today?

CHAPTER **Five**

# The Gospel According To The Apostle Paul

I GREW UP believing the cross of Jesus to be the central pillar, if not the complete basis for Christian theology. Jesus died for me, and that expression of God's love was all I needed. To believe it, and to accept it, granted eternal life. Running rampant through the prayers of fellow worshippers, through hymns I knew by heart, and through the preaching of countless men and women of God was the confession of glory in the sacrifice and death of Jesus. Jesus died for me. That's all I needed to know, and it all stopped there.

The person most often quoted was the apostle Paul. I became convinced it was Paul's words that provided the proof for the centrality of the cross. The testimonies of countless believers incorporated the following verses,

> For I decided to know nothing among you except Jesus
> Christ and him crucified. (I Corinthians 2: 2 ESV)

> But far be it from me to boast except in the cross of our
> Lord Jesus Christ, by which the world has been crucified
> to me, and I to the world. (Galatians 6: 14 ESV)

Even that most solemn moment each month, the sacrament of Holy Communion, resounded with the words I came to believe were among the most important Paul ever uttered:

> For as often as you eat this bread and drink the cup, you
> proclaim the Lord's death until he comes. (I Corinthians
> 11: 26 ESV)

Resurrection word weren't completely avoided, but they always seemed to slide backwards into the cross. Sermons on Galatians 2: 20—'I have been crucified with Christ. It is no longer I who live, but Christ who lives in me'—always concentrated on the first sentence.

Later, as I matured in the faith and grew more familiar with Scripture these verses became confusing to me. In one place Paul said, in effect, 'I glory only in the cross of Christ'. But in II Timothy 2: 8, he said, 'Remember Jesus Christ, risen from the dead…as preached in my Gospel.' Which is it, Paul? Is it the cross or the resurrection? Are you speaking out of both sides of your mouth? Aren't these verses contradictory in their emphasis? They are, unless we understand the title Christ as a resurrection word; only then is the contradiction re-solved. Paul is saying, in Galatians 6: 14, that he wants only to glory in the cross of Christ, that is, the one validated as the Christ in the resurrection. And in I Corinthians 2: 2 he wants to bear witness of the Christ, the risen One, who was also crucified. Seeing the word Christ as a resurrection title is the key that answers the question. The Good Friday and Easter events are fused in Paul's mind, inseparable! He embraces the efficacy of the sacrifice, the cross and the crucifixion only because there was a validating resurrection! Potential contradic-tion resolved!

I became convinced through this interpretation that Paul was not a death-minded person! His emphasis was placed very solidly on the resurrection of Jesus first and foremost. All he says of the cross is root-ed in the power of the resurrection. Resurrection is the soil; out of it grows a theology of the cross. Take away the resurrection soil and the tender plant of the cross has no meaning, no support, no vindication, and dies. To treat Paul as a theologian who sees the cross without the eyes of the resurrection is to do his thinking a great injustice.

We, the Church, have made a mess of Paul's resurrection thinking; essentially, we have ignored it. Let me try to outline a brief argument in support of the thesis that Paul is above all a life-minded and resurrection-centered believer.

## The Damascus Road Conversion of Saul

Paul, as Saul, was completely aware of the crucifixion, yet he continued to persecute the followers of Jesus. Saul had even heard the resurrection witness of the early believers, but evidently considered it a foolish tale. He stood by and watched the stoning of Stephen that resulted from the martyr's resurrection witness. I wouldn't be surprised if it was Saul who, with a nod of his head, set the stoning in motion. Saul had ample opportunity to become a believer in the crucified One and the power of the cross, but didn't. It took the assault by the risen Christ to convert him!

Paul's theology must have grown out of that conversion experience—and what an experience it was. As he traveled toward Damascus to continue his persecution of the Christians, he was struck down by the blinding light and deafening voice of the risen Christ:

> [Paul's defense before King Agrippa]... *I journeyed to Damascus with the authority and commission of the chief priests. At midday, O king, I saw on the way a light from heaven, brighter than the sun that shone around me and those who journeyed with me. And when we had all fallen to the ground, I heard a voice saying to me in the Hebrew language, 'Saul, Saul, why are you persecuting me? It is hard for you to kick against the goads.' And I said, 'Who are you, Lord?' And the Lord said, 'I am Jesus whom you are persecuting. But rise and stand upon your feet, for I have appeared to you for this purpose, to appoint you as a servant and witness to the things in which you have seen*

*me and to those in which I will appear to you, delivering
you from your people and from the Gentiles—to whom I
am sending you to open their eyes, so that they may turn
from darkness to light and from the power of Satan to
God, that they may receive forgiveness of sins and a place
among those who are sanctified by faith in me.' (Acts 26:
12-18 ESV)*

His conversion, from the most feared enemy of the early Church
to the boldest messenger for Christ dates to that instant. How could
he ever forget it? It is foolish to think such an incredibly explosive
encounter with the risen Christ could ever recede into the shadow of
emphasis on the crucified Jesus. His vision of the resurrected Christ
and the transforming power of that experience must have illumined
every word he ever spoke to the Church.

That this experience was important in the life of Paul is evidenced
in the *Acts of the Apostles* where it is stated in great detail three times!
Apart from Gospel accounts of Jesus' life and ministry no other event
is reiterated like this one. The fact that Luke, the author of Acts, spun
out the story three times is ample evidence Paul was continually talking about it. If Luke had recorded every instance of Paul's Damascus
road retelling, I'm certain the book would be much longer! Three
times is enough to convince us of the centrality of that transforming
event in Paul's life. As Paul relates it, Ananias spoke the word of the
Lord to him:

*"The God of our Fathers appointed you to know His will,
to see the Righteous One and to hear a voice from his
mouth; for you will be a witness for him to everyone of
what you have seen and heard." (Acts 22: 14-15 ESV)*

In this command Ananias was referring to the blinding light and
deafening voice of the resurrected Lord.

In his own retelling of the event we see that Paul considered his calling to be one of witnessing to the risen Christ who had confronted him. Further, he seemed convinced that forgiveness of sins came through confession of the name of the resurrected One. There are no words in his testimonies in Acts that give salvific significance to the Good Friday event. Such words are completely absent.

It isn't only in the *Acts of the Apostles* that Paul is pictured as being convinced of the saving power of the resurrection Gospel. In the following passages from Romans (a passage recounted in the previous chapter and worthy of reiteration) and I Corinthians Paul is just as clear and unequivocal. Read them with the resurrection words from the previous chapter in mind:

> *Paul, a servant of Christ Jesus* [stop: Christ, that is, validated as Christ the anointed One through the resurrection power of God], *called to be an apostle* [stop: one who has seen the risen Christ and testifies about him], *set apart for the gospel of God* [stop: the 'good news' of the resurrection] — *which he promised beforehand through his prophets in the holy Scriptures, concerning his Son, who was descended from David according to the flesh and was declared to be the Son of God in power according to the Spirit of holiness by his resurrection from the dead* [emphasis mine], *Jesus Christ* [stop: validated as Christ the anointed One through the resurrection power of God] *our Lord* [stop: validated as the sovereign Lord through the resurrection power of God].... *For I am not ashamed of the [resurrection] gospel, for it is the power of God* [power manifested in the raising of His Son] *for salvation to everyone who believes...* (Romans 1: 1-4, 16 ESV)

> *Now I would remind you, brothers, of the gospel* [the good news of the resurrection] *I preached to you, which you received, in which you stand, and by which you are being saved... And if Christ* [validated as the Christ through

> **the resurrection]** *has not been raised, then our preaching is in vain and your faith is in vain. We are even found to be misrepresenting God, because we testified about God that he raised Christ, whom he did not raise if it is true that the dead are not raised. For if the dead are not raised, not even Christ has been raised. And if Christ has not been raised, your faith is futile and you are still in your sins. (I Corinthians 15: 1-2, 14-17 ESV)*

# Paul declares his Apostleship

His Damascus road vision of Christ in his risen glory was considered by Paul to be a substantiation of his apostolic calling. Only those who had seen the resurrected Christ had the right and the authority to be called *apostles*. Apostleship and resurrection are therefore solidly and permanently linked, as we discussed in detail in the previous chapter. Paul's authority as an apostle is derived exclusively from his experience with the resurrected Jesus, and he knows it! In Galatians, chapter one, he brings it again to the attention of his readers. It seems Paul went out of his way in his writings to verify and substantiate his claim to apostleship through that Damascus road confrontation with the risen Lord. He must have known that unless he could be accepted as a legitimate *apostle* his message would not carry the weight and authority necessary for its proclamation.

The growing Church wanted words from those who had had experiences with the risen Christ; such persons could be trusted because the searing fire of the resurrection experience would certainly have observably transformed their existence. Paul knew full well the authority that was commanded by the title *apostle*, and he knew of the early Church's respect for such witnesses. An apostle was responding to the highest calling, the calling of the actual presence of the risen Christ. If one were to be introduced as an apostle, the audience knew immediately that his words would be spoken in the light of that remarkable experience. They would be inclined to accept the words of such a witness, knowing the ordination of God's resurrection power stood behind them. Paul knew unless he could speak as one 'ordained' in this way he would have no credibility in the emerging Church. He was convinced that only the power attained through the actual appearance of the risen Christ would make one bold enough, audacious enough to speak this resurrection message which to the pagan world was so absurd, illogical and unreasonable. He *had* to establish his resurrection credentials. He understood the way to salvation was via the resurrection of Jesus following and linked to his crucifixion. He may not have had the opportunity to be one of the original followers of Jesus who ate and drank with him following his resurrection, but Paul believed his interception by the resurrected One on his way to Damascus certified his apostleship. He may have been 'untimely born', as he said, but he was certain of his calling nonetheless.

The command and will of God was that he should witness and testify to what he had seen and heard, that is, the blinding light and deafening voice of the risen Christ on the Damascus road. If we knew that Paul disobeyed God's commandment—speaking only of Jesus' sacrifice at the expense of the resurrection—would we trust him? Would we believe anything he said? In effect, our lack of witness to the resurrection witness of Paul is an act of disobedience and a denial of the life-changing vision behind his ministry.

## The Two Faces of Transformation

In categorizing Paul's words several themes emerge. One of the more prominent is that of *transformation*. Paul's personal transformation resulted from the intervention of the risen Lord. The Damascus road experience was the bridge by means of which Paul was able to move from the old life governed by sin to the new life filled with the power of the Holy Spirit. The Christ-event forced Paul to make two decisions. First, he had to put away the old life, and his own 'old life' was one of murder and mayhem against the fledgling community of Christians. As he said, put it to death, a fate that it deserved. Paul's letters contain many references to the crucifying of the old person. He spoke of dying to sin, to the law, to the world. He knew that only through this dying could he be transformed or resurrected to a new life. The purpose of dying, then, was to live. It wasn't enough just to die. The death of Jesus is important for Paul in this process because it is only through the his death on the cross that Jesus,

> …[forgave] us all our trespasses, by canceling the record of debt that stood against us with its legal demands. This he set aside, nailing it to the cross. He disarmed the rulers and authorities and put them to open shame, by triumphing over them in him. (Colossians 2: 13-15 ESV)

We have no power or authority in ourselves to put our sins to death. The cancellation of them is already complete in Jesus' obedient sacrifice. We must only claim the forgiveness. It is the love of Christ, expressed in his willingness to be obedient even unto death that compels us to make that claim:

> …and he died for all, that those who live might no longer live for themselves but for him who for their sake died **and was raised** [emphasis mine]…. that is, in Christ [**proved as Christ in the resurrection**] God was reconciling the world to himself, not counting their trespasses against them, and entrusting to us the message of reconciliation. Therefore, we are ambassadors for Christ [**the risen One**], God making his appeal through us. We implore you on behalf of Christ [**the name of the risen One**], be reconciled to God. For our sake he made him to be sin who knew no sin, so that in him we might become the righteousness of God. (II Corinthians 5: 15, 19-21 ESV)

If, contrary to what this passage tells us, the mission and the purpose of Jesus were completely fulfilled in his dying, we would have every reason in the world to concentrate on that sacrifice. We would be compelled to think on it, to emphasize it, to make it the center of our theology. It would be reasonable to perpetually contemplate the ugliness of our sins in order that we might thereby begin to comprehend the magnitude of Jesus' sacrifice. This is in fact what we do.

I remember as a young boy how thrilled I was to hear the testimonies of visiting speakers who had lived lives of sin much more horrible than I, an innocent small town boy, could ever imagine. These stories of wretched lives circulated throughout our church long before the speakers arrived—the greater the life of debauchery to be told, the greater the numbers of those who came to listen. Usually the speaker would go on for nearly an hour reciting episode after episode of wretchedness while the listeners sat in rapt attention on the edges of their seats. We young boys would sit in the front with wide eyes and gaping jaws. We had never heard of such sins before! I remember how often I was slightly jealous and envious. "Why couldn't I have been saved from a life as wretched and miserable as that?", I uttered. Then, at the end of an hour of recounted and remembered horrors, he would give one minute or less to the good news of God's transforming power—"But God saved me", he would say, and then sit down. I shouted my 'hallelujahs' along with everyone else at these words of deliverance from sin, but it was the lurid details of the life of sin that were remembered and talked about, in the same way they had been emphasized by the speaker.

We heard all about being rescued from the old life of sin. But what about the nature of new life made possible by the transformation? There was never any elaboration on the meaning of the new life that had replaced the old life. I often wondered, "Are we only transformed *from* something and not *for* something?" What kind of Christian life is it if we are only forgiven sinners not set upon the promised path of a truly *new life*? We spend immense energies leading people to the forgiveness offered by the sacrifice of Jesus, and rightly so. If only we would spend equal energies shepherding them into the abundant life, the truly redeemed and resurrected life promised by the risen Lord!

It seems as if we are in a prison of our own making. Christ the Judge has granted us full pardon. The record of our trial is torn to shreds. Our fingerprints and mug shots are destroyed. The computer memory of our misdeeds is erased and cancelled out. The hard drive backup has crashed. Nowhere is there anymore a record of our previous life. A new memory has been installed to record our transformed existence. We have become completely free to begin a new life totally unencumbered by remembrances of the past. The jailhouse doors have been thrown open. We, however, refuse to leave. We like life there. We have chosen to remain forever apologetic, contrite and consumed by guilt even though the Judge has said, *"I have forgiven you.... I have pardoned you.... Go and sin no more.... Your sins are as far removed as the east is from the west.... I don't even remember them."*

Imagine, the Omniscient One, Mind of very mind—who knows the number of hairs on our heads and keeps a running account of the shifting grains of sand on every wind and surf swept beach—no longer remembers our sins! Think for a moment about the biblical metaphor of 'east' and 'west'. If God had said our sins were removed as far as the north is from the south, that wouldn't have been far at all: I could stand at the equator with one foot in the northern hemisphere and the other in the southern hemisphere. My sins wouldn't be removed any further than one foot is from the other. But if I go east, west is always behind me, and if I go west east is always ahead of me. No matter where I am, east or west always remain beyond me. So are our sins in the mind of God.

If God chooses to cancel our sins out of his memory, and he does, why do we persist in them? If God commands us to be loosed from the power of sin doesn't he also desire that we, like him, be loosed from the memory of it as well? As Paul said:

> *...forgetting what lies behind and straining forward to what lies ahead. (Philippians 3: 13 ESV)*

Even though the final judgment is still a coming reality, isn't it counter-productive to keep our sins at the forefront of our minds? Paul would have us put them to the side and move on.

Transformation, then, is more than being changed or delivered *from* something. Jesus affected that first stage when he died, when he took our sins to their grave. But because God raised Jesus to new life, transformation itself takes on a second stage; we become changed or delivered *for* something. The resurrection of Jesus sealed the *'from'* of the old world of sin and opened the pathway *'for'* the new order of abundant and everlasting life.

> *Therefore, if anyone is in Christ* **[the risen One],** *he is a new creation. The old has passed away; behold, the new has come. (II Corinthians 5: 17 ESV)*

It is not enough merely to claim the forgiveness of our sins, which was accomplished in the crucifixion of Jesus; we must also embrace the new life, which was made possible through the resurrection.

> *If then you have been raised with Christ, seek the things that are above, where Christ is, seated at the right hand of God. Set your minds on things that are above, not on things that are on earth. (Colossians 3: 1-2ESV)*

Why is it we are professionals when it comes to claiming forgiveness, but rank amateurs in the practice of embracing new life? Why do we live in the *'from'* and not in the *'for'* of transformation? Why are we content with the 'forgiven' life divorced from the fullness pledged and sealed by the resurrection of Jesus? Why are we more intrigued with death than life?

Paul's entire message can be summed up in the two-faceted nature of transformation, both the *'from'* and the *'for'* of it. He never leaves us in doubt of the latter. His absolute certainty of the resurrection colors his entire attitude toward the Christian life of faith. There can be no disputing that for Paul the resurrection was,

> ...central to his whole approach to Jesus Christ. He provides
> a full exposition of the Easter faith, which is nevertheless
> expounded in such a way as to leave no doubt that for him
> the resurrection was a fact of history. This central position
> of the resurrection is in full accord with the Acts narrative
> about the apostle's experience and preaching. [1]

It is simply a gross distortion of human emotion and psychology to think that Paul could have had the Damascus road experience with the risen Christ and not have it dominate his heart and mind for the rest of his life.

Paul knew a miserable 'from' and he also rejoiced in his glorious 'for'. He was convinced not only of forgiveness but also of purpose, the former through the death of Jesus and the latter through his resurrection. Search his writings and you will find the two together:

> ...put off your old self, which belongs to your former man-
> ner of life and is corrupt through deceitful desires, and be
> renewed in the spirit of your minds and put on the new
> self, created after the likeness of God in true righteousness
> and holiness. (Ephesians 4: 22-24 ESV)

One cannot escape the movement in these verses from the event of the cross toward the event of the resurrection. The phrase, *new nature of God's creating,* is used by Paul as a rather beautiful way of saying that it was by the power of God that Jesus was raised to begin the new order filled with promise for all humankind. It is this new nature toward which we who believe are heading. It is as if creation has begun again, a new Genesis so to speak.

If I could choose one passage from the entire New Testament that accurately describes the proper procedure of Christian faith and witness it would be this:

*...that I may know him* **[the One validated as Christ through the resurrection]** *and the power of his resurrection, and may share his sufferings, becoming like him in his death, that by any means possible I may attain the resurrection from the dead. (Philippians 3: 10-11 ESV)*

Notice the order. Paul begins with the resurrection: to know Christ, the risen One, and then to experience resurrection power. Only when he has placed himself firmly in the hands of the risen One and experienced the power derived from him is he enabled to move back and share in the suffering and death of Jesus. Why is he willing to suffer? Because he knows that God, through Christ, has made his own resurrection possible. For Paul the resurrection is the starting block of the Christian faith. It is the pathway to the cross. For him the doorway to 'cross carrying' is resurrection power promised by God in the Easter event. This precise ordering of things is exactly the way it should be done in our corporate worship as well as in all the activities of our spiritual lives.

## The Supremacy of the Resurrection

Beyond what we have said of the two-fold act of Jesus—his death and resurrection—and Paul's corresponding idea of the dual nature of transformation—the *'from'* and the *'for'*—there remains still another Pauline concept. It regards the supremacy of the resurrection, and can be summed up in the words, *'much more'*. Each time I read Paul's letters I become increasingly convinced that he attaches much more importance, power and authority to the resurrection of Jesus than to his death. Not that he underplays the significance of Jesus' death, but rather, he senses it is the resurrection that ennobles and empowers the sacrifice and gives it meaning. I have found I am not alone in this view. Everywhere I turn in my research I find theologians of every persuasion saying the same thing. Even those who do not themselves accept the historical fact of the resurrection confess it is the central pillar of Paul's theology. As Neville Clark says, speaking of Paul's view,

> 'Without the resurrection the cross remains tragedy and defeat....'[2]

Another author writes,

> '...instead of the cross being the defeat of righteousness, it is God's victory through the resurrection.'[3]

The new world has dawned, not in the death, but in the resurrection of Jesus. Albert Schweitzer warned that Paul's theology becomes thoroughly tangled and unintelligibly chaotic unless viewed from a single position, one unifying center,

> '...and that center is the raising of Christ from the dead.'[4]

Paul indeed speaks of the cross. We, however, have tended to be selective in our view of Paul's writings, creating a distortion of the 'theology of the cross' which almost completely overlooks or at the very least diminishes the importance of the resurrection in the doctrine of salvation. It is important to realize that,

> 'It is only because of the attestation of the Risen One that the death of Jesus becomes an essentially theological problem.... Thus cross and resurrection stand in the relation of riddle and interpretation—and indeed in such a way that the very raising of the theological question is conditioned by the answer of the resurrection.'[5]

Said another way, the answer provided by the resurrection of Jesus *preceded* the question of Good Friday. Would any of the disciples have been able to answer the eternal question, *"Why do good persons die?* "All the speculation in the world would not have provided either a satisfactory answer or solace. Only the resurrection allows a satisfactory answer to the question.

This appears to be the way it was for Paul. The new life began for him with a resurrection experience. It is only over the years of his ministry that the question of theological meaning was raised regarding the cross. But never did his view of the importance of the cross grow to outweigh or overshadow his sense of the pre-eminence of the resurrection. The latter was always *'much more'*. Examples of this attitude are numerous. In his great exposition on the resurrection, I Corinthians 15, references leap off the page:

> And if Christ has not been raised, then our preaching is in
> vain and your faith is in vain. (I Corinthians 15: 14 ESV)

This verse leaves no doubt that in Paul's mind the sacrifice accomplishes nothing without the Easter event, thereby intimating that the latter has *'much more'* importance. Some translations substitute the phrase *null and void* following the words *preaching* and *faith*: "And if Christ has not been raised, your preaching and your faith are null and void.* "I once asked an attorney for a definition of the legal term *'null and void'*. His answer brought home to me in a powerful way the true and deep meaning of the verse: *"As if it never existed".* I have heard this exact definition from many in the legal profession. If Christ was not raised it would be as if our faith and the good news never existed! The crucifixion by itself is not the fount of good news or faith. The same can be said of verse 17:

> And if Christ has not been raised, your faith is futile and
> you are still in your sins. (I Corinthians 15: 17 ESV)

Wait a minute! I thought the death of Jesus cancelled out sin! According to Paul, not until the death was accepted and validated by the resurrection power of God did Jesus' death have any significance. Can you see how lacking in biblical truth it is to persist in our often-heard testimony, "I'm so glad Jesus died for me so that I could have forgiveness for sin and eternal life"? To talk about the cross of Jesus without continuing on to the resurrection power of God that authenticated it is wrong! These verses truly accord supremacy to the resurrection. Even the words, *'Death is swallowed up in victory' (I Corinthians 15: 54)* render death subservient to life. Romans 5: 10 continues the emphasis:

> *For if while we were enemies we were reconciled to God by the death of his Son, **much more** [emphasis mine], now that we are reconciled, shall we be saved by his life.*

The capstone verse, the one which leaves no doubt as to where Paul stands, is found in Romans 8: 34:

> *Who is to condemn? Christ Jesus is the one who died— **more than that, who was raised** [emphasis mine]…*

Paul could have said, 'also was raised', 'in addition was raised' or 'and was raised'; such wording would suggest equality between the two events. However, he chose to say 'more than that', who was raised. Doesn't Paul's choice of words here indicate where he stands regarding the supremacy of the resurrection?

How can we read these passages and persist in our practice of placing the Good Friday event at the center of human history? How can we believe the cross to be the fulcrum point of theology? How can we honestly spend such incredible energies in our worship practices on attitudes related primarily to the sacrifice while at the same time, perhaps unconsciously, we keep resurrection-mindedness in extremely low profile? If we take Paul at his word we must come to the conclusion that the cross and the death of Jesus have no power to cancel sin unless the resurrection follows (I Corinthians 15: 17). Only the resurrection gave meaning and power to the submission of Jesus to the cross. The crucifixion can only stand in tandem with and supported by the resurrection; it cannot stand by itself, as if it alone is all we need, the way Christians for more than thirteen hundred years seem to have treated it. In our preaching, witnessing, singing, and praying, in all our clichés and liturgical formulas, the cross must be approached only in union with or through the words and eyes of the resurrection event. To do otherwise is to rob the crucifixion of any power and authority it has. As Paul has said, without the resurrection of Jesus we remain controlled by the power of sin.

## The Death and Resurrection of Jesus are Inseparable

With these two Pauline concepts in mind—*transformation* and *the pre-eminence of the resurrection*—is it thereby possible to postulate that Paul considers resurrection the key to liberation from sin? Does he link forgiveness with the risen rather than the crucified Jesus? As we noted in a previous chapter, the book of Acts tends to substantiate this position (Acts 2: 38; 5: 31; 10:43; 13: 38; 22: 16; 26: 18). Many other passages take a stance parallel to Acts, including the following:

> *For I am not ashamed of the Gospel* **[the good news of the resurrection]**, *for it is the power of God for salvation to everyone who believes. (Romans 1: 16 ESV)*

> *...God was able to do what he had promised. That is why his faith was counted to him as righteousness. But the words "it was counted to him" were not written for his sake alone, but for ours also. It will be counted to us who believe in him who raised from the dead Jesus our Lord, who was delivered up for our trespasses and raised for our justification. (Romans 4: 21-25 ESV)*

> *But if Christ* **[the risen One]** *is in you, although the body is dead because of sin, the Spirit is life because of*

*righteousness. If the Spirit of him who raised Jesus from the dead dwells in you, he who raised Christ Jesus from the dead will also give life to your mortal bodies through his Spirit who dwells in you. (Romans 8: 10-11 ESV)*

We would be unfair to Paul's theology, however, if we discounted his understanding of the sacrifice as a vital part of the plan of salvation. While it is true that Paul places the resurrection in a position of supremacy, it is nonetheless only as a validation and acceptance of the sacrifice, and, as such, can have no meaning without that sacrifice. The same can be said of the sacrifice without the resurrection. Herein lays another concept found in Paul's writings: *the death and resurrection of Jesus are fused, inseparable events, each deriving its meaning from the other.* Theologian Künneth refers to it as, *'indissoluble unity'*[6]. Together, and only together do they provide forgiveness for the sinner. If salvation is promised in the crucifixion, it is delivered in the resurrection. If sacrifice is the obedient offering of Jesus, the resurrection is the thankful acceptance by God. If the cross is condemnation of sin, the resurrection is vindication of the Sinless One. We have said that the death of Jesus has absolutely no meaning apart from the resurrection. We have also stated that the reverse is also true. If nothing had been accomplished by the death of Jesus nothing would have resulted from the resurrection, save God's reclaiming of his son. To minimize one is to minimize both. If the crucifixion was no great sacrifice, then the resurrection was no great victory. Take away one and the other vanishes into meaninglessness. Power is derived only from their union. 'Death' and 'Resurrection' cannot be separate words when referring to Jesus. They must become hyphenated in our theology: *Death-Resurrection, one new word.* They are at the same time, however, equal and unequal: equal in the sense that they together create the possibility of forgiveness and new life; unequal because, while resurrection implies that a death was involved, death without resurrection is only unrequited death. This, I believe, is the basis for Paul's placing the resurrection of Jesus, *'in principle above the cross'*.[7]

I have read Paul's letters with three questions in mind: first, how often does he talk about the death of God's son without mentioning the resurrection; second, how often does he mention Jesus' resurrection with no word of his death; and third, how often are the two words and events 'hyphenated', that is, death and resurrection in sequence together? Answers to these questions constitute a rather startling revelation of Paul's belief.

The fewest references are given to 'death' alone. 'Resurrection' by itself is used only slightly more often. 'Death-Resurrection', the unified force, greatly outnumbers the other two. In all of Paul's writings as well as those thought to be 'Pauline', the 'death' of God's son is mentioned by itself as related to salvation only fifteen times. 'Resurrection' and 'Death-Resurrection' create a combined total of nearly ninety references! 90 to 15: the ratio of *Life* to *Death* is six to one in favor of Life. Interestingly, this is just the reverse ratio of death hymns versus life hymns in the standard hymnal.

This is not the last word, however. These verses need further examination, particularly those focusing on the 'death' of God's son. Paul indeed speaks of the importance of the cross, as we have said. While these passages are greatly outnumbered by resurrection passages they are important nonetheless.

If Paul says, on the one hand he prefers not to know anything save the crucified Christ (I Corinthians 2: 2), and then says he wants to know the power of Christ's resurrection (Philippians 3: 10-11), how do these verses fit his statement that the resurrection of Christ is the theme of his gospel (II Timothy 2: 8)? As we asked earlier, is Paul contradicting himself? The answer, as we have said, lies in how we understand the use of the title *'Christ'*. If we accept that *'Christ'* is a resurrection word/title, that Jesus was validated as the Christ by God's resurrection power (Acts 2: 36; Romans 1: 4), we must confess that Paul is not contradictory at all. I am convinced that in the New Testament Church those who heard or read the letters of Paul would have understood the title *'Christ'* as a reference to the risen One.

With this in mind we must re-read every Pauline passage where 'sacrifice', 'shedding of blood', 'suffering and death', 'cross', 'crucified', or any words related to the death of Jesus are used. Amazingly, we will find that the title *'Christ'* is used in place of or along with his earthly name 'Jesus' every time! The context is that it was Christ—the One raised to life by God's resurrecting power—who had been subjected to suffering and death. Paul has infused even those passages that attempt to understand the meaning of the sacrifice of God's son with the halo or light of the resurrection! If Paul had used his earthly name 'Jesus' instead of his sovereign, resurrection title 'Christ', our understanding would have to be different. The numbers we used in the previous paragraph, then, are not at all accurate in the deepest sense. All fifteen references in the 'death' column now move to the 'death-resurrection' column because he imbues Jesus' earthly name with at least one of his resurrection titles—*Lord* or *Christ*. Paul is consistent. There are no passages focused exclusively on the death of Jesus. Paul is centered on the risen 'Lord' or 'Christ' and is *looking back through the event of the resurrection to the death that preceded it*. The two events are fused. Paul is saying, 'I want to know nothing less than that the One who was raised by God's power was also given in sacrifice.' Paul stands on Easter and embraces Good Friday. Only in this light can the contradictions be resolved. Our conclusion has to be that Paul never separates 'Death' from 'Resurrection' anywhere in his writings. If there is any single message to be heeded in this book it is this: *we can concentrate on the sacrifice of Jesus as much as we want as long as we consistently approach it through the resurrection event which gave it meaning and validation.*

What does this mean? First of all, if my experience in the Christian faith is at all typical, we've been unconsciously or inadvertently misrepresenting the apostle's theology. We have emphasized his preaching of the cross completely isolated from his own view of his calling, based on his experience with the resurrected Christ on the Damascus road. We have taken him completely out of context, ignoring the weight of his resurrection teaching as well as his passion for it.

We have lost sight of key resurrection-minded words such as 'Lord', 'Christ', 'witness', 'apostle' and 'gospel', which in the early Church would have been properly understood as linked to the risen One, and which we have reduced to a watered down, imprecise, 'generic' interpretation. It also suggests that we have not traced our traditions back far enough, stopping somewhere between St. Augustine and Luther, when we should have recaptured the spirit of the *Acts of the Apostles* and Paul's missionary journeys. In so doing, we are no longer 'witnessing' in the biblical sense of the word, nor do we deserve the privilege of being called modern day apostles.

Second, we have rendered Jesus' sacrifice on the 'cross' impotent because of our shabby treatment of his resurrection. We have stripped God of his power manifested in the raising of his son. Let's be honest—most churches haven't grown, nor have they effected change in their neighborhoods or communities, possibly because they have forgotten that first message which turned the world upside down almost overnight. Our preaching has created legions of lukewarm believers who wallow so much in the guilt of forgiven and cancelled debts that new life in the risen Christ escapes them. We have forfeited the right to be called 'witnesses' because we have denied the resurrection authority by which the honor was given.

The words of Paul have much to tell us about our hope, our power, and our resources in the kingdom of God. There can be no mistaking Paul equates them with the resurrection of Jesus that he holds aloft as the measuring standard. His words have been our concern in this chapter; let them also be our guide and challenge:

> …*having the eyes of your hearts enlightened that you may know what is the* **hope** *to which he has called you, what are the* **riches of his glorious inheritance** *in the saints, and what is the* **immeasurable greatness of his power toward us** *who believe, according to the working of his great might that he worked in Christ* **when he raised him from the dead** *and seated him at his right hand in the heavenly*

*places, far above all rule and authority and power and dominion, and above every name that is named, not only in this age but also in the one to come [emphases mine]. (Ephesians 1: 18-20 ESV)*

## CHAPTER SIX

# What Is The Cross Without The Resurrection?

THE NEW TESTAMENT emphasizes the two-fold act of Jesus: his death *and* resurrection. Not even a casual reader would disagree. What has been missed is how strongly the Scriptural texts suggest their inseparability. In essence death and resurrection constitute one event, taking place over a period of three days. They are two sides of the same coin. The risen Lord is the crucified Jesus, and the crucified Jesus is the risen Lord. There is no alternative to this thinking. In spite of our practice—emphasizing Jesus' death with little regard for the imbalance thus created—we must finally confess that it is wrong to speak of one without speaking of the other.

It can also be stated that within this single two-faceted event one of the facets is pre-eminent: the resurrection of Jesus. Much more verbal activity surrounds it throughout the New Testament than surrounds the crucifixion, though neither facet has any possibility of spiritual merit without the other. It is theologically correct to say that only through the resurrection is the sacrifice of Jesus on the 'cross' validated. The crucifixion cannot validate itself; no evidence exists in the New Testament to support such a claim. Our practice has been to view the crucifixion as a single event containing in itself its own efficacy. We must abandon that approach and encounter and examine everything the New Testament says about the crucifixion through the resurrection side of the coin.

Remember as a child how you would put a coin on its edge, flick it with your finger and watch it spin? Heads and tails became blurred; you couldn't distinguish one from the other. They became fused while the coin was spinning. This is a good picture of the Death-Resurrection fusion we have been talking about: the spinning coin. While it would be best to keep the coin spinning perpetually it inevitably falls, exposing only one side. In the first centuries of the Christian era the coin figuratively fell resurrection side up. The last 1300 years have seen the reverse.

Even with the resurrection side up, the cross is not to be ignored. Jesus' suffering and death must not be minimized. He paid a horrible price when he submitted to the cross. That price was the measure of our personal and collective sin-guiltiness. For one man to die for another would be sacrifice enough, especially when the manner of the sacrifice is crucifixion. But for one man to die in the place of the entire population of history compounds and exceeds our sense of the tragedy and suffering he was called upon to endure. Jesus died because of the sin of the entire human race, and that must never be forgotten. No wonder he asked in the garden if there was another way, if the cup could be taken from him. No wonder he fell under that enormous weight of our sin as he made his way to Golgotha!

Furthermore, to minimize Jesus' death also minimizes the power of the resurrection. When God sent Jesus to take the entirety of humankind's sin to the grave, and then shattered the chains of 'all Death' for 'all Time' when he raised him from the dead, it was an incredibly mighty act. If sin and death are small enemies of the human race, then the resurrection is only a small victory. To gloss over the power of sin and death reduces God's mighty resurrection act to comprehensibility, whereas it should always remain beyond the scope of our minds to fathom it.

Wrong as it is to focus so single-mindedly on the cross—as we have—if we move from our obsession with the cross to an equal obsession with the resurrection we will be just as wrong. Contemporary

Christianity has made Jesus too human by over-emphasizing his suffering and death at the expense of his victory over them; by so doing we have, in effect, robbed him of his Deity. The world has wanted to view Jesus as just a man, though a very good man. However, there cannot be a man-Christ who provides salvation. On the other hand if we, like the *Docetists* of old, rob Jesus of his humanity by over-emphasizing his Deity at the expense of his sacrifice, we make him into a God-Christ, and salvation eludes us again. What makes Christianity different from all other religions is the existence of Jesus in 'Time' as both God *and* Man inseparably. Only as God-Man, only as the one who died and was raised can he be the Christ who forgives sin and grants eternal life.

This balancing act seems so easy. But I have been amazed at the confusion over the question: 'What did Jesus' death accomplish?' I have been surprised how many Christians are of the opinion that Jesus' death provided forgiveness for sin, and that *that is all we need.* They seem to equate forgiveness for sin with eternal life.

I want to be careful here, because the ground is rather treacherous. On the one hand I know from my own experience and from talking with others how much emphasis has been given to the idea that the death of Jesus by itself brought about our salvation. All the time-worn phrases that populate our preaching, prayers and testimonies lead to this faulty conclusion: "Jesus died that we might have forgiveness for sins and eternal life". That phrase has been part of my own testimony, I confess, and I hear it constantly, even on Christian radio and television.

On the other hand, in my examination of the New Testament I have found only one passage out of the many that attempts to make sense of Jesus' death that could, on its surface, suggest such an attitude:

> *For God has not destined us to the terrors of judgment, but to the full attainment of salvation through our Lord Jesus Christ. He died for us so that we, awake or asleep, might live in company with him. (I Thessalonians 5: 9-10 ESV)*

However, notice that it is not 'Jesus' who died for us, but 'the Lord Jesus Christ'. What distinction is being made? 'Jesus' is his earthly name. In the phrase 'Lord Jesus Christ' his earthly name is book-ended by titles indicating his sovereignty, titles bestowed on him by virtue of his being raised from the dead. This distinction is also made in Peter's first sermon after the resurrection and ascension of Christ, a sermon preached in front of the enemies of Jesus, those who had demanded his crucifixion.

> *Let all the house of Israel know for certain that God has made him both Lord and Christ, this Jesus whom you crucified. (Acts 2: 36 ESV)*

It is critical that the titles 'Lord' and 'Christ' be seen as 'resurrection centered'. In that context Peter is fusing the crucified Jesus and the resurrected Lord-Christ into an inseparable union. It is the risen One, obedient even unto death, through whom we have eternal life. Take away the resurrection and we are left with an incomplete and tragic tale of a good man who was unjustly put to death, nothing more. As I read it the New Testament says the death of Jesus accomplished something, but not everything. Without the response of God's resurrection power, even that *something* becomes *nothing*. The sad truth is that without the resurrection of Jesus his crucifixion accomplished absolutely nothing (I Corinthians 15).

The danger in this thinking is being accused of driving a wedge between the death of Jesus and the resurrection of Jesus, then downplaying the former in favor of the latter. I am not interested in wedges. Rather, balance. If any wedge has been driven, it has been by the western Church over the last 1300 years. The crucifixion of Jesus has taken center stage. The crucifixion dominates almost every category of Christian teaching and worship: our sermons, our Sunday School materials, our clichés, our hymns and worship music, our art. Our focus on the crucifixion has driven the resurrection of Jesus to the sidelines where we activate it basically at Easter and funerals. This wedge must be removed. It would be wise to keep the following quote by Karl Barth in mind as we proceed: *"Christianity without the resurrection is a lie and a deceit."*[1]

Human wisdom often reaches its limits before finding itself able to comprehend a particular theological question. When that happens the usual tendency is to alter the question, stripping it of its identity or mystery, until it is reduced to fit the limits of our ability to reason. So it has been with our treatment of the biblical account of the resurrection. We haven't gone so far as to eliminate all references to the event, but we have sapped it of its redemptive power. We have been diverted into thinking that in the crucifixion of Jesus—a rationally acceptable and believable event—lay both the initiation and completion of our salvation. In other words, we have unwittingly located all that is necessary for eternal life in the crucifixion, making theological difficulties with the resurrection of less consequence. We take pride in our orthodoxy when we 'preach the crucifixion'. We 'glory in the cross'. We surround ourselves with signs of the cross like so many pickets in a gigantic spiritual fence. Jesus would not have done this. Whenever he mentioned the cross it was always preceded or followed by words of his coming resurrection. The two facets were always linked:

> *And he began to teach them that the Son of Man must suffer many things and be rejected by the elders and the chief priests and the scribes, and be killed, and after three days rise again. (Mark 8: 31 ESV)*

> *"See, we are going up to Jerusalem, and the Son of Man will be delivered over to the chief priests and the scribes, and they will condemn him to death and deliver him over to the Gentiles. And they will mock him and spit upon him, and flog him and kill him. And after three days he will rise". (Mark 10: 33-34 ESV)*

He said, "I lay down my life, *in order that* I might take it again" (John 10: 17-18); and, "The Son of Man must die, but will rise on the third day." In his mind it appears that the resurrection was the completion or ultimate purpose of his death; that whatever was to be fulfilled in his death could not be accomplished without his resurrection.

What we fail to realize, and even now it may make us uncomfortable to say, is that the only power invested in the cross was the power to kill, the power to maim, the power to destroy:

> *This Jesus, delivered up according to the definite plan and foreknowledge of God, you crucified and killed by the hands of lawless men. (Acts 2: 23 ESV)*

> *The God of our fathers raised Jesus, whom you killed by hanging him on a tree. (Acts 5: 30 ESV)*

> *And though they found in him no guilt worthy of death, they asked Pilate to have him executed. And when they had carried out all that was written of him, they took him down from the tree and laid him in a tomb. (Acts 13: 28-29 ESV)*

We are forced to admit that the cross, whether empty or hung with a grotesque image of a dying Jesus, is no more than two pieces of wood with the cruel power to bring death. The cross, an instrument of destruction, has never had the power to bring life, and not even Jesus, the Son of God, survived it. The proliferation of crosses on steeples, sanctuary walls, necks and lapels marks a sad commentary on how we have substituted the object of destruction for the 'Person of Life'.

My wife Doy created a powerful analogy: imagine if you will, that you are involved in a military battle. The fighting is intense. You and your buddies are entrenched in a bunker. All of a sudden a live grenade lands right in the middle of your group. One of your squad instinctively throws himself over the grenade to smother its impact, taking the full force of the explosion into his own body. He is killed, but in his sacrificial act the rest of you are spared and given a new lease on life. How absurd it would be to carry in your wallet for the rest of your life a picture of a grenade! The honorable thing would be to honor the one who gave his life for you rather than commemorate the instrument that led to his death. While it is true the grenade was part of the story it certainly was not the most important part, nor did it have anything to do with the extension of your life.

When I was a young boy, and a Protestant, I often heard it said that the Roman Catholics didn't believe in the resurrection, because their Jesus was still on the cross. In my mind, and seen in the light of what was just said, the Roman Catholic crucifix is more justifiable than the Protestant empty cross. The crucifix, Jesus on the cross, points to the figure, the person who took on himself the ultimate penalty of sin, our sin. The empty cross really points to itself, and while we think it infers new life or resurrection it really holds aloft its own power. If Jesus had been hanged would we wear nooses around our necks? If he had been electrocuted would electric chairs abound in Christendom? By our fixation with the cross we unintentionally speak of the power of evil men and what they were able to accomplish on Friday while relegating Jesus' willing, bodily sacrifice and God's superior resurrection power to a secondary position. There is a sort of human arrogance in this emphasis on what we did in the crucifixion rather than on what God did in the resurrection.

The empty cross is really an 'in-house' sign. For those of us who already believe in the resurrection the empty cross can be held aloft as a reminder of that wonderful event. But to the unbelieving world the empty cross is nothing more than a sign of our death-mindedness.

Even for the disciples the empty cross was not a sign of a risen Christ. It was empty mid-afternoon on Friday and the disciples were hiding. It was empty all day Saturday, and they remained trapped in fear. It was empty early Sunday, and the women went to the tomb to anoint the body. For them the empty cross was only a sign that the body of a dead Jesus had been removed from it.

Remember that Paul said the 'preaching of the cross' was folly to the Greeks. Why? Because the rational and logical Greek mind couldn't conceive of a dead man being brought back to life; death was death and there was nothing more. Who else but Christians believes in the resurrection? The sign we hold up to the world is one only we as believers can understand. Unfortunately, it signals something entirely different to the unbelieving world.

To perpetuate a 'cross-minded religion' accomplishes absolutely nothing. Jesus' Good Friday legacy was weeping, sadness, emptiness, denial, fear, resentment and loneliness—hardly jewels of the kingdom of God. Would any minister develop a series on the virtuous qualities in these conditions? Would they be advocated as necessary to a Christian lifestyle? They seem to me to be more in keeping with the workings of Satan, who is after all the ruler of the kingdom of Death. Our Good Friday death-mindedness plays right into his hands. Satan is not as wise as God, but he is certainly wiser than mortals. He knows he can't easily take away the sum total of our faith. What a cruel trick he has played by allowing us half the pie, the crucifixion half, enough to make us think we are devoted followers of Christ, while we invest the majority of our 'spiritual' energies in the world over which he is master and lord. He has deceived us by making us comfortable with the theology that we have life because of Jesus' death. The theologian Walter Künneth writes,

> *Death is the curse of sin....Every glorification and idealiza-*
> *tion of death is unrealistic and pointless, because in it God*
> *executes His annihilating judgment.*[2]

In 1983 I was asked to speak at the American Club in Ostia, Italy, the ancient seaport city of Rome. The American Club is a Christian way station for people caught in a holding pattern between countries. In 1983 Soviet Jews lived there while in transit from the Soviet Union to Israel. The group I spoke to that night was a mixed group including a number of Soviet Jews. My topic was 'The Art of the Roman

Catacombs and its Emphasis on Resurrection and Deliverance'. After my presentation the director introduced me to a young Soviet Jew to whom he had been witnessing, and left us alone. He confirmed the director had tried to convince him about the merits of the Christian faith. He had good reason to reject it, he said. Where he had come from, the Soviet Union, it was the Christians who throughout Russian history had been responsible for the death-like existence of his people. It was they who visited actual death upon them time after time, burning their villages in periodic pogroms. Why, he asked, should he embrace the religion of his persecutors? Furthermore, he said, when he thought of Christianity death came to mind. Did not the Christians worship a dead man? His cross was everywhere to be seen. But, he continued, if what I was saying was true, that Jesus was actually raised from the dead, and that his resurrection was the central pillar of the Christian faith, then he would be willing to consider it. He had enough of death, he said. He didn't need any more. What he was seeking was life, and if that truly was at the heart of Christianity it would be better than anything he had ever experienced.

His words gave me pause; they were convicting. Paul was right! The 'preaching of the cross' *is* foolishness to the non-believing world. I wonder if by giving in to the power of death we have rendered even our present condition of life meaningless. Have we, in our practices if not in our hearts, admitted that death has the upper hand? In spite of what we think, have we been sending the wrong signal to the world? It seems that whatever separation existed between Christians and the unbelieving world—our hope and promise provided by the resurrection of Jesus—has been breached, marginalized, or abandoned. We seem no longer to be in possession of Christ's intended and fulfilled alternative. The gospel of Freud has replaced the Gospel of Christ:

> Freud sees in death an omega which brings us back completely to our alpha.... 'If we are to take it as a truth', says Freud, 'that knows no exception that everything living dies for internal reasons—becomes inorganic once

> *again—then we shall be compelled to say that the goal*
> *of all life is death, and, looking backwards, that what was*
> *inanimate existed before what is living....Thus death is not*
> *'accident' or 'chance' but a remorseless law of nature; it*
> *is 'ananke', from which no living being can escape....In*
> *short, our real pleasure is death itself, for life is always*
> *dominated by a fascination, never fully got rid of, with its*
> *opposite; it is a refinding of death after having been for a*
> *moment, and inadvertantly, an avoidance of death.'[3]*

The only alternative we have is to resurrect the second half of God's plan, the reverse side of the coin, the resurrection of Jesus. Without it not only is the 'cross' meaningless, but also Jesus' incarnate life and the eternal existence of his Father. If Jesus is not 'raised' in our religious and worship practices, then we cannot claim that God is the God of the living (Mark 12: 27) nor can we suggest we worship a living God. If Jesus is not 'raised' in our Christian lives then death is more powerful than God and God's truthful word appears in practice to be a lie.

To say, then, that Jesus died as atonement for our sin is true, but it is an incomplete truth. In I John 2: 2 we see that it is the Christ, the risen One, who is the propitiation for our sins. No mere mortal can redeem the sins of another. While many have given their lives in order that others might live on for a time, they did not have the power to bestow an eternity without death. Nor were they able to offer a life, however brief, where all transgressions of the law—present and future—were counted as forgiven without penalty. For Jesus to come to his death, and nothing more, renders him a man, and nothing more. All mortals die. What about Jesus' death would have made him unique? Walter Künneth states it well:

> *The possibility of a theological inquiry into the saving*
> *character of the cross does not exist at all apart from the res-*
> *urrection, but is given only in the light of the living Christ.* [4]

*It is the resurrection that first makes apparent the unique
quality of this death of the Son of God.* [5]

Unless Jesus had been invested by God with the power to rise from
the dead, his God-ness, his claim that he and his Father were one,
would have been a bald-faced lie. He would have been a charlatan
with no more power to cancel debts that a piggybank has of rectifying
the national deficit. Only in Jesus' resurrection does he manifest the
God-ness that imbues his sacrificial death with the power to cancel
sin. As Paul said,

> *And if Christ has not been raised...you are still in your sins.*
> *(I Corinthians 15: 17 ESV)*

Even if Jesus' death by itself without the resurrection had the power to forgive sins (and Paul destroys this argument in I Corinthians 15)
what good would it have done? Our sins would be forgiven, but we
would remain enslaved by the chains of Death. We would go to the
grave sinless, but eternal decay would be no respecter of persons; sinners and forgiven sinners alike would be subject to the same natural
law of disintegrating flesh. Karl Barth wrote:

> *Whence do we lay claim to the arrogance that dying
> means redemption? Dying is pitilessly nothing but dying,
> only the expression of the corruptibility of all finite things,
> if there be no **end** of the finite, no **perishing** of the corrupt-
> ible, no **death** of death* [emphasis mine].[6]

I, for one, would be tempted to say, "What's the point of living a
life according to the teachings of the Bible, or even according to the
highest codes of human, moral endeavor? If, in the end, death is the
final victor, why not struggle for as much power, money and control
as possible in the few short years available to me?" When Christ is
not 'risen' in the hearts and minds of humanity chaos often results
because flesh becomes the master of whatever little spirit is left in the

world. History, trapped in the stranglehold of time, marches toward its bleak conclusion. The 'cross' alone, with its death-power, changes nothing. The history of the world is the same with or without the single event of the crucifixion of Jesus; only the resurrection of Jesus validated the sacrifice, intersected the path of history, and redeemed it from its inevitable dissolution.

The cross of Jesus is responsible only for part of salvation, not all of it. The New Testament, while continually emphasizing the importance of their union, is very clear about separating what was accomplished on the cross from what was accomplished by the resurrection. Nearly seventy times the Epistle writers speak directly to the death of Jesus by using words such as 'blood', 'cross', 'sacrifice', or 'suffering'. Tracing these thoughts through their letters an interesting picture develops. Nearly half the references (27) state that 'forgiveness for sin' is accomplished through the death of Jesus. Another fifteen state only that Jesus died for us, with no suggestion as to what that dying meant. Other references reveal that we are 'reconciled', 'acquitted', 'bought', 'brought near' and 'consecrated'. *None ascribe eternal life to the crucifixion of Jesus.* According to the Epistle writers the death of Jesus cancelled the bondage of sin. Forgiveness for sin is a tremendous gift, but is it enough? I don't think so, and neither do the New Testament authors. They speak often and powerfully about how it was the resurrection of Jesus that cancelled the power of death. In the first letter to the Thessalonians several verses address themselves to this issue of fusion:

> *For they themselves report concerning us the kind of reception we had among you, and how you turned to God from idols to serve the living and true God, and to wait for his Son from heaven, whom he raised from the dead, Jesus who delivers us from the wrath to come. (I Thessalonians 1: 9-10 ESV)*

> *But we do not want you to be uninformed, brothers, about*

*those who are asleep, that you may not grieve as others do who have no hope. For since we believe that Jesus died and rose again, even so, through Jesus, God will bring with him those who have fallen asleep. (I Thessalonians 4: 13-14 ESV)*

Only through the annihilation of death can we have eternal life. We must come to realize there are two powers to be overcome: the power of sin, and the power of death. The Church must claim both forgiveness *and* eternal life that are ours through both the death *and* resurrection of Jesus.

Some years ago, early in my study, a new friend of mine, a chemist for Exxon, suggested the perfect analogy for inseparability. He had participated in my week-long seminar and set about trying to make sense of the message in a manner which would speak to him in the world of his profession. As we ran around Swanzey Lake in southern New Hampshire he said he'd let me know if he ever found the solution. I received a letter from him some months later written on a church bulletin; the answer must have come to him in the middle of a sermon. The perfect analogy, he said, was *salt*. I laughed at the appropriateness of it. How often have we heard sermons preached on the words, 'Ye are the salt of the earth'! Jesus, with his Father the creator of elements and atoms, was speaking far more authoritatively than anyone knew! My friend explained: Salt is composed of two elements, sodium and chlorine. Each, by itself is a killer: explosive, destructive and deadly. The same can be said of the cross and resurrection when separated from each other: the edifice of Christianity crumbles into meaninglessness and Faith is destroyed. But when sodium and chlorine become fused their new property, completely the opposite from their old separate natures, is that which preserves and keeps from decay! Salt heals! Salt gives flavor! (Preachers, there are sermons buried in this analogy). The most interesting part of the analogy, my friend said, is that once sodium and chlorine become chemically bonded, nothing can ever permanently separate them into their original properties. The elements of salt cannot be separated by fire—what a wonderful image, one the early resurrection-minded Christians suffering under Roman persecution came to believe unswervingly. Emperor Nero burned Christians at the stake to light his night-time orgies. The flames did not separate them from their Faith. The elements of salt can be separated in water, but when the water is evaporated they are bonded together again.

Salt simply has a stability about it that defies any return to its original components once they are united. So it must become with the death and resurrection of Jesus. God in his wisdom put them together like salt and created a new order of spiritual healing, flavored lives, and eternal preservation. The two together provide all we need. Separated we have nothing. Once bonded by God, he had no intention of seeing them exist ever again in isolation. The New Testament writers knew this very well. The whole message coming from their diverse pens is the 'union' of Jesus' death and resurrection.

We live in the flesh in the tide of history's continuation. But we also live in the spirit between the end of history brought about by the resurrection of Jesus, and the beginning of eternity beyond the arena and scope of history. As Neville Clark put it,

> ...The last day at the end of history [has] taken place on the third day in the midst of history.[7]

Because of the resurrection we live, says the biblical scholar Künneth, in a 'consummated time, a time fulfilled.' [8]

Therefore, only the resurrection of Jesus rescued the crucifixion from the curse of history and rendered the sacrifice eternally 'atoning'. It was a two-fold act.

> 'It will be counted to us who believe in him who raised from the dead Jesus our Lord, who was put to death for our trespasses and raised for our justification'. (Romans 4: 24-25 ESV)

Even in these verses we see indivisibility.

Death had to give way to resurrection or we would be, as Paul said, without hope. That very fact makes it mandatory that we come to the belief that the resurrection is the absolute pivot point of history and, even more than that, the knife-edge of our theology. It must become the basis for Faith, the model for living, the theological superstructure in our corporate worship, and the spiritual force underlying our witness. We do not have a choice. We cannot have the crucifixion without the resurrection. A word of caution: it will not be enough to add a few resurrection words here and there, like pinning a resurrection-tail on a crucifixion-donkey. Too much of that kind of 'tokenism' already exists. Sorry to say, Easter Sunday may be a good example, for apart from that one day resurrection preaching and attitude hardly exist any other time during the year in most churches.

We must also stop 'assuming' the resurrection while we speak effusively about the crucifixion. It appears we think that when we talk about the crucifixion of Jesus people simply understand that a resurrection followed. As we have continually said, this is foolish thinking. We can't assume that resurrection follows death; it only happened once in the entire history of the world. 'Death-Resurrection' fusion is mandated. If we make any mistake at all let it be in emphasizing the 'right side of the hyphen', not the left. Death does not imply resurrection, but to speak of the resurrection implies that a death preceded it.

Here is the mandate: Stand on Easter and embrace Good Friday; that is the theology of Paul. To stand on Good Friday and give a casual, occasional wave to Easter is dead wrong and not what the New Testament teaches. Let's put it another way. We stand on the near side of the resurrection. All of history was changed by that event. We can now refute the inevitability, the *Omega* of death as claimed by Freud. If the beginning of our salvation, our *Alpha* is concentrated in the crucifixion of Jesus, all our hope, all the hope of the entire world finds its *Omega* in the event of the risen Lord.

From our point in time in the 21st century we have to travel 2000 years back in time through the *Omega* to get to the *Alpha*. The road back to the cross of Jesus goes through the portal of the resurrection; that towering, history changing and life changing event stands between us and the cross. Therefore, the resurrection of Jesus is the lens or the telescope through which we must see his crucifixion—every time.

Resurrection is the maypole of Faith and all else must be attached to it, including the preaching of the crucifixion. Take away the maypole and all the streamers flutter aimlessly and pointlessly. Or as Calvin said,

> *If the hope of the resurrection be removed, the whole edifice of piety would collapse, just as if the foundation were withdrawn from it.*[9]

Linkage is called for. We must make a certain decision. If we continue to concentrate our energies on the meaning of the crucifixion, as we have done, we are in a manner of speaking suggesting that the 'death' of Jesus is more powerful, more pregnant for our faith than the 'resurrected life' of Jesus. In our heart of hearts we know this is not true. We must confess, like Paul, that,

> *The resurrection of Jesus stands in principle above the cross.*[10]

When we acknowledge that Scriptural truth our work begins. Perhaps first, a change of heart is needed. Without this there is no launching pad for our new understanding. We must first allow the power of the resurrection to fill us with the truth of living the life ordained by the risen Christ. Out of that transformation all our corporate and individual spiritual activities will begin to reflect the powerful hope we possess, a hope firmly established by God's powerful act of raising his son on the 'third day'.

## What Symbol Tells the Complete Story?

As we continue to say, the death of Jesus on the cross absolutely cannot stand by itself; it needs the resurrection. The reverse is also true. If this is the theological case, then it should also become true in our symbolism. Just as the resurrection provides for the crucifixion a theological validation, some visual sign needs to be added to the sign of the cross if it is to be aesthetically validated. Our crosses are empty and, as we have said, the empty cross speaks to the unbelieving world only of the absence of a dead Jesus. For them the empty cross is an emblem of the power of death over life. It needs a resurrection sign attached to it. If the death and resurrection of Jesus are two facets of a single event, or like the two chemicals bonded eternally in salt, then the symbol for the Christian faith must embody the same concept.

Wherever I have spoken on this subject people have suggested some possibilities. Two Roman Catholic couples told me that in their churches the crucifix had been altered; rather than Jesus hanging on the cross he stood in front of the cross, resurrected. That for me was exciting news; it marked a return to one of the first images in Christian art—the wood carved doors of Santa Sabina Church in Rome, a time of emphasis on the risen Christ. I think, though, that some Protestants might have difficulty with an actual figural representation of Jesus in this manner. There are other possibilities. At Easter a number of churches hang a white cloth over the arm of the cross as a symbol of the shed grave clothes. Why not leave the cloth permanently? A minister from Texas, who later became a church planter in Georgia, said that his parishioners came up with the idea of wheat attached to the cross, giving visual witness to Jesus' words: 'I am the bread of life'. These are all good suggestions.

My personal preference is for the incorporation of the 'sign of the Fish'. These days the 'Fish', *Ichthus*, is common in Christian circles, but not for the same reason I would use it. Most Christians treat *Ichthus* as a generic Christian symbol and are not aware how it was used in the early Church. We simply believe that the first Christians drew signs of the Fish in the sand as a form of secret code identifying their Christian belief.

The true reason for the 'sign of the Fish' has its basis in the New Testament. When Jesus ate a piece of fish in the presence of the unbelieving disciples on Easter night, their eyes were opened and they recognized him as the risen Christ. On only three occasions in the New Testament did Jesus eat fish with his followers, and all three were after his resurrection (John 21). *Ichthus* for the early Christians became a symbol for the resurrected Christ. If the cross is a sign of Jesus' sacrificial death, *Ichthus* is a sign of his triumph in the resurrection, his victory over death. To superimpose *Ichthus*, the 'sign of the Fish', over the cross, or to enclose the cross within the 'sign of the Fish' would be the perfect symbol, the most accurate visualization of Paul's words: *'Death is swallowed up in victory'* (I Corinthians 15: 54). Here too the sign already exists; it appears on necklaces, lapel pins, and car bumpers. The problem is that we simply see it as two generic Christian symbols rather than the representation of Paul's words. For those who believe Paul's words, the history of the world, governed as it is by the fall of Adam, has come to an end. We would do well to give the proper sign to the world, one that would convince them that Life is at the center of our Faith. We can make of the empty cross what we will, trying to imbue it with resurrection significance whether or not it is wise or even accurate to do so. But as we have said, to those who perish the cross is foolishness and speaks only of our death-mindedness. Have you ever thought what signal the cross on your church steeple is really giving to the surrounding community? Encircling our crosses with *Ichthus*, 'the sign of the Fish', might cause people to ask what it is all about. We then would have the opportunity to explain our faith in a fresh, completely biblical and balanced way. On our lips would be the confession, the biblical injunction: 'Jesus, who died, is Lord and Christ, the promised Messiah, the risen One'. In these words is hope for a despairing, hopeless world.

CHAPTER **Seven**

# The Words Of Jesus

JESUS KNEW THE eternal purpose behind his incarnation. We would do well to consider his words. Taken in total there appear to be two significant goals in Jesus' mind: the quality of life here and now, and the promise of life eternal.

Our hymnals are filled with texts focusing on the release from the travails of this life and a longing for the world beyond. Often we are guilty of pinning all our hope on eternal life, while God's promise to us in the life we now live remains secondary. To the unbelieving world, Christians often appear to be long faced and joyless. To be honest, we must confess that all too frequently the Christian life as we live it leaves unbelievers with the impression that what has to be 'given up' to be a Christian is not worth the price. Additionally, the phrase, 'By their deeds you shall know them', too infrequently captures the desired difference between believers and non-believers. This is not a problem inherent in Faith itself, or in the model lived by Jesus. I feel it has resulted from our own pre-occupation with the sacrificial aspects of Jesus' earthly calling at the expense of his resurrection, the imbalance that has been the concern of this book. The 'terrible price' Jesus paid possesses our thinking and determines the character of the life we live. Unfortunately, this attitude has in great measure shut out the intrusion of joy stemming from God's gift of new life for his son in the resurrection.

By standing to one side and observing people in their normal everyday activities it is nearly impossible to determine who is a Christian and who is not. The term 'Christian' itself has become watered down to the point where it is more a cultural term (as in 'this is a Christian nation') than a spiritual one. One is 'Christian' if not Muslim, Buddhist, Hindu, Jew, Atheist or any of a number of 'others'. In this context, then, it might be preferable to make a distinction between the identifiers 'Christian' and 'Christ-filled', the latter much more defining and descriptive. Even making this distinction, can we observe any outstanding quality in those who profess to be 'Christ-filled' that is absent in others?

In my own profession as a teacher in a Christian institution of higher learning students were given the opportunity to evaluate their teachers. One question asked was, 'How does the teacher give evidence to the Christian faith?' With very few exceptions the answers were no more pointed than, 'Shows respect and concern for students'. I would expect that of any good teacher—atheist, Buddhist, Hindu or Christian. This is not to say that my colleagues were not Christian. It is only to suggest that Christians are not always looking for the 'distinctives' that should be identified with the Faith. It might also point out that Christians have a very hard time expressing the difference that God through his son Jesus Christ intended for us. If we are truly 'Christ-filled', shouldn't the difference be evident and call attention to itself?

## Jesus and Abundant Life

Jesus intended that life here and now have a distinctive quality about it. Much of his earthly ministry was given to miracles of revitalization, rejuvenation and rebirth. How many people had the quality of their lives reclaimed for them through the miraculous work of Jesus? The blind, the lame, the sick, the palsied, the demon-possessed, society's outcasts—he changed them all. Jesus is intent on life being lived to the fullest. The purpose of Jesus' healings was to lead to a new, more fulfilled life immediately.

In the account of the man crippled for thirty-eight years (John 5) Jesus was not deterred by the fact it was the Sabbath. He could have come back the next day. After all, the man had been lying by the Sheep Pool for years; what difference would one more day have made? But Jesus seized the opportunity and healed him then and there, and by so doing set his action against the Jewish laws concerning the Sabbath. No contingent factors could keep him from immediately bestowing the intended quality of life where it had been absent. To the charges of the Jewish authorities he replied,

> *For as the Father raises the dead and gives them life, so also the Son gives life to whom he will. (John 5: 21 ESV)*

Jesus was not content simply with fulfilling his mission leading to eternal life; he was determined that there be a 'resurrected' life now. Believers have the future gift of eternal life—and we long for it—but Jesus says we have already 'passed from death to life' (John 5: 24). If so, where is the evidence that we are truly alive? Jesus wants us to live a life of quality ordained by God, and he intends for us to have it at this moment. He is our example and we are enabled to be reflectors of his glory.

> *I am the light of the world. Whoever follows me will not walk in darkness, but will have the light of life. (John 8: 12 ESV)*

Again He says,

> *I came that they may have life and have it abundantly. (John 10: 10 ESV)*

Over and over again in the Gospels Jesus' miracles are recounted. Jesus teaches us how to live and demonstrates God's concern for our wholeness. The miracles of Jesus give evidence of his life-changing power. Each of us who believes has had just such a miracle performed on our behalf. The miracle cannot be revoked. Beyond the point of miracle, however, we are commanded to live it out in daily activity. It is at this point where Jesus provides clues, through his parables, to govern our living. Many of them enumerate varying responses to a single idea, experience or event. We are then asked to respond by making the proper choice. By confronting the parables, and by heeding the advice of Jesus, we are led to understand what it means to choose the Christ-like way in a world choked by confusion and enticed by temptations. We know, through the miracles of Jesus, through his teaching and by his example, how he intends for us to live a life of the highest quality, set apart from the world around us by our deeds as well as our words.

## Jesus and Eternal Life

Jesus' words also point toward eternal life. Jesus makes absolutely clear that there will be a resurrection from the dead. To the Sadducees, who maintained that there was no resurrection, Jesus threw the words of their Scriptures back at them:

> And as for the resurrection of the dead, have you not read what was said to you by God: 'I am the God of Abraham, and the God of Isaac, and the God of Jacob'? He is not God of the dead, but of the living. (Matthew 22: 31-32; also Mark 12: 27 and Luke 20: 38 ESV)

Again he said:

> For this is the will of my Father, that everyone who looks on the Son and believes in him should have eternal life, and I will raise him up on the last day. (John 6: 40 ESV)

In John 12: 50, Jesus stated that he spoke on the authority of his Father who had commanded him what to say and how to say it: his

Father's commands are eternal life.

Throughout the Gospels Jesus was approached by people asking what they must do to be saved, or to have eternal life. Rich and poor, rulers and servants, they all came to him. They had evidently heard what he had to say about a life beyond this one, promises contrary to the accepted position of the authorities, and were concerned about it. That many authorities as well as the citizenry were questioning him regarding the idea of resurrection seems evidence enough that Jesus was speaking widely and often about it.

Jesus equated the new life, the resurrected life, with himself. He was not only going to be the example, he was himself that *Life* and *Resurrection*. To the Samaritan woman's question Jesus replied that he was the *Living Water*.

> The woman said to him, "Sir, you have nothing to draw water with, and the well is deep. Where do you get that living water? Are you greater than our father Jacob? He gave us the well and drank from it himself, as did his sons and his livestock." Jesus said to her, "Everyone who drinks of this water will be thirsty again, but whoever drinks of the water that I will give him will never be thirsty again. The water that I will give him will become in him a spring of water welling up to eternal life." (John 4: 11-14 ESV)

To the crowd that gathered around him following the 'miraculous feeding' Jesus responded:

> Jesus then said to them, "Truly, truly, I say to you, it was not Moses who gave you the bread from heaven, but my Father gives you the true bread from heaven. For the bread of God is he who comes down from heaven and gives life to the world." They said to him, "Sir, give us this bread always." Jesus said to them, "I am the bread of life; whoever comes to me shall not hunger, and whoever believes in

*me shall never thirst." (John 6: 32-35 ESV)*

To Martha in Bethany, upon the death of her brother Lazarus, Jesus said:

> *I am the resurrection and the life. Whoever believes in me,*
> *though he die, yet shall he live, and everyone who lives*
> *and believes in me shall never die. (John 11: 25-26 ESV)*

Jesus did not say he would show people the way, or reveal to them the truth, or lead them to the life; he said without equivocation that he himself *was* the way, the truth, and the life, and that no one would come to the Father except by him (John 14: 6). He never said he was the way, the truth, and the sacrificial death leading to life. Even though his suffering and death were the penultimate part of the eternal plan his words reveal constantly that the redeemed life of his creation through resurrection was the ultimate purpose behind his mission.

## Jesus and His Sacrificial Death

Jesus is interested in life now and the life hereafter. The essential message of his earthly ministry was one of *Life* with a capital 'L'. But what did he have to say about his sacrificial death? What significance did he place on it? How often did he talk about it? Does our infatuation with Jesus' death have any grounding in his attitude toward it?

Here we must reiterate what has been said in an earlier chapter. Jesus referred to himself most often as the Son of Man. Jewish interpretation of this title was that of a figure coming from Heaven to set up his Kingdom, throw out the evildoers, and reign forever. Jesus, however, referred to himself as the Son of Man who would die. But he didn't stop there. He always went on to say that on the third day he would rise from the dead. Jesus seems not to treat these two events with any particular emphasis given to either one, but rather couples them together as a single act that must be accomplished for the salvation of the human race. Jesus simply does not separate the fact of his coming resurrection from the fact of his coming sacrificial death.

When the authorities asked for signs of his Son-ship Jesus condemned them for asking and said the only sign would be the sign of the prophet Jonah. Three days and three nights would the Son of Man spend in the bowels of the earth (Matthew 12: 38-41; also Luke 11: 29-32). By this he pointed toward his death that would result in his resurrection.

Even when Jesus spoke of his being 'lifted up' (John 3: 14) we must be careful not to let our 'cross predisposition' cloud the wider meaning of the phrase. To examine the Greek word, *Hupsoun*—meaning 'to lift up'—clarifies the context:

> *The strange thing is that it is used of Jesus in two senses. It is used of his being lifted up upon the cross; and it is used of his being lifted up into glory at the time of his ascension into Heaven…There was a double lifting up in Jesus' life— the lifting on the cross and the lifting into glory. And the two are inextricably connected. The one could not have happened without the other. For Jesus the cross was the way to glory. Had he refused it, had he evaded it, had he taken steps to escape it, as he might so easily have done, there would have been no glory for him.*[1]

When Jesus entered into his glory, he did so as the Christ, the One raised by God's power. It is apparent that Jesus' followers did not expect his resurrection (it was not even in their minds though he told them of it) because they had not understood the Hebrew Scriptures' prophecies that the Son of Man was ordained to die. In their encounter on the Emmaus road Cleopas and his friend were chastised by the risen Christ because they had not believed all that the prophets had said:

> *Was it not necessary that the Christ should suffer these things and enter into his glory? (Luke 24: 26 ESV)*

It was in the mind of Jesus that his death was his chosen path to glory, that his death in and of itself was not a stopping point. His words in the previous passage included both his dying and rising. His glory was not in his suffering and dying on the cross. That was an act necessary for the cancellation of the power of sin. It was a tragic necessity. The Son of Man paid a tremendous ransom for our souls kidnapped by sin (Matthew 20: 28; Mark 10: 45). The price was his blood, an awful price brought about by the condition of our sinful and wicked state. But to glory in the cross of Christ, as the familiar hymn suggests, is the wrong response. Humble and penitential thanksgiving would be suitable, but not glory. Nowhere does Jesus glory in his sacrifice, nor does he ever suggest that 'glory' should be our response. The purpose in his dying was to put an end to the age governed by sin. The purpose of his resurrection was to bring us into the new era where life in its fullest meaning, to its fullest extent, could be realized. The Good Shepherd gave his life for the sheep willingly because he knew that once he laid it down he would take it up again.

> *I am the Good Shepherd. I know my own and my own know me, just as the Father knows me and I know the Father; and I lay down my life for the sheep…. For this reason the Father loves me, because I lay down my life that I may take it up again. No one takes it from me, but I lay it down of my own accord. I have authority to lay it down, and I have authority to take it up again. This charge I have received from my Father." (John 10: 14-15, 17-18 ESV)*

Jesus came into his glory when God raised him from the dead. Our glory should have its focus in the same event. We can and should be filled with thankfulness for his willing sacrifice while at the same time we glory in his resurrection.

It is true that Jesus saw himself as a ransom, as the One whose blood would be shed for the remission of sins, whose sacrifice would be once for all, putting an end to the law and to continual rituals of purification. We must confess, however, that in searching his words we will find he spoke about this aspect of his mission only on rare occasions. While he mentioned the fact of his death (always coupled with the fact of his resurrection) he gave little, if any, emphasis to the meaning of it.

Jesus seemed concerned primarily with life—its quality here and now and its eventual immortality. He preferred to speak of himself as the *living water*, the *true bread from Heaven* which gives life to the world, the *light of life*, the *One who quickens*, the *One who brings eternal life*, the *One who is the resurrection*. He knew the meaning of the fusion of death-resurrection we have been talking about. The supremacy of the resurrection, the theme of this book, is rooted in his words. His Good Friday sacrifice shed no new light on what it meant to die. He understood full well that there could be no meaning, no purpose, no joy, no glory in suffering and death apart from and detached from the significance brought to bear in them through the resurrection. He came to teach us living. He came also with a promise of eternal living, and in delivering that promise in his own unique way, through his sacrifice and resurrection, he revealed to us what it means to die to sin, to die to the world, and to live with the light of the living Christ in our hearts.

According to Jesus' life and words, his death and resurrection, dying is the path to living. In that context we have no choice but to sacrifice our death-mindedness on the altar of his life and live as Jesus ordained us to live—as people who have already passed from death to life.

CHAPTER **Eight**

# The Power Of God

AMONG HIS MANY attributes, God is the essence and apotheosis of power, and the nature of his power is beyond imagining. Try as we may no one can truly understand its fullness. Yet in our age of infatuation with the power of Science we have been led to believe that in time all the secrets of the universe will be unlocked by our self-exalted minds. Who needs God when we are all-sufficient! We now have the awesome power to heal, to manipulate, and to destroy. We can create something new out of an existing something. The foolish result has been to think we have attained enough authority and ability to usurp God's power. In this process our arrogance has attempted to divest God of his creative power thus demoting him to the role of stationary engineer, or master mechanic of the universe, if indeed he is recognized as existing at all! I remember the magazine cover caption in the middle '60's which asked a question that to my mind represents the epitome of our self-absorption: 'Is God dead?', suggesting that perhaps we don't need him anymore, if we ever did. This exaltation of humankind and diminution of God is one of the great tragedies of history, and the resulting myth of our own 'god-ness' is the supreme hoax of modern times.

While it would be a mistake to belittle human capabilities and achievements—we were after all created 'a little lower than the angels'—we should recognize the finite limits of our prowess.

Are we able to create something out of nothing? God did. Can we place even one puny star in its eternal place? God did in numbers beyond reckoning. Can we develop a sense of order and logic that will keep the universe ticking like one gigantic clock for billions of years? God's majesty alone could do that. As the Scriptures tell us, God can do far beyond anything we ask or even in our most brilliant moments think or dream.

Thankfully, though at great professional risk, some from the scientific community are beginning to abandon their inherited theories of the advent of the universe in favor of a single event, a 'prime mover', an 'Intelligent Designer', or as some have dared to say, a 'Creator God'. There is a growing awareness that the grand order we observe in ever-greater detail is more than a random accident.

Apart from the sheer splendor and wonder and manifestations of God's power we see around us, it all pales when compared to the power he exercised when he brought his son back from death never again to suffer corruption or decay. Everything else God had created in perfection seems to have been subjected to the laws of disintegration and time, those laws God put in place as a result of man's disobedience in the Garden of Eden. Instead of the perfection and incorruptibility of his creation grass withers, flowers fade, and flesh is as the grass. Even stars are born and die. It is almost as if God, in his establishment of these principles following the disobedience of the first Adam, was setting us up for a single, spectacular event.

In the middle of history, in the center of the passing of time God, in the *Incarnation,* subjected his only son to that same universal law which leads inevitably to death. We know the immense power there is in loving. That Jesus, God's son, should have died for us was God's supreme manifestation of a kind of love far beyond human understanding. But God's love, as seen in Jesus' life and sacrifice alone, was not considered by him to be enough. It was only the beginning, the *alpha* of love. If Jesus was God's son and was subjected to eternal death, then darkness would surely have overcome the light, banished love and overwhelmed the world. It is God's refutation, in the resurrection, of that one universal law of decay he had created which absolutely forces us to stand in awe of him, praise him for the immensity of his love and exult in his omnipotence. When we recognize this beneficent act of God we ourselves become part of that 'new creation', the *omega* of his love:

> The old has passed away; behold, the new has come. (II Corinthians 5: 17 ESV)

God's intervening power, refuting his own basic laws of nature, has given us a foretaste of what will be the reward of those who believe. Paul says in Romans:

> If you confess with your mouth that Jesus is Lord **[that is, validated as Lord through the resurrection]** and believe in your heart that God raised him from the dead, you will be saved. (Romans 10: 9 ESV)

God's resurrecting power is the great theme of the New Testament. It marks the end of the old age governed by the universal laws of death and decay, and marks the first step in the 'death' that will be brought to Death itself.

Jesus' death on the cross by itself did not have the power to destroy Death and the Church is in error when it ascribes such power to that event. Rather, we are mandated to bear witness to the power of God manifested in the resurrection of his son. His resurrection power in answer to the crucifixion of his son constitutes our gospel and finalizes our salvation. Even the proof of the 'Son-ship' of Jesus came through God's action in the resurrection:

> ...was declared to be the Son of God in power according to the Spirit of holiness by his resurrection from the dead, Jesus Christ our Lord **[His Lordship having been established through the resurrection power of God]**. (Romans 1: 4 ESV)

This is the 'good news', and those that accept it and ascribe the power to God will be saved:

> *For I am not ashamed of the Gospel* **[the good news of the resurrection of Jesus]** *for it is the power of God for salvation to everyone who believes....* (Romans 1: 16 ESV)

Reading the Epistles, one finds numerous references to the resurrection power of God. On approximately fifteen occasions the word 'power' itself is used. It must be made clear that the Greek word for God's power is *dunamis* (from which our word dynamite is derived), and is set against temporal or lesser power, Satan's power, referred to as *exousia*. Thus the Epistle writers made it abundantly clear that God's dynamite power is vastly superior to all other powers, including the more frail power of Satan. Let's state it another way: while Satan's power is vastly superior to our power, it is vastly inferior to God's power.

Other passages use the words 'grace of God', 'gift of God', 'God's act', 'God's creating', 'splendor', or 'glory', all in the context of God raising his son; it is immensely important to understand how context is crucial to understanding those words. Applying this resurrection context wherever these words are found reveals the core of resurrection faith intended by the writers but obscured by our 'cross' predisposition. Words and phrases that originally had been given specific resurrection meaning, over the course of centuries have been rendered 'generic'; we have lost the power and intent of their original purpose resulting in a tragic loss of the importance given to the resurrection in the New Testament. For that reason and in order to reclaim what I believe to have been the original 'resurrection intent' of the Epistle writers I am inserting parenthetic similar to statements put forth in an earlier chapter to reinforce that intent.

> *For all have sinned and fall short of the glory of God, and are justified* **[he was raised for our justification]** *by his*

*grace as a gift* **[his act of raising his son]**, *through the redemption that is in Christ Jesus. (Romans 3: 23-24 ESV)*

*Now the law came in to increase the trespass, but where sin increased, grace abounded all the more* **[in this instance identified with his resurrection power]**, *so that, as sin reigned in death, grace also might reign through righteousness leading to eternal life through Jesus Christ our Lord. (Romans 5: 20-21 ESV)*

Sin condemned us. God's power, or free grace, liberated Jesus and justifies those who believe, granting eternal life. While the death of Jesus destroyed the power of sin (Romans 3: 25)—even though Paul said we were still in our sins until the resurrection—it appears the resurrection power of God resulted in the possibility of life everlasting. We need both. It is not enough to be forgiven sinners, a condition achieved through the crucifixion of Jesus (though again, Paul said if there was no resurrection the crucifixion would accomplish nothing).

Sin is only one of our enemies; the other is our mortality. Unless our mortality is 'forgiven', our death abolished, we will still die eternally and be fodder for worms. Our mortal enemy Death was destroyed through God's resurrection power. Jesus' sacrificial death, by itself, changed nothing and equals nothing. The willing and sacrificial death of Jesus coupled with the resurrection power of God provides everything.

If there were a 'Christian' mathematics it would suggest that, 'one (the crucifixion) plus nothing (no resurrection) equals nothing; one (the crucifixion) plus one (the resurrection) equals everything we need'.

If we continue to concentrate only on the first half of the equation, as I believe we have, we in effect will be negating the very event that gave meaning, purpose, and the power to forgive sin to Jesus' death. It is God's 'free gift', given in the resurrection of Jesus, which issues in eternal life (Romans 6: 23). Only God has the 'power **[as seen in the resurrection of Jesus]** to make our standing sure' (Romans 16: 25).

I would like to suggest that we look at the following verses without making the cross the central theme of the salvation message. Rather, let us look at them through the eyes of the resurrection. At the heart of Paul's words lies the thought that it was what God did in answer to the cross, not the working of Jesus on the cross that is important in these verses. First of all, we must admit that Paul's gospel is a message of the good news of the resurrection: he says, 'Remember Jesus Christ, risen from the dead...this is the theme of my gospel' (II Timothy 2: 8). In this spirit these verses will be interpreted. We will again add parenthetic statements following key words, words that in the heart of the author and ears of the listeners or readers would have resounded with resurrection connotations.

> For Christ **[the risen One]** did not send me to baptize but to preach the Gospel **[the good news of the resurrection]**; and not with words of eloquent wisdom **[which would accept death as the final event]**, lest the cross of Christ **[the risen One]** be emptied of its power. For the word of the cross is folly to those who are perishing but to us who are being saved it is the power of God **[manifested when he raised Jesus from the dead]**. (I Corinthians 1: 17-18 ESV)

Only by proclaiming the resurrection as the central issue can Jesus' submission to the cross bear its full weight. The partial weight of the cross, exclusive of the resurrection, is destructive. Full weight comes through the acceptance of the sacrifice by God in the resurrection. The 'language of worldly wisdom' would deny that anyone could survive the death-power of the cross. No one had ever come back from a crucifixion before. For Paul to preach about a man destroyed by the power of the cross would have indeed been folly. What would have been special about such a person? What would set him apart from any others of the countless number of zealots crucified by the Romans for subversion? God's wisdom and resurrecting power made all the difference in the world. Those who don't believe in the resurrection don't know the 'power of God'. Those who believe know that the 'full weight' of the cross is what happened on Sunday when the sacrifice was accepted, the story was completed, and the mystery resolved.

> For Jews demand signs and Greeks seek wisdom, but we preach Christ **[the risen One]** crucified **[the risen One who also was crucified]**, a stumbling block to Jews **[Messiah doesn't die]** and folly to Gentiles **[there is nothing beyond death]**, but to those who are called, both Jews and Greeks, Christ the power **[dunamis]** of God **[the recipient of God's resurrecting power]** and the wisdom of God. (I Corinthians 1: 22-24 ESV)

> And because of him you are in Christ Jesus **[the risen One, validated as Christ through the resurrection]** who became to us wisdom from God **[Acts 2: 36: 'God has made this Jesus, whom you crucified, both Lord and Christ']**, righteousness and sanctification and redemption, so that, as it is written, "Let the one who boasts, boast in the Lord" **[the one proved to be Lord through the resurrection]** (I Corinthians 1: 30-31 ESV)

Jesus' death on the cross, by itself, couldn't possibly have been a stumbling block to the Jews or folly to the Greeks. Death was something they knew full well. After all, the Jewish leaders had seen to it that Jesus was crucified. However, the Sadducees, who had trouble comprehending the idea of a general resurrection at the end of time would certainly have been in a state of confusion over the resurrection. The Pharisees, who believed in a general resurrection at the end of time, would be baffled by the resurrection of a single person in the middle of time, especially one who had so astounded their sensibilities and confused their understanding of Jewish law and ritual.

As for the Greeks, their rationality and reason had come to grips with death and its meaning in countless ways. Greek wisdom did not accept an afterlife; such talk would be folly to them. These words of Paul set all three groups on edge, then, for different reasons. Only those who had heeded the call of the risen One could really know that the wisdom and power of God were manifested in his mighty Easter Sunday act. The proclamation of Christ (that is, the risen One) on the cross was made, but only from the standpoint of the exercise of God's power, God's act in making Christ our 'wisdom' through the resurrection. The preaching of the cross would not have elicited Jewish anger and confusion or Greek derision. Only the preaching of the resurrection did that. The message is that Jesus succumbed to the cross:

> ...*In weakness, but lives by the power* **[the resurrection dunamis]** *of God. (II Corinthians 13: 4 ESV)*

Those who put Jesus to death boasted of their power in doing away with him. Are we to boast of the same crucified Jesus—or of the 'Lord', the risen One? Our boasting, our faith should be in Christ Jesus who was the recipient of the resurrection power of God.

We cannot build faith upon our own wisdom, which would keep us from expecting anything beyond death. Death is a fact of existence; it doesn't take faith to accept it. Unless we move beyond death there is no need for faith. And the only way to fully embrace faith is to transcend 'worldly wisdom' and accept the resurrection power of God. This was God's great secret. No one other than his son knew of God's marvelous plan. If those who attempted to kill Jesus had known what God had in mind—raising his son from the dead—they wouldn't have played into his hands like they did. Why would the forces of Satan have done the very thing—crucifying God's son—that would provide God with the opportunity to destroy them and their power? God allowed them to put Jesus to death so that his 'hidden wisdom', his 'secret purpose' framed from the foundation of the world could be revealed: the intervention in the law of death and decay, bringing about the promise of life forever with him.

I submit to you that our cross-centered theology is incomplete theology, for it all-too-often turns a deaf ear to the divine goal and purpose of the crucifixion: that is, the movement from the 'age of sin and death' now covered by the blood of Jesus, to the 'age of Life' accomplished in God's resurrecting power, accepting and validating his son as the Christ, the risen One. Only because of the Death-Resurrection fusion we have been talking about is our theology of salvation complete. Perhaps the most vivid statement describing this transformation is that of Ephesians 1: 18-23; how could anyone want to rob Jesus of such magnificent authority, which, in effect, we do by concentrating so single-mindedly on his pre-resurrection sacrifice:

> ...having the eyes of your hearts enlightened, that you may know what is the **hope** to which he has called you, what are the riches of his glorious inheritance in the saints, and what is the **immeasurable greatness of his power** toward us who believe, **according to the working of his great might that he worked in Christ when he raised him from the dead** and seated him at his right hand in the heavenly places, far above all rule and authority and power and dominion, and above every name that is named, not only in this age but also in the one to come. And he put all things under his feet and gave him as head over all things to the church, which is his body, the fullness of him who fills all in all **[emphases mine]**. (Ephesians 1: 18-23 ESV)

Jesus, having submitted to the corruption of the flesh, having suffered its defilement, shed it like a worn out garment. Through the resurrection he became 'the effulgence of God's splendor' (Hebrews 1: 3), so that, by God's power, he could transform,

> ...our lowly body to be like his glorious body... (Philippians 3: 21 ESV)

Like Christ, we too are called to leave our 'former way of life' and,

> ...put off your old self, which belongs to your former manner of life and is corrupt through deceitful desires, and to be renewed in the spirit of your minds, and to put on the new self **[the possibility of the 'resurrected life']**, created after the likeness of God in true righteousness and holiness. (Ephesians 4: 22-24 ESV)

We must live the resurrected life even now so as to,

> ...obtain the glory **[the God-ordained radiance promised to us through the resurrection]** of our Lord Jesus Christ. (II Thessalonians 2: 14 ESV)

That means moving beyond Good Friday, planting our- selves firmly in Easter Sunday, and viewing all things, including Jesus' earthly flesh-bound existence and his will- ing sacrifice, from the standpoint of the presence of the risen Christ. Even as Jesus' sacrifice on the cross led the way to a demonstration of God's power, so must our the- ology of the sacrifice become completely and eternally linked to the greater power brought to bear in the resur- rection. That power, or strength, has brought us salvation by breaking the power of death and bringing life and im- mortality to light (II Timothy 1: 8-10).

> His divine power [resurrection dunamis power] has granted to us all things that pertain to life and godliness, through the knowledge of him who called us to his own glory and excellence **[a reference to his radiance and authority given by God in the resurrection]**, by which he has granted to us his precious and very great promises **[at the final resurrection]**, so that through them you may become partakers of the divine nature, having escaped from the corruption that is in the world because of sinful desire. (II Peter 1: 3-4 ESV)

What, then, of Jesus' sacrifice? If the resurrection power of God is the central pillar of the New Testament are we to ignore Jesus' submission to the cross altogether? Does the crucifixion count for nothing? Let me suggest some answers here.

The New Testament presents a two-fold plan for salvation: Jesus' death on the cross providing forgiveness for sin, and the resurrection making possible eternal life for those who believe. We need both. What has also been stated is that, while both are interlocked, the resurrection stands supreme because it alone validated the work of Jesus on the cross. Death without resurrection is purely and simply death, something we all know and witness daily. Death does not by itself imply a resurrection will follow. Conversely, to speak of resurrection without mentioning death still implies that a death preceded it. The early Church assumed the latter position, focusing on resurrection. The Church for the last 1300 years has proclaimed the former, implying resurrection in a feeble way at best, but preferring to emphasize the atoning work on the cross. Of the two positions, that of the contemporary Church is the most lacking in New Testament truth, but both in principle are wrong. We place the greater power in the cross, in the 'wonder-working power in the blood of the Lamb' as the old gospel hymn proclaims. The New Testament certainly does speak of the purchase made by the 'precious blood' (I Peter 1: 19), for example, but we must be careful to acknowledge that the words 'precious blood' are followed by, 'of Christ', his resurrection title, and thus create fusion between his death and resurrection. When the New Testament speaks of power, that power which in and of itself brings us life, it is God's power in the resurrection that stands alone.

As has been stated several times, we must be careful not to misunderstand the crucifixion words Paul uses, because his intent is to bring both the crucifixion and resurrection together:

> But far be it from me to boast except in the cross of our
> Lord Jesus Christ... (Galatians 6: 14 ESV)

Paul's intentional use of the resurrection titles 'Lord' and 'Christ' create the fusion of the two events. If Paul had boasted in the cross of 'Jesus', his earthly name, that would draw complete focus to the crucifixion event. But Paul is always clear by using Jesus' resurrection titles 'Lord' and 'Christ' when referring to the sacrifice. Our own inclination to 'preach Christ crucified' must then be tempered to reflect the fusion Paul suggests. We have shown that the inclusion of the title 'Christ' imbues the passages with resurrection meaning, creating a bond between the two events. The statement must be interpreted as follows: "We preach Christ, that is, the one who was validated as the Christ by the resurrection power of God, who was crucified." Fusion results. Furthermore, a similar posture is amplified many times by passages like the following:

> ...that I may know him [the risen One] and the power [dunamis] of his resurrection, and may share his sufferings, becoming like him in his death, that by any means possible I may attain the resurrection from the dead. (Philippians 3: 10-11 ESV)

As we recounted in an earlier chapter, Paul begins with the risen One and then moves back to embrace his suffering and death. Paul shows us that he knows balance is called for, but he also reveals he knows where the power is, and where the Christian faith begins.

Baptism may serve as an analogy. It, too, is a two-fold act. We are immersed or submerged in water as a sign of our sin-corrupted bodies being buried with Christ, who took the sins of the world to their grave. We rise from the water completely cleansed, freed from sin and death, as a sign of being raised to new life and eternal life with the resurrected Christ. Paul says,

> If with Christ [the risen One] you died to the elemental spirits of the world... (Colossians 2: 20 ESV)

and is careful to link Jesus' death with his resurrection by use of the title 'Christ'. A few verses later Paul reinforces the fusion by saying,

> If then you have been raised with Christ **[the risen One]**...
> (Colossians 3: 1 ESV)

It is unfortunate that chapter designations, applied long after the letter was written, separated these two verses. In truth, they belong together, almost in the same breath. It isn't as if we are to die now with Christ and remain dead with him until the final trumpet call. We are immediately raised to new life! We are to live the resurrected life here and now; we already live in the resurrection promise.

Stopping after the first half of the baptismal rite, especially in immersion, waiting for the 'final call' would be disastrous! Here is a sad truth: if we performed baptisms the way we have exercised our theology, most believers for the last 1300 years would have drowned! The New Testament very clearly uses baptism as a sign of its double-edged theology: death cancels sin, resurrection cancels death. The latter follows on the heels of the former: for Jesus, three days—for us, immediately.

> We were buried therefore with him by baptism into death, in order that, just as Christ was raised from the dead by the glory of the Father, we too might walk in newness of life. For if we have been united with him in a death like his, we shall certainly be united with him in a resurrection like his. We know that our old self was crucified with him in order that the body of sin might be brought to nothing **[not sin and death both]**, so that we would no longer be enslaved to sin. For one who has died has been set free from sin. Now if we have died with Christ, we believe that we will also live with him. We know that Christ, being raised from the dead, will never die again; death no longer

*has dominion over him. For the death he died he died to sin, once for all, but the life he lives he lives to God. So you also must consider yourselves dead to sin and alive to God in Christ Jesus* **[validated as Christ in the resurrection]***. (Romans 6: 4-11 ESV)*

Not only is the fusion between the death and resurrection obvious in the previous Scripture, taken from Paul's letter to the Romans, so also is the delineation between what the death of Jesus accomplished and what was accomplished as a result of the resurrection. Paul clearly wants the entire Christian community to be aware of the linkage epitomized by baptism, as he again emphasizes it in his letter to the Colossians:

*...having been buried with him in baptism, in which you were also raised with him through faith in the powerful working of God* **[a dunamis resurrection phrase]***, who raised him from the dead. And you, who were dead in your trespasses and the uncircumcision of your flesh, God made alive together with him* **[the risen One]***, having forgiven us all your trespasses, by canceling the record of debt that stood against us with its legal demands. This he set aside, nailing it to the cross. He disarmed the rulers and authorities and put them to open shame, by triumphing over them in him. (Colossians 2: 12-15 ESV)*

Did Jesus' death discard those cosmic powers, or was he too at that moment subject to them? Had he remained dead, who would have been the victor: God, or Satan, Prince of the cosmic powers? In his triumphal procession from the tomb, Jesus, enabled by the resurrection power of the Father, trampled down Death, sealed the eventual fate of Satan, and made a laughing stock, a public spectacle of them. Eastern Orthodox Christianity has incorporated this image in frescoes and icons that adorn many if not most of its sanctuaries. In these works Christ leaps with great energy from the grave using the skull of death as his launching pad. With his hands he pulls Adam and Eve to life with him. This powerful resurrection fresco is always used as a counter balance to another fresco, equally prominent, which depicts the crucifixion of Jesus. Western Christianity would do well to provide similar balance between these two essential components of our salvation.

Can there be any doubt regarding the salvific resurrecting power of God and its place of authority in New Testament thought, that power which provided, through the death and resurrection of his son,

*…a ransom for all. (I Timothy 2: 6 ESV)*

To continue to speak of the Jesus of the cross, as we have done for thirteen centuries, without interfacing with the resurrection each time, places Jesus figuratively in the hands of the cosmic powers and in effect constitutes a denial of the resurrection power of God. Without that where would we be?

Jesus' death by itself accomplished nothing, not even the forgiveness for sin; the apostle Paul said it (I Corinthians 15: 17). By the same reckoning there could be no resurrection unless there had first been a death. The promise of life eternal could not be fulfilled without Jesus' crucifixion, his death. As sin and death together are our mortal enemies, so the crucifixion and resurrection together constitute our only hope for immortality.

We must not continue to rob the resurrection 'peter' to pay the crucifixion 'paul'. God's resurrection power can be loosed in our lives only through our acknowledgement of its authority and our insistence on its fusion with the crucifixion in our daily witness. The New Testament is clear. The choice is ours. Will we refuse it or reclaim it?

## CHAPTER Nine

# The Resurrection Difference

AS WE COME to the end of our discourse one final question begs an answer: 'What difference does the resurrection of Jesus make?' This is both the easiest and most difficult question. It is entirely possible for us to appease our intellects on this matter and still come up short when it translates into how we live our lives in light of the resurrection. As I have shared my thoughts and concerns for this research with Christians from across the country and around the world one of the most common responses is, 'You are right, generally speaking, but we don't have a problem with the resurrection in our church. The resurrection is really at the center of all that we do.' It is not easy to counter such responses. Obviously, I would be delighted if it were true, but I can't help wondering if their churches really have different hymns than those I know, if they have different symbols than those I see surrounding worshipers everywhere, if the clichés they use in prayers and testimonies really stand apart from those I have heard all my life. I'm curious about visual evidences of the risen Christ they might have in their sanctuaries. You see, my concern is not that people don't believe in the resurrection of Jesus—most people I have met do. I am concerned about balance, equal play, and the fusion or inseparability of Jesus' death and resurrection. If they do indeed exist in tandem, does the resurrection occupy the position of supremacy that seems to be called for in the New Testament? My experience in Christian worship settings is that whether we are conscious of it or not we give very little evidence to the risen, living Christ in our corporate gatherings. We know full well what the crucifixion of Jesus means, and live our lives in response to the forgiveness we have accepted and received. We live the 'crucifixion difference' daily. We are witnesses to the myriad ways that difference has been manifested in our hymns, our church art, our clichés and our testimony. But 'resurrection difference' is another matter; it is more elusive, less tangible, and we find it difficult to articulate. Hence it has not become a significant part of the life we live and the testimony we share.

I suppose one rebuttal could be that the Church has done well for itself. It has lasted almost two thousand years. People are still converted to the Christian faith. The institution pays its bills. Congregations grow. Buildings spring up everywhere. We support all kinds of charitable agencies and send missionaries all over the world. The Church must be fulfilling the command of Jesus and the Gospels or it wouldn't be in existence.

I too believe the legalized Church has loosed God's power in the world, but nothing like that first power unsheathed by the first century Christians. Even the simplest comparison leaves us humbled. That small band of believers set out in sailboats and on foot from Jerusalem. Paul himself walked almost two thousand miles over barren, desolate terrain as well as mountains, through all kinds of weather, in the face of untold hazards. In the nearly thirty years covered in the *Acts of the Apostles* there grew up Christian communities throughout the Greco-Roman world with believers numbering in the tens of thousands, some estimates suggest over one hundred thousand. Increasing from a relative handful of believers in Jerusalem to nearly one hundred thousand? In less than thirty years? Preaching a resurrection message? Astounding!

We Christians today, numbering nearly a billion, barely balance deaths and transfers in our churches with new members in a given year. In spite of mass communication networks, ease and rapidity of travel, the Christian Church becomes a smaller percentage of the

world's population every day. The Christians of the first three centuries exercised such power and influence through their message
and lives that they effected, in addition to the thousands of converts
to the Christian faith, tremendous change in the moral structure of
their day. Today's churches are hardly able to keep from being affected by the pluralistic and often immoral conditions surrounding
them in the world. We affect less and are affected more. The 'world's'
problems have become ours. The message of 'Good News' has been
replaced by the pop psychology of 'good feelings', even in some of
our churches. In many people's minds one is Christian by birth into
a so-called 'Christian' environment or nation rather than by rebirth
through choice into God's Kingdom. Those who profess to be 'born
again Christians' are often ridiculed and belittled by other members
of the wider 'Christian' community. In the early years of the Christian
era there was such a thing as a Christian distinctive—it was obvious
who was Christian by the manner in which life was lived, decisions
were made, words were spoken, and the manner in which they responded to their persecutors. Even the way in which Christians faced
death was 'different' and prompted in many hearts the first stirrings
leading to faith in the Christian God. The dividing line is much fuzzier
today.

Something is wrong. We are not exercising God's power the way it
once was manifested. Reasons for the diminution are complex, elaborate and perhaps even undeterminable, but allow me one simplistic
answer: we are not preaching the same message. We may think we
are, but we're not. The early Church's witness was first and foremost
centered on the resurrection of Jesus. The *Acts of the Apostles* leaves
absolutely no doubt about that, as we discussed in an earlier chapter.
Now we can go for weeks without hearing it, and often ministers feel
sheepish about preaching resurrection sermons when it isn't Easter.
Congregations feel the same way about singing resurrection hymns.
Its funny how we feel comfortable spreading the Good Friday message across the entire Church calendar year, while limiting the Easter
message to its 'special day'. Yes, there is power in preaching the Jesus

of the cross. And yes, Jesus' sacrifice must be told forthrightly. But the New Testament tells us there is even greater power in preaching the Christ of the resurrection.

So let's rephrase our initial question: 'If the resurrection were to become central in our thinking—as the New Testament suggests—what would the results be?' I, like you, am just beginning to comprehend the meaning of the resurrection, having struggled under the same cross-centered messages and interpretations of Scripture that have prevailed for more than a thirteen hundred years. The list I will share with you is by no means complete—I'm sure there is more to be discovered—but it will at least be a point for departure into the spirit I feel permeates the entire fabric of the New Testament. As we proceed it is important to realize that these benefits of the resurrection would not be ours without it; they are distinctives exclusively linked with God's power manifested in the raising of his son. I think you'll agree that if we were to take these distinctives away the Christian life would be greatly diminished, if indeed it could even continue to exist.

## Eternal Life

Take away the resurrection of Jesus and we have no possibility of eternal life. First and greatest of the distinctives, the resurrected Christ offers a life that is eternal. The promise of the Father is this—what he has done for his son he will do for us. God destroyed the power of death on that first Easter. Jesus became the *first-fruit* from the dead. Notice the phrase *first-fruit*; it implies there will be further fruit. God has promised his *first-fruit* Jesus will not be the last, but merely a fore-taste of his promise extended to us.

Christians should not make the mistake of believing that the death of Jesus opened the door to eternal life. We hear this often in Christian circles and conversation. The familiar refrain of a much-loved hymn is absolutely wrong when it says: 'that by his death he has opened heaven.' Nowhere in the New Testament can we find such a concept. The writings are extremely clear on this matter: Jesus' death conquered the power of sin, and his resurrection destroyed the power of death. If God has not raised his only son, what human arrogance would assume he would extend that favor to us? We need to be forgiven of our sin; God be praised that he gave his son to die for that purpose. We also desire eternal life. Praise to God for the exercise of his resurrection power. To the question, "What must I do to be saved", we need only respond in the words of Paul:

> ...if you confess with your mouth that Jesus is Lord **[validated as Lord through the resurrection]** and believe in your heart that God raised him from the dead, you will be saved. (Romans 10: 9 ESV)

How would Paul have responded if Jesus had not been raised? Jesus would not have been who he said he was. His followers would have silently dispersed after his crucifixion. Paul as Saul would have had no need to persecute them because they wouldn't have mentioned the name of Jesus again in the company of strangers. As a consequence he would not have encountered the risen Christ on the Damascus Road. He would have remained faithful to the Law, and all thoughts that Messiah had come would have disappeared in a generation. Not a word of the New Testament would have been written. The author of Hebrews had this to say:

> …but he holds his priesthood permanently, because he continues forever. Consequently, he is able to save to the uttermost those who draw near to God through him, since he always lives to make intercession for them. (Hebrews 7: 24-25 ESV)

Jesus was declared to be Son of God by the mighty resurrection power of the Father. What greater witness could there be to the truth of Jesus' claims than that? If we believe in this resurrection witness of God we are to carry it in our hearts. If we refuse to accept God's

THE EASTER JESUS AND THE GOOD FRIDAY CHURCH

resurrecting witness we make him out to be a liar.

> *And this is the testimony, that God gave us eternal life,*
> *and this life is in his Son. Whoever has the Son has life;*
> *whoever does not have the Son of God does not have life.*
> *I write these things to you who believe in the name of the*
> *Son of God that you may know that you have eternal life.*
> *(I John 5: 11-13 ESV)*

The scripture is clear: without the resurrection of Jesus we have no hope of eternal life. As Paul said,

> *If in Christ* **[validated as Christ-Messiah through the res-**
> **urrection power of God]** *we have hope in this life only,*
> *we are of all people most to be pitied. (I Corinthians 15:*
> *19 ESV)*

## A Transformed Life

The resurrected Christ offers a life that can be transformed. I have often wondered what the lives of the disciples would have been like if Jesus had not risen from the dead. They, after all, had forsaken their friend in the time of his greatest need. Even if Jesus had not been who he said he was it is difficult to forgive them for deserting him. Friends deserve better. Not only did they flee from him; one denied he had ever known him, and all, save one, were nowhere near the scene of the crucifixion. Only the women were willing to honor him by preparing spices to take to the tomb, but even they were expecting to anoint the dead body of Jesus, not be confronted with his risen presence. How would these men have lived with themselves? Imagine the darkness and despair of their thoughts as they absentmindedly tossed their nets into the Galilee waters. Think of the humiliation. Would they have been able to look comfortably into each other's eyes? How would they regard strangers? Is it possible that fear of discovery might have plagued their presence among new faces? Whatever their doubts and behaviors toward Jesus before his crucifixion would have been amplified following his burial; doubts and denials would not have given way to any suggestion of transformation.

And what about Jesus? Knowing their fickleness, denial, disbelief and flight, wouldn't it be more reasonable to assume he would have chosen others to carry out his purposes following the resurrection? Why think you could build a community of belief with untrustworthy rascals like them? That's what we would do, and who could blame Jesus if that had been his choice? Thank God it wasn't. One of the remarkable characteristics of Jesus the Christ is his power to do the unexpected and reclaim and transform those whom society, as well as human nature would reject.

Take Peter. When crowds gathered around Jesus, when it was wonderful to bask in the glow of miracles, when palm branches and hosannas fluttered in Jerusalem breezes Peter was willing to ac-knowledge that Jesus was indeed the Christ. Fair weather breeds easy friendship. One could cope with the wrath of the authorities when it was evident the people sided with Jesus. But when the soldiers came to Gethsemane on that infamous Thursday the mood of the night had a certain snarl about it. Jesus was led away to his ultimate persecu-tion leading to death. Peter, the boldest of the disciples, fearing for his own life, disowned him. For doing so he deserved repudiation and contempt.

Yet Jesus, upon his resurrection, singled him out. To the women at the tomb he said, "Go and tell the disciples, and Peter". It was Peter that Jesus asked, "Do you love me?", thereby giving him a chance for reconciliation and transformation. Jesus healed Peter's transgressions. For the three denials, three questions. For each of Peter's replies there was a profession of confidence by Jesus in his disciple's ability to lead: "Feed my sheep...feed my lambs". Even when Jesus foretold Peter's crucifixion (John 21: 18) Peter didn't flinch. Several days earlier the very thought of suffering and death had turned him into a coward.

What a difference the resurrection of Jesus made! No longer a coward, Peter became bold. Peter it was who took charge of the gathering at the ascension of Jesus and set the framework in place for replacing Judas with a resurrection witness. Peter it was who preached the very powerful resurrection sermons on the day of Pentecost (Acts 2 and 3) in the face of the enemies of Jesus. Peter it was who was the conduit for the first miracle in the name of Jesus the Christ, the risen One (Acts 3), and astonished the authorities with his boldness, coming so quickly after his demonstration of cowardice. Ascribed to Peter are the beautiful and powerful letters written to give encouragement and to strengthen those about to suffer persecution following the terrors of Emperor Nero. Think of it! The vacillating one who cringed at the very thought of suffering had been made steadfast and bold to write as well as live out in his own suffering and death this magnificent exhortation of the promise of God:

> *Blessed be the God and Father of our Lord Jesus Christ* **[validated as sovereign Lord and Christ through the resurrection]***! According to his great mercy, he has caused us to be born again to a living hope through the resurrection of Jesus Christ from the dead, to an inheritance that is imperishable, undefiled, and unfading, kept in heaven for you, who by God's power are being guarded through faith for a salvation ready to be revealed in the last time. In this you rejoice, though now for a little while, if necessary, you have been grieved by various trials, so that the tested genuineness of your faith—more precious than gold that perishes though it is tested by fire—may be found to result in praise and glory and honor at the revelation of Jesus Christ. (I Peter 1: 3-7 ESV)*

Peter would not, and indeed could not have done any of these things were it not for the intersection of his gloomy path by the brilliance of the risen Christ.

It is interesting to note that in our own day the strongest Christian communities in the world, those who stand out in their witness and experience tremendous growth thereby, are the churches suffering under severe restrictions and persecutions: Africa, China, the Middle East. As we have said, it was also true in the first three centuries. Perhaps the worst thing that ever happened to Christianity was its legalization! But in 'catch-22' fashion, such a powerful witness was bound to be victorious. Then, when risks are removed and we are no longer truly accountable in a life and death manner for our faith, complacency sets in. Watered down witness does not elicit persecution, for the would-be persecutors then have nothing to fear; and without persecution there is nothing to purge our weakness and make us strong. In a way we need persecution, but our luke-warm witness doesn't provoke it.

James, the brother of Jesus, is another witness to the resurrecting and transforming power of Christ. Even this member of Jesus' own family, it appears, was not convinced his brother was who he claimed to be (John 7: 5). Early in Jesus' ministry (Mark 3) James and the rest of the family acted in the following manner:

> And when his family heard it, they went out to seize him, for they were saying, "He is out of his mind." And the scribes who came down from Jerusalem were saying, "He is possessed by Beelzebul," and "by the prince of demons he casts out the demons." (Mark 3: 21-22 ESV)

As Paul recounts the post-resurrection appearances of Jesus in I Corinthians 15, he says in verse 7, "Then he appeared to James..."Through this encounter James, the skeptical and unsympathetic brother of Jesus, was transformed and became the undisputed leader of the Jerusalem Church. Under his direction (Acts 15) the Council of Jerusalem opened the doors of the fledgling Church to Gentile converts. He remained a stalwart servant of the Gospel and one who willingly preached the risen Lord even as he breathed his last breath in martyrdom:

> *So the aforesaid Scribes and Pharisees set James on the pinnacle of the Temple and called to Him: 'O thou, the Just, to whom we all ought to listen, since the people is going astray after Jesus the crucified [notice that the religious leaders mentioned the crucifixion rather than the resurrection] tell us what is the door of Jesus?' And with a loud voice he answered: 'Why do you ask me concerning the Son of Man? He sitteth himself in heaven on the right hand of the great Power, and shall come on the clouds of heaven.' And when many were convinced and gave glory for the witness of James, and said, 'Hosanna to the Son of David', then again the same Scribes and Pharisees said to one another, 'We were wrong to permit such a testimony to Jesus; but let us go up and cast him [James] down, that through fear they may not believe him'....Accordingly they went up and cast the Just down. And they said to one another, 'Let us stone James the Just', and they began to stone him, since he was not killed by the fall, but he turned and knelt down saying, 'I beseech thee, Lord God Father, forgive them, for they know not what they do'.... And a certain one of them, one of the fullers, taking the club with which he pounds clothes, brought it down on the head of the Just; and so he suffered martyrdom.* (The witness of Hegesippus, preserved in Eusebius' *Ecclesiastical History* 2: 23, as found in William Barclay's *The Letters of James and Peter*, revised edition, pp. 13-14).

Not only was the transformation of James remarkable—it had profound, far-reaching implications for the Church in the world. It is entirely possible that without the transforming power of the resurrected Christ the message of Jesus would have died in Jerusalem and been lost to the world.

If James presided over the Jerusalem Church's decision to allow Gentile converts into its body, it was Paul who became the chief witness for the risen Christ throughout the non-Jewish world. Certainly no prolonged elaboration need be given to the transformation in the life of Christianity's greatest spokesman. It is enough to say how important Paul considered his Damascus Road encounter with the resurrected Lord, in that it is stated in detail four times in the New Testament, three times in Acts and once in Galatians. For Luke, the author of the *Acts of the Apostles*, to state the experience three times, Paul must have spoken of it every time he gave his witness. Beyond any doubt Paul's transformation by the risen Christ is the focal point and inspiration for everything he preached or wrote throughout his ministry. It is astounding how God, through the power of his risen son, was able to take the most feared persecutor of the Christians and make of him the chief witness for the Gospel of Jesus Christ.

The message is clear: we, whose legacy from Adam was death, have been given the priceless inheritance of eternal life through God's act of raising his son from the dead. This is the greatest transformation of all. And if God can turn death around imagine what he can do with a wayward or misdirected life. Paul, James, and Peter are but three of the countless men and women of the New Testament whose lives were radically altered by the risen Christ.

To those who constitute the unremarkable, anonymous sea of humanity, whose lives remain somewhere near the plain center between the heights and the depths, Jesus spoke words of transforming power in the Beatitudes (Matthew 5): the poor in spirit receive Heaven; the mournful are comforted; the meek inherit the earth; those hungry for righteousness are filled; those who grant mercy receive it. Even in these seemingly simple gifts are the seeds of radical transformation.

Those who follow Christ are led from darkness to light (John 8: 12), and this light is *Life*. Because Christ knew death, yet was raised never to know it again, the promise is given that we also can become one with his resurrection:

*We were buried therefore with him by baptism into death, in order that, just as Christ was raised from the dead by the glory of the Father, we too might walk in newness of life. For if we have been united with him in a death like his, we shall certainly be united with him in a resurrection like his. (Romans 6: 4-5 ESV)*

## Abundant Life

Jesus not only promises a transformed life, he desires for us a life that is abundant.

*I came that they may have life and have it abundantly. (John 10: 10 ESV)*

Christianity is not intended to be a life of 'giving up'—it is meant to be a life of 'living up'. 'Living up' in the Christian sense is much more exalted and fulfilling than 'living it up', which is the errant cliché of worldly living. We often think of the Christian life as one of sacrifice. Worldly wisdom to the contrary, to taste of God's Kingdom of *Life* is to make all the world has to offer bland by comparison, like week old uncapped ginger ale. To genuinely follow Christ puts fizz into life, it doesn't take it out.

Unfortunately, for many the Christian uniform seems to be 'sackcloth and ashes'. Standard countenance is 'pale and wan'; faces are drawn 'vertically' rather than 'horizontally'. We shuffle close to the wall blending into the woodwork like so many mice. Anything beyond subdued pleasure is looked at askance. Life is more akin to meatloaf than lobster. This would be understandable and even acceptable if a crucified Jesus was intended by God to occupy the central position of the Christian faith. Death and suffering would be our lot both in this life and the next (if indeed there was one). Perhaps without our really knowing or acknowledging it, our countenance is the outward manifestation of our inward belief, if not the deeply hidden reality of it.

And conversely, perhaps our unbalanced belief is the reason so many Christians fit the sorry description just stated. If Jesus is truly alive, and if we honestly believe it, life cannot possibly be dull or mundane or deprived. The risen Christ commands us to "be healed", "receive our sight", "go our way and sin no more", and "rejoice". Paul tells us that it is not enough simply to acknowledge the fact of our salvation—exultation is called for:

> For if while we were enemies we were reconciled to God by the death of his Son, much more, now that we are reconciled, shall we be saved by his life. More than that, we also rejoice in God through our Lord Jesus Christ **[the risen One]**, through whom we have now received reconciliation. (Romans 5: 10 – 11 ESV)

Eliminate the resurrection of Jesus and life is left with an abundance of sorrow, meaninglessness, and purposelessness. Only a life that is buoyed by an eternal hope can truly be called 'abundant'.

## A Joyful Life

The abundant life is a life that is joyful, and exults in the risen Christ. Of all the fruits of the Spirit—love, joy, peace, patience, kindness, goodness, fidelity, gentleness and self-control (Galatians 5: 22)—joy seems the most difficult to come by. I often feel that carrying the cross of Jesus aloft in the spirit of Good Friday tends to render our exuberance, enthusiasm and joy somewhat inappropriate. We occasionally bask in the magnificence of the resurrection but continually reach back to Good Friday as the inspiration for our demeanor. There is never a quieter quiet than when we sit hushed in the presence of the cross, overcome with emotion at the enormity of Jesus' sacrifice. Would that we could experience an equivalent joy when basking in the glow of the resurrection! We are called to be Easter people. We live on the near side, not the far side of the resurrection. When we look back through history the resurrection stands between us and the cross. Shouldn't that color our response to it? Isn't joy an appropriate response to the death of Jesus, knowing what happened on the third day?

Jesus, with the cross ahead of him, moved toward it resolutely and with confidence because he knew what lay beyond it. His life radiated an attitude of resurrection certainty. He was propelled through his last days by the joy held in store for him on Easter:

> …looking to Jesus, the founder and perfecter of our faith, who for the joy that was set before him endured the cross, despising the shame, and is seated **[because he was raised from the dead]** at the right hand of the throne of God. (Hebrews 12: 2 ESV)

The shame of the cross was completely scorned in the resurrection. No resurrection, no joy. No resurrection, the shame of the cross remains. If there was ever a more greatly vexed, morose group of people than the followers of Jesus on Good Friday, I have yet to hear of one. They had nothing left in them of happiness. Life had come to an abrupt, shattering chasm of joyless darkness. Then came the resurrection. The women were the first to be transformed through the words of the angel:

> "Do not be afraid, for I know that you are seek Jesus who was crucified. He is not here, for he has risen, as he said. Come, see the place where he lay…." So they departed quickly from the tomb with fear and great joy and ran to tell his disciples. (Matthew 28: 5–6, 8 ESV)

The response of Cleopas and his friend along the Emmaus road, recognizing that the stranger who had been with them was Jesus, said to each other, "Did not our hearts burn within us?" (Luke 24: 32). Joyful, burning hearts are proper responses for those who come to believe in the risen Lord. The disciples, however, believed neither the women nor Cleopas. Then, into the gloom of the upper room, came the risen Jesus. Joy overwhelmed them completely; it seemed too good to be true (Luke 24: 41). After Jesus led them to Bethany, blessed them and departed,

> ...they worshiped him and returned to Jerusalem with great joy, and were continually in the temple blessing God. (Luke 24: 52–53 ESV)

Jesus had known what their response to his death would be. He said,

> "Truly, truly I say to you, you will weep and lament, but the world will rejoice." (John 16: 20 ESV)

Satan himself must have been ecstatic; he loves dour Christians. As long as he can keep Christians in the arena of Friday, he obscures the fact of his own destruction that took place on Sunday. Death is the kingdom over which Satan is lord and master. Good Friday piety without the transforming power of Sunday plays right into his hands. But Jesus had also anticipated Easter, and predicted their reaction:

> You will be sorrowful, but your sorrow will turn into joy. When a woman is giving birth, she has sorrow because her hour has come, but when she has delivered the baby, she no longer remembers the anguish, for joy that a human being has been born into the world. So also you have sorrow now, but I will see you again, and your hearts will rejoice, and no one will take your joy from you. (John 16: 20–22 ESV)

Think for a moment. What excuse do we have for lack of joy when Jesus in his resurrection has overcome both Satan and the world? What conditions, thoughts or events rob us of joy? The new era has been born; why not put away the anguish and gloom more closely identified with the old order? Any joy we think we have through the incarnation, life, miracles, suffering and death of Jesus is incomplete, un-enhanced joy if the resurrection is left out of the mix. God wants for us 'complete joy', joy in which nothing is missing; joy which so totally fills us there is no room for anything else; joy which has such power and dominion in our lives that it cannot be discarded, abandoned or shoved aside even in our moments of pain and need; joy thoroughly convinced of the Easter side of Friday and impossible without it.

## A Spirit Filled Life

There is no indwelling of the Holy Spirit if Jesus was doomed to an eternity in the grave. It was the resurrection of Jesus that prepared the way for a life infused with the Holy Spirit.

The Spirit of God has been active in the world from the very beginning of creation when it moved upon the face of the abyss. Throughout the Old Testament God's Spirit continued to be active. Each 'abyss' of men's lives was intercepted and encountered by the Spirit of God moving upon it. The Spirit 'moved upon them', 'entered them', 'fell on them', 'lifted them up', was 'poured upon them'. God activated, or loosed the Spirit upon men each time they were in need of it. The Spirit returned to the Father when his work was accomplished.

In the resurrection, however, we arrive at a point of demarcation and difference. Whereas the Spirit resided in God's temple in the Old Testament and came to our aid in times of need, the risen Christ promised upon his departure that the Holy Spirit would come to dwell permanently in our hearts and become a constant companion and guide:

> *Nevertheless, I tell you the truth: it is to your advantage that I go away, for if I do not go away, the Helper will not come to you. But if I go, I will send him to you. And*

*when he comes he will convict the world concerning sin and righteousness and judgment: concerning sin, because they do not believe in me; concerning righteousness, because I go to the Father, and you will see me no longer; concerning judgment, because the ruler of this world is judged.... When the Spirit of truth comes, he will guide you into all the truth... (John 16: 7–11, 13 ESV)*

We know the Holy Spirit of God dwells within us. The verses we have committed to memory from childhood are constant reminders:

*Do you not know that you are God's temple and that God's Spirit dwells in you? (I Corinthians 3: 16 ESV)*

*Or do you not know that your body is a temple of the Holy Spirit within you, whom you have from God? (I Corinthians 6: 19 ESV)*

*In him you also, when you heard the word of truth, the gospel of your salvation* **[the good news of the resurrection]**, *and believed in him, were sealed with the promised Holy Spirit, who is the guarantee of our inheritance until we acquire possession of it, to the praise of his glory. (Ephesians 1: 13–14 ESV)*

We acknowledge the Holy Spirit's presence. What we find more difficult is to become conduits for the Spirit's purpose. It is interesting that Jesus coupled the Holy Spirit's power with his command to witness his death and resurrection to the world—"you will receive power after the Holy Spirit comes upon you, and you will be my witnesses" (Acts 1: 8). Stephen, the first Christian martyr, is a good example of this fusion. He was enlisted by the disciples because he was 'full of faith and of the Holy Spirit' (Acts 6: 5). Full of grace and power, he began to work 'great miracles and signs among the people' (Acts 6: 8). In his first recorded sermon it was the tremendous power of the Holy Spirit that made Stephen bold, even unto his death. He spoke with inspired wisdom. The Holy Spirit's infilling empowered Stephen, and he saw the glory of God. His preaching of this new gospel was more than words; it was made dynamic by God's indwelling force. The Spirit empowers our speech if we let him. As it says in I Thessalonians 1: 5,

> ...*because our gospel* [**the good news of the resurrection of Jesus**] *came to you not only in word, but also in power and in the Holy Spirit and with full conviction.*

Beyond our witness, which is an outpouring of what we have so graciously received, we are also promised several wonderful qualities for ourselves: peace and joy, singled out from the long list of the Spirit's fruits mentioned in Galatians 5: 22. God fills us with peace and injects us with joy as a reward for our faith. Only to the extent we live out these qualities will the Holy Spirit bring to us an overflowing of hope:

> *May the God of hope fill you with all joy and peace in believing, so that by the power of the Holy Spirit you may abound in hope. (Romans 15: 13 ESV)*

Without the resurrection of Jesus would any of this be ours? Because of the Easter event the Holy Spirit is now permanently within us. All we have to do is claim the promises of God who says that the Spirit is to be and can be the source of our life. What a fantastic gift the risen Christ has given to us.

## A Life of Equivalent Resurrection Power

God's mighty act of raising his son from the dead has given us a life of equivalent resurrection power. In the New Testament the phrase '*power of God*' is most often linked with the bringing of life to his crucified son,

*...and was declared to be the Son of God in power according to the Spirit of holiness by his resurrection from the dead, Jesus Christ our Lord. (Romans 1: 4 ESV)*

*For he was crucified in weakness, but lives by the* **[resurrection]** *power of God. For we also are weak in him, but in dealing with you we will live with him by the power of God. (II Corinthians 13: 4 ESV)*

The second law of thermodynamics states that everything moves from order to chaos. Stars are born and die. Plants grow and decay. All life moves from birth to death. How immense God's resurrection power must have been, refuting the very laws of nature he himself had put in place. God's saving resurrection power is the heart of our Gospel; Paul declares:

*For I am not ashamed of the gospel* **[the good news of the resurrection]***, for it is the power of God for salvation to everyone who believes, to the Jew first and also to the Greek. (Romans 1: 16 ESV)*

And in another letter Paul states that faith must not be built on human wisdom. If it was, no one could understand or even accept the notion of an intervention by new life into the final judgment of death. Faith, he says, can only be based upon the power of God—that is, the incredible fact of the resurrection. Human wisdom would be insufficient:

*...that your faith might not rest in the wisdom of men but in the* **[resurrection]** *power of God. (I Corinthians 2: 5 ESV)*

Furthermore, Jesus is only the *first-fruit* of that power which will be exercised again on our behalf:

*And God raised the Lord and will also raise us up by his* **[resurrection]** *power. (I Corinthians 6: 14 ESV)*

The Greek word for this resurrecting power is *Dunamis*, from which our word 'dynamite' is derived. This same word is used over and over again to describe the power not only manifested for us, but given for our use in the world! The resource of God's power available to those who believe, the Bible says:

*…is the immeasurable greatness of his power toward us who believe, according to the working of his great might that he worked in Christ when he raised him from the dead…. (Ephesians 1: 19–20 ESV)*

The entire verse should be highlighted! Clearly, the power given to us is equated with that same *Dunamis* power God put to the raising of his son. Can we wrap our minds around this gift of the Holy Spirit? Do we realize its vastness? What purpose did God have in mind when he determined to make that investment in us? Can we comprehend the incredible challenge and responsibility we have to exercise this power in our world?

Paul was aware of the immeasurable vastness of God's resurrecting power. He desired it above all else, for he knew if he could ever come into complete possession of it, nothing would be immune to its force. If he could experience that power equivalent to Christ's resurrection, which God promised, he could then, and only then be equipped to share in Christ's suffering and death, thereby arriving at his own resurrection from the dead; notice the order of the process in the passage from Philippians—Paul begins with the risen One and proceeds to his own willingness to suffer, even die, because he knows what awaits him. We have written of this in previous chapters, but it bears repetition here. It is, I believe, God's precise model for the journey from weakness to strength:

*...that I may know him* **[Christ, the risen One]** *and the power of his resurrection, and may share his sufferings, becoming like him in his death, that by any means possible I may attain the resurrection from the dead. (Philippians 3: 10–11 ESV)*

Paul knew that it was necessary to first of all make a commitment to the risen One. That would be followed by resurrection power made available through the Holy Spirit (Paul is careful to use the same word *Dunamis* for both God's resurrection power and the power given to us by the Holy Spirit). Then, he says, suffering for Christ would be akin to fellowship with him; the fellowship of suffering seems in Paul's mind to be a joyful experience, even if it leads to death, for he knows that his own resurrection is sure to follow. In my opinion this is the only way, indeed the most profound way to enter into Christ's service.

How do we receive this resurrection power? By declaring faith in the risen Christ, by confessing that our strength is insufficient to do anything, and by offering up our weakness to the Lord who says:

*..."My grace is sufficient for you, for my power is made perfect in weakness." (II Corinthians 12: 9 ESV)*

Paul preferred to find his joy in the very things that rendered him weak: contempt, persecution, hardship, frustration, even weakness itself, because he knew Christ's resurrection power would be his at the very ragged edge of his weakness. Hence one of the most baffling paradoxes ever spoken:

*For the sake of Christ, then, I am content with weaknesses, insults, hardships, persecutions, and calamities. For when I am weak, then I am strong. (II Corinthians 12: 10 ESV)*

*Dunamis* power was also at the heart of the first preaching. The Jewish authorities were amazed at the boldness of Peter and John, and confessed to each other that, indeed, they could not deny the noticeable miracle that had come about through them. Nonetheless, cautions and threats were leveled against them. Invoking the Lord to give them boldness and work signs and miracles in his name, the Spirit burst upon Jesus' followers and,

> *And with great power the apostles were giving their testimony to the resurrection of the Lord Jesus, and great grace was upon them all. (Acts 4: 33 ESV)*

No wonder the book of Acts reveals that thousands confessed Christ as Lord and Messiah—there is no stopping resurrection 'dynamite' once it is turned loose.

The acts of the apostles were literally explosive because they had been armed with the power from above, the *Dunamis* of the Holy Spirit as promised by the risen Christ (Luke 24: 49). As we have stated, the same power manifested in God's resurrection of Jesus is given to us when the Holy Spirit comes upon us! (Acts 1: 8). I find that absolutely astounding: the same *Dunamis* power exercised in the resurrection is ours through the Holy Spirit. I can barely comprehend the magnitude of power available to me. Knowing God's promise of this incredible power source, why is it the Church has had so little impact on the world in recent centuries? If we ever were able to harness and focus this spiritual energy can you imagine the transformation that would take place? Remember, it all began with the resurrection of Jesus!

Some years ago I was in a situation where I felt the power of Satan at work all around me. Never before had I encountered anything like it. I had always believed that Satan existed, but in my mind he was a rather nebulous force existing 'out there somewhere'. It was possible to observe evil in the world, and Satanic influence, but I simply had never considered the possibility that Satan could actually dwell inside someone and work through them seemingly with their full consent. Even now I find it difficult to actually say that I was in the presence of such a person, but I believe it to be true. I had great plans during that time to engage in writing this book, but I became so entangled and distraught because of the influence of Satan in that person's life, affecting not only him but also the young, impressionable people around him, that I was totally bound. It was frightening, debilitating and depressing. I was possessed with trying in my own power to counteract his influence. Try as I might, I failed miserably. Talking to the person did no good—my words were only twisted by his convoluted rebuttals. At the point of my greatest despair over the situation I was trying to sort out the meaning of the phrase *power of God* in the New Testament and its relationship to the resurrection of Jesus. The Greek word *Dunamis* leaped off the page as I came to realize that the word used for God's resurrection power was the same word used for the power available to us through the Holy Spirit. I began to take courage.

But what of Satan's power? Wasn't it also incredible? Look at its force in the world. Was the same *Dunamis* at work through him? To my amazement, and joy, I discovered that the Greek word most often used to describe Satan's power was *Exousia*—not 'dynamite', but instead a certain 'temporal authority', a power nowhere near the vastness of *Dunamis*. When Jesus said, "In the world you will have tribulations; but be of good cheer, I have overcome the world", he knew what he was saying. The temporal authority of the world has already been overcome by the dynamite power of the risen One. When Christ was raised from the dead and enthroned in Heaven he was given a power—*Dunamis*:

> ...*far above all rule and authority and* **[exousia]** *power and dominion, and above every name that is named, not only in this age but also in the one to come. (Ephesians 1: 21 ESV)*

> ...*and you have been filled in him, who is the head of all rule and authority. (Colossians 2: 10 ESV)*

> *He disarmed the rulers and authorities and put them to open*

*shame, by triumphing over them in him* **[that is, by Jesus' victory over death and the grave]**. *(Colossians 2: 15 ESV)*

Satan's power in the world has been overshadowed and over-come by the death and resurrection of Jesus. Satan has already been defeated! His is an inferior power, greater than our human power but far lesser than God's *Dunamis* power. I claimed that superior power through the Holy Spirit and in so doing discarded the sorry influence and control my adversary had exercised against me. It was as if a shroud of gloom had been lifted. Those who had been swayed and mesmerized by this person began to see how they had been deceived. His influence dissipated. The truth of his falseness was unmasked. When he left, only a minor remnant of his domination remained. This would not have been possible without the resurrection of Jesus. Praise and thanksgiving justly belong to God for his freeing, overwhelming *Dunamis* power.

## A Life Without Fear

Jesus having been raised from the dead has made possible a life without fear. This is particularly good news in our day, where fears come at us from every angle and from a multitude of sources. We live in an age almost totally absorbed by fear.

Those who live in constant fear are most to be pitied. How often have we observed people who shrink from human contact because of fear, or who weave a protective cloak of isolation or silence to envelop themselves. Haven't you known someone whose fear was almost irrational? People have phobias about heights, the dark, other people, human touch, flying, death, certain colors, just about every-thing imaginable. I don't know if I've ever met a person who wasn't afraid of something. The trouble with fear is that, once possessed by it, the spectre of it looms ever larger and more ominous, eventually imprisoning us and freezing us into inactive, unproductive, stagnant lives.

Dimitri Shostakovitch, the Soviet Union's most famous twentieth century composer and one of the great composers of history, lived a life ensnared by fear of Stalin and his cohorts in power. In his memoirs he said that he slept every night for the last thirty years of his life with a packed suitcase by his bed, even long after the death of Stalin. He feared that the authorities would carry him away in the middle of the night for some artistic indiscretion or musical statement alien to Soviet policy. This from a man so famous in his own country and around the world that a great shout of protest would have come from every corner had any harm come to him. His very real fear was a tragic condition, but not an isolated one.

My beloved wife, before we met each other, lived a number of years imprisoned by fear. She had been awakened in the darkness of her bedroom by an intruder pressing a pair of scissors against her throat and was raped by him. Fear so dominated her life that suicide would have been a distinct possibility as a way out had she not felt taking one's own life was immoral. Counseling, psychotherapy and hypnosis made her life a bit more livable, but fear continued to dominate her existence. Then one day several years later she came upon a simple Sunday school poster with a single verse inscribed on it:

*The Lord is my light and my salvation; whom shall I fear?*
*(Psalm 27: 1 ESV)*

It was, she said, as if it immediately penetrated to the very core of her being. God's powerful, healing hand freed her from fear instantaneously and she has not been tormented by fear for a single moment since.

Joseph of Arimathaea kept his belief in Jesus a secret because he feared what the Jewish authorities might do to him (John 19: 38). On Maundy Thursday the disciples, with Jesus in the garden following the Last Supper, ran away out of fear. Peter denied he knew Jesus out of fear. They all gathered behind locked doors for several days for fear of the religious authorities. Would they have ever escaped their fear if Jesus hadn't been raised from the dead? I can see them, years later, still looking over their shoulders as they walked the shore of the sea of Galilee. I can almost feel their sweaty palms when approached by strangers. I can hear their hearts pound when someone mentioned the name of Jesus, for fear that someone would identify and associate them with the crucified One.

I think Jesus knew their fears and chose his first resurrection words carefully. To the startled women in the garden he said, "Be not afraid" (Matthew 28: 10). It is also important to realize that in all but one of the Gospel accounts the disciples did not heed the words of the women and hasten to the garden to see for themselves. Their doubt gave Jesus the opportunity to provide a model for healing from which we can all take hope: he invaded their sheltered, hidden, inconspicuous, protected upper room space with words of peace!

> And he said to them, "Why are you troubled, and why
> do doubts rise in your hearts? See my hands and my feet,
> that it is I myself. Touch me, and see. For a spirit does not
> have flesh and bones as you see that I have." (Luke 24:
> 38-39 ESV)

Wherever we are, huddled against our fears, Jesus comes to us. The risen Christ places his hand upon our fears and says:

> "Fear not, I am the First and the Last and the Living One.
> I died, and behold I am alive forevermore...." (Revelation
> 1: 17–18 ESV)

The love of God in Christ is liberating, but we must fully understand that it would not be so if it were only given in the sacrifice of Jesus. Human love is manifested to its fullest extent in one's being willing to die for that which he loves. The love of God, if it is to be a superior love, must reach beyond death. The offering up of Jesus in his death is only half the story—love remains incomplete. As Paul says:

> *And if Christ has not been raised, your faith is futile and*
> *you are still in your sins. (I Corinthians 15: 17 ESV)*

And if that is so—that we are stilled trapped in our sins—what was accomplished in the sacrifice? The love of God is initiated in the sacrifice and completed in the resurrection. It is the added dimension of the resurrection which separates Godly love from human love and thereby transforms the world. Jesus and his Father's love are brought to completion and are perfected in the resurrection:

> *Although he was a son, he learned obedience through*
> *what he suffered. And being made perfect [raised to his*
> *original perfection], he became the source of eternal sal-*
> *vation to all who obey him… (Hebrews 5: 8–9 ESV)*

This is the fully complete love that leaves no room for fear.

> *There is no fear in love, but perfect love casts out fear…(I*
> *John 4: 18 ESV)*

Once delivered from fear we have the promise of being released from it forever, through the working of the Spirit of God.

> *For you did not receive the spirit of slavery to fall back into*
> *fear, but you have received the Spirit of adoption as sons,*
> *by whom we cry, "Abba! Father!" (Romans 8: 15 ESV)*

That the disciples were completely delivered from their fears is attested to in the *Acts of the Apostles*. In the face of adversity, threats and physical abuse they continued with power (*Dunamis*) to witness to the resurrection of Jesus. They were fearless. Nothing could stop them. These were men who but a few weeks earlier wouldn't have even whispered the name of Jesus to anyone outside their circle. Now they were the living embodiment of Paul's words to the Philippians:

> *Only let your manner of life be worthy of the gospel of Christ* **[that is, the good news regarding the risen One]**, *so that whether I come and see you or am absent, I may hear of you that you are standing firm in one spirit, with one mind striving side by side for the faith of the gospel, and not frightened in anything by your opponents. (Philippians 1: 27-28 ESV)*

They remained faithful to the message of the risen Christ even though, according to tradition, all but one of them suffered martyrdom at the hands of God's enemies (see the Chapter "The Anticipated Messiah"). In light of the evidence that God's resurrection power obliterates fear these words found in the book of Revelation make infinitely more sense:

> *'The words of the first and the last, who died and came to life....Do not fear what you are about to suffer... Be faithful unto death, and I will give you the crown of life.' (Revelation 2: 8–10 ESV)*

## A Life of Spiritual Growth

Continuing our list of resurrection benefits, the risen Christ has also become our foundation upon which to grow and be built up. The Psalmist, in words clearly prophetic, wrote:

> *The stone that the builders rejected has become the cornerstone. (Psalm 118: 22 ESV)*

Jesus knew these words well, and understood that he himself was that cornerstone. He also must have known that the term 'builders' was used in reference to the religious leaders. When he used it in response to questions intended by the Jewish authorities to trip him up, the religious leaders of his day must have been cut to the quick.

The authorities as well as his own followers may not have understood how it was that Jesus used these words. That they came to be regarded as important is evidenced by the fact that all three Synoptic Gospels record them, and in essentially the same way:

> Jesus said to them, "Have you never read in the Scriptures: 'The stone that the builders rejected has become the cornerstone; this was the Lord's doing, and it is marvelous in our eyes'? Therefore I tell you, the kingdom of God will be taken away from you and given to a people producing its fruits. And the one who falls on this stone will be broken to pieces; and when it falls on anyone, it will crush him." When the chief priests and the Pharisees heard his parables, they perceived that he was speaking about them. (Matthew 21: 42–45; also Mark 12: 10, and Luke 20: 17–18 ESV)

Writing in the lingering glow of the resurrection, Matthew, Mark and Luke came to understand how these prophetic words were fulfilled in the Christ who was raised from the dead. The phrase must have become a litany, a rallying cry, a hymn of triumph in the early Christian community. Peter is quoted by Luke in the *Acts of the Apostles* as saying them, this time with knowledge and elaboration, in response to the question why they had healed the lame man:

> ...the priests and the captain of the temple and the Sadducees came upon them, greatly annoyed because they were teaching the people and proclaiming in Jesus the resurrection from the dead **[remember, the Sadducees did not believe in any kind of resurrection]**.... They inquired, "By what power or by what name did you do this?" Then Peter, filled with the Holy Spirit, said to them, "Rulers of the people and elders, if we are being examined today concerning a good deed done to a crippled man, by

> *what means this man has been healed, let it be known to all of you and to all the people of Israel that by the name of Jesus Christ of Nazareth, whom you crucified, whom God raised from the dead—by him this man is standing before you well. This Jesus is the stone that was rejected by you, the builders, which has become the cornerstone. And there is salvation in no one else, for there is no other name under heaven given among men by which we must be saved." (Acts 4: 1-2, 7–12 ESV)*

Even though the Jewish leaders had rejected Jesus of Nazareth, by giving him over to death they unwittingly played a part in God's master plan of creating the colossal edifice of salvation brought to completion in the resurrection. Peter's testimony used the biblical phrase they all knew to indicate that the prophecy had become fulfilled in the living Christ. Paul wrote to the Churches at Corinth and Ephesus,

> *According to the grace of God given to me, like a skilled master builder I laid a foundation and someone else is building upon it. Let each one take care how he builds upon it. For no one can lay a foundation other than that which is laid, which is Jesus Christ* **[validated as Christ through the resurrection]**. *(I Corinthians 3: 10–11 ESV)*

> *...built on the foundation of the apostles and prophets. Christ Jesus himself being the cornerstone, in whom the whole structure, being joined together, grows into a holy temple in the Lord. In him you also are being built together into a dwelling place for God by the Spirit. (Ephesians 2: 20–22 ESV)*

Paul may be suggesting that Jesus is not only the foundation—he is the mortar bonding all the stones (believers) into a single unit. Jesus has become the replacement for the temple in Jerusalem, a movable feast of the glory of God. Those who profess the risen Lord are more than stones in the edifice—they each have a life of their own though mortared together in common purpose. They live; they constitute a new priesthood of believers spoken of by Peter:

*As you come to him, a living stone rejected by men but in the sight of God chosen and precious, you yourselves like living stones are being built up as a spiritual house to be a holy priesthood, to offer spiritual sacrifices accept- able to God through Jesus Christ. For it stands in Scripture: "Behold, I am laying in Zion a stone, a cornerstone chosen and precious, and whoever believes in him will not be put to shame." (I Peter 2: 4–6 ESV)*

While we have unified purpose in this 'resurrection sanctuary', our missions are varied and distinctive. Each has a role to play, and none is subservient to the others. In this spiritual cathedral the door handle is as important as the flying buttress. God calls us according to our abilities. Whether great or small he desires for us to play out our roles completely, sacrificially, lovingly, enthusiastically, and joyfully. As the widow's mite was given, we also must give. All that we are and have belong to him, and is to be offered without immaturity and vacillation. In so doing we,

*…grow in the grace and knowledge of our Lord and Savior Jesus Christ. (II Peter 3: 18 ESV)*

Paul offered the following challenge with full knowledge of the diversity of living stones:

*And he gave the apostles, the prophets, the evangelists, the shepherds and teachers, to equip the saints for the work of ministry, for building up the body of Christ [the risen One], until we all attain to the unity of the faith and*

*of the knowledge of the Son of God, to mature manhood,
to the measure of the stature of the fullness of Christ, so
that we may no longer be children, tossed to and fro by
the waves and carried about by every wind of doctrine,
by human cunning, by craftiness in deceitful schemes.
Rather, speaking the truth in love, we are to grow up in every way into him who is the head, into Christ. (Ephesians
4: 11–15 ESV)*

If we are to grow and be built up we must be rooted in Christ, the
one validated as both Lord and Christ on Easter (Colossians 2: 6-7).
The only things that grow in darkness are moss and mushrooms. If we
don't grow spiritually it isn't the fault of God or God's son. It may be
because we dwell most often on the far side of the shadow cast by
the cross or in the darkness of the tomb. We are to walk in the light as
he is in the light. Our call is to be raised to life with Christ, to aspire
to the realm where Christ lives (Colossians 3: 1). Only the resurrection gives life, and when we claim that resurrected life there most
certainly will be spiritual growth.

## A Life of Cross Carrying

With all that has been said in pursuit of developing an attitude
of resurrection-mindedness, for me to now advocate 'cross-carrying'
may seem a paradox. Yet, the resurrection of Jesus gives us the courage
to live a life unafraid to carry the cross. To suggest that 'cross-carrying'
is made possible by the resurrection of Jesus is not paradoxical nor is
it out of place. Precisely because we have come to the point of granting the resurrection the central position of the New Testament, we are
now able to pick up the cross of Jesus and carry it in good conscience
and with the proper spirit. We are enabled because we know that
Jesus was crowned with glory and honor on Easter for carrying his
cross.

*But we see him who for a little while was made lower than the angels, namely Jesus, crowned with glory and honor* **[through the resurrection]** *because of the suffering of death, so that by the grace of God he might taste death for everyone. (Hebrews 2: 9 ESV)*

In light of the resurrection 'cross-carrying' becomes a joyful experience. Jesus made a mockery of the cross on Easter, scorning its shame. Though our own 'cross-carrying' may be physically taxing, the spiritual yoke of the cross is easy, its burden light—we know the portal of suffering leads beyond the grave to life with Christ. 'Cross-carrying' is folly only for those who do not understand or even believe the truth of the resurrection. For us who know the outcome on 'the third day' carrying the cross can be a sign of the resurrection power (*Dunamis*) of God (I Corinthians 1: 18), but only if we carry it in a resurrection spirit.

A word of qualification is necessary here. As long as Christians focus primarily on Jesus' sacrifice and death—and I believe this is a universal problem in the Church—'cross-carrying' does not fulfill the commands of the New Testament. It is done, then, in the wrong frame of mind and for the wrong purpose. Then the tendency is to say, "I have brought my life to the grave, just as he did." God's purpose for his son was not to bring him to Friday. It was intended to deliver him through Friday to Sunday. Friday was only one step, albeit the necessary first step on the way to Sunday. Therefore, we are compelled to carry the cross in the spirit of Easter. Only then will it make the proper statement to the world. Only then will it speak of the superiority of the Christian faith over all other philosophies and religions that do nothing more than make us content in living and comfortable in dying.

Jesus commanded his followers to take up the cross:

*"And whoever does not take his cross and follow me is not worthy of me. Whoever finds his life will lose it, and whoever loses his life for my sake will find it." (Matthew 10: 38–39 ESV)*

The Gospels record these words a total of five times (also Matthew 16: 24; Mark 8: 34-35; Luke 9: 23; Luke 14: 27). These words, along with Jesus' words that he would die and rise on the third day, had to have been puzzling to the disciples. We must realize how they were unprepared through their understanding of the Scriptures for a Son of Man, Davidic King or Messiah who would die. So what was all this talk of 'cross-carrying'? Peter, who had just said, "Thou art the Christ, the Son of the living God" (Matthew 16: 16), responded to Jesus' first words of his coming death by rebuking Him (Matthew 16: 22), even though Jesus, in the same breath, had talked about his rising from the dead on the third day. Obviously, his disciples were also baffled by his talk of 'rising'. After all, if the Messiah they were looking for was not supposed to die, any sort of rising or resurrection would be unnecessary. However one interprets their response to his talk of dying, it appears Peter did not refer to Jesus as the Christ or Messiah again. Though he and the others were uncertain about who Jesus was, there were enough signs and miracles to keep them wondering. On Palm Sunday the disciples were elevated to the heights of emotion by vast crowds shouting their 'hosannas'. But four days after Jesus' triumphal entry into Jerusalem Peter would deny that he ever knew him. When Jesus carried the cross on Good Friday who volunteered to carry it for him—none of the disciples, for they were nowhere to be found. They had forsaken him and were in hiding. Each of the eleven had become in his own way a kind of Judas. There were no volunteers to carry the cross for this man who, if he were nothing more than a man, deserved at least some kind of sympathy for what he had done to improve the quality of life for so many.

When Jesus stumbled on the way, Pilate's soldiers corralled someone from the crowd to assist him. Not a single person came forward willingly. Poor Simon, a visitor from Cyrene: in the wrong place at the wrong time! Staring headlong into the death of Jesus no one was willing to identify with his coming suffering and death. A Good Friday spirit, acting as if there never was a Sunday, not only disallows 'cross-carrying', it also deems the act irrational and the volunteers unworthy.

But there was a Sunday! Everything changed, from the lives of the disciples to the course of history. The resurrection of Jesus Christ from the dead emboldened the disciples and gave them joy in his service regardless of the perils they encountered. Contrast the attitude of Acts 5: 41 with what you know of the disciples' responses between Maundy Thursday and Easter night:

> *Then they* **[the apostles]** *left the presence of the council, rejoicing that they were counted worthy to suffer dishonor for the name* **[referring to the Name which is above every name: Jesus the Christ, the risen One].**

As it says in Philippians 2: 8-12:

> *And being found in human form, he humbled himself by becoming obedient to the point of death, even death on a cross. Therefore God has highly exalted him and bestowed on him the name that is above every name, so that at the name of Jesus every knee should bow, in heaven and on earth and under the earth, and every tongue confess that Jesus Christ is Lord, to the glory of God the Father.*

In the Name of the One validated as both Lord and Christ by God's resurrecting power the apostles carried the cross, an action not even remotely considered before the Easter event. Think of the enormity of this transformation, and realize that it took place in a matter of days, a few weeks, not months or years. It was nothing short of radical metamorphosis.

The suffering of the One who was made alive, not the One brought to death, has become our example. That may seem a very thin line of distinction, but we would do well to ponder its immense implications. Try to imagine the profound complexity involved in the transformation from a broken spirit on Good Friday to the heart stopping joy of the upper room Sunday evening. Transformation was not subtle, not gradual, but truly so wrenching that there could never be a return to their pre-resurrection world. When we finally are able to wrap our minds and hearts around that immense shift of spirit we'll be able to understand why the proper attitude for 'cross-carrying' is one of life changing joy and privilege. Whatever suffering is encountered is greatly ameliorated by resurrection confidence:

> For it has been granted to you that for the sake of Christ **[the risen One]** you should not only believe in him but also suffer for his sake... (Philippians 1: 29 ESV)

Such a privilege can only be entered into by 'living' stones offering up to God their 'living' sacrifices. If Christ, the chief cornerstone referred to earlier, is not living, it would be impossible for us to be living stones and living sacrifices:

> I appeal to you therefore, brothers, by the mercies of God, to present your bodies as a living sacrifice, holy and acceptable to God, which is your spiritual worship. (Romans 12: 1 ESV)

We can be 'alive' in our sacrificial living because,

> The Spirit himself bears witness with our spirit that we are children of God, and if children, then heirs—heirs of God and fellow heirs with Christ **[the risen One]**, provided we suffer with him in order that we may also be glorified with him. (Romans 8: 16–17 ESV)

Paul goes on to say that in no way does the suffering compare to the splendor that shall be ours. We are to carry the cross as ones already marked by the splendiferous resurrection of Jesus Christ.

'Cross-carrying' should not take out of context the words of Paul in Galatians 6: 14:

*But far be it from me to boast except in the cross of our Lord Jesus Christ* **[validated as Lord and Christ through the resurrection]**, *by which the world has been crucified to me, and I to the world. (Galatians 6: 14 ESV)*

Paul is referring to the cross of the risen One. He makes a practice of approaching the crucifixion through the eyes of the resurrection. This is evidenced by his use of the resurrection titles 'Lord' and 'Christ'. As we have said throughout this book, to view the Galatians passage as cross-minded exclusively, without its resurrection connotation, bends and distorts Paul's theology.

The verses which reveal the proper path for cross-carrying are found in his letter to the Church at Philippi, used several times earlier:

*...that I may know him and the power of his resurrection, and may share his sufferings, becoming like him in his death, that by any means possible I may attain the resurrection from the dead. (Philippians 3: 10–11 ESV)*

It is fitting that we use these words here, for the third time in the book, as we come to the end of this treatise. I have suggested this passage to be perhaps the most profound roadmap for living the Christian life. For that reason it is the last issue you'll read, with the hope that it will characterize the resurrected life God calls us to embody. I believe that Paul was very careful to give us a precise and well-ordered model for living and worshiping, and for true understanding of his sense of the Gospel. His model has four points, and, as we have suggested, it is the order of these four points that is most striking and most important.

First and uppermost is the desire to know the One raised by God's resurrecting power. We approach the Christian faith through the risen Lord. From this doorway, once opened, stretches the vast horizon of faith possibility.

Second, once we have entered the doorway of the resurrection, we not only embrace Christ, the risen One, but are imbued with that same resurrection power manifested on his behalf; in other words, we, too, are given *Dunamis* power through the Holy Spirit.

Third, having been duly gifted with this promise of eternal life and resurrection power, we are enabled to suffer with and for Christ. Sharing in the suffering of Christ is no longer to be feared, because we have the assurance of being pulled from its consequences by our newly gained resurrection hope.

Fourth, even if we are called to die for our faith in the risen Christ, we can do so with joy and thanksgiving, knowing that when this life is ended the brilliance of the resurrected, eternal existence with the Triune God awaits us.

Facing his coming death, the disciples of Jesus were not able to suffer with him. They went to great lengths to distance themselves from his fate, even denying they had ever known him. Why? They had seen what a truly remarkable person he was. They had seen his supernatural powers displayed. They had even heard his words of eternal life and Son-ship. Where was the problem? I feel they responded the way they did because they had not yet known the risen One, experienced his resurrection power, or for that matter, even understood his words of resurrection. The first two points of the Philippians model were not yet available to them. Therefore, they had to begin with suffering, and in this absence of hope, who would be willing to suffer and die for a dead man? Before the crucifixion Jesus' disciples turned cowardly, but after basking in the presence of the risen Christ for forty days they became unbelievably bold. Daily they stared death itself in the face without batting an eye. They were willing to die for the cause of the risen One because they were convinced that same resurrection would be theirs. *The path to 'cross-carrying' may lead us into the valley of the shadow of death, but the path of 'cross-carrying' also leads us into the deep, sure channels of the resurrection.*

Paul knew this. His transformation began, after all, with a confrontation with the resurrected One on the Damascus road. For him, everything proceeded out of his encounter with the risen Christ. Sufferings and hardships, imprisonment and beatings were no deterrent to his witness. Paul was certain that living for the living Christ, or dying for the living Christ, both led to an eternity with the living Christ.

> *Our hope for you is unshaken, for we know that as you share in our sufferings, you will also share in our comfort…. Indeed, we felt that we had received the sentence of death. But that was to make us rely not on ourselves but on God who raises the dead. (II Corinthians 1: 7, 9)*

We know Jesus was raised from the dead, step one. We know that same *Dunamis* power has been made available to us through the Holy Spirit, step two. How tragic it would be to proceed in our Christian walk with the third step, that of suffering, as if the first two steps did not exist. That is the history, past and present, of the Church. It should not be the future of the Church! Our activities and desires for the Christian life must begin with the risen Lord—first—and then reach back to embrace his sacrifice.

Carrying the cross comes last, after first holding aloft the standard of Christ's resurrection and planting it in the center of our being. New Testament style 'cross-carrying' is a sign of our being touched by the risen One. This kind of 'cross-carrying' is a mark of a life that, by the power of the resurrection, is eternal, transformed, abundant, Spirit-filled, empowered by *Dunamis*, joyful, fearless, and nurtured into continued growth. Life-certain 'cross-carrying' is made possible by the knowledge that none of these qualities and characteristics of the Christian life would be fully possible had not Jesus been raised from the dead.

Ours is a desperate world seeking hope. We who believe have been made clean by the sacrificial and atoning death of Jesus. We have been made alive with him through his resurrection. We who live the resurrected life possess the answer to our culture's deepest needs.

It is the resurrection of Jesus, and that above all, that is the seed bed of the life which is truly Christian and which stands in stark and vivid contrast to those of the unbelieving world through its remarkable, life-empowering difference.

# End Notes

## Chapter Three

Frend, W.H.C., *Martyrdom and Persecution in the Early Church: A Study of a Conflict from the Maccabees to Donatus*, Oxford, Basil Blackwell, 1965, p. 80

## Chapter Four

1. Fuller, Daniel, *Easter Faith and History*, Wm. B. Eerdmans, Grand Rapids, Michigan, 1965, p. 230-31.
2. *Ibid.*, p. 232.
3. Marshall, I. Howard, *The Acts of the Apostles*, an Introduction and commentary, Inter-Varsity Press, Leicester, England, 1980, p. 25.
4. Frend, W.H.C., *Martyrdom and Persecution in the Early Church: A Study of a Conflict from the Maccabees to Donatus*, Oxford, Basil Blackwell, 1965, p. 88

## Chapter Five

1. Guthrie, Donald, *New Testament Theology*, Inter-Varsity Press, 1981, p. 387.

2.  Clark, Neville, *Interpreting the· Resurrection*, SCM Press, Ltd., London, 1967, p. 55.
3.  Jansen, John Frederick, *The Resurrection of Jesus Christ in New Testament Theology*, Westminster Press, Philadelphia, 1980, p. 58.
4.  Künneth, Walter, *The Theology of the Resurrection*, SCM Press, Ltd., London, translated J. W. Leitch, 1965, p. 143.
5.  *Ibid.*, p. 151.
6.  *Ibid.*, p. 151.
7.  *Ibid.*, p. 153.

## Chapter Six

1.  Barth, Karl, *The Resurrection of the Dead*, translated by H. J. Stenning, Fleming H. Revell Co., N.Y., 1933, p. 153
2.  Künneth, Walter, *The Theology of the Resurrection*, translated by J. W. Leitch, SCM Press, London, 1965, p. 223
3.  Martelet, Gustave, *The Risen Christ and the Eucharistic World*, A Crossroad Book, The Seabury Press, N.Y., translated 1976, pp. 49-50
4.  Künneth, Walter, *op. cit.*, p. 151
5.  *Ibid.*, p. 154
6.  Barth, Karl, *op. cit.*, p. 159
7.  Clark, Neville, *Interpreting the Resurrection*, SCM Press, London, 1967
8.  Künneth, Walter, *op. cit.*, p. 186
9.  Barth, Karl, *op. cit.*, pp. 211-12
10. *Ibid.*, p. 212

# Resurrection Meals As A Model For Eucharist

WE BEGIN OUR discourse with a brief recounting of the disciples' psychology leading up to the Last Supper and continuing until joy overtook them at Jesus' appearance on Easter night. First of all, can anyone doubt that the mood that Passover night was one of sorrow, fear, doubt and despair? It was supposed to be a remembrance of the deliverance from the bondage of Egypt. Instead, Jesus talked about betrayal, denial, and death. The Old Testament scriptures were not understood by the Jewish scholars to suggest that Messiah would die. Very few believed in the possibility of a resurrection at the end of the age, and no one believed Messiah would need it in the middle of time; Messiah wouldn't die. If Jesus, whom they thought was Messiah, was going to die, how could he be the One they had hoped for? No catacomb art works, much less any of the Eucharist portraits found there, seem to be characterized by the somber mood we associate with Maundy Thursday.

I feel what happened in the hearts and minds of the disciples at the Last Supper was the beginning of a series of experiences they would later come to regret. They fell asleep in the garden, and ran for their lives when Jesus was taken captive. Peter denied him. Jesus died on the cross with only one of the remaining eleven disciples by his side. They didn't believe the report of the women or of Cleopas on 'the third day'. They were slow to recognize Jesus even when he

appeared in their midst on Easter night. All these responses, beginning perhaps with their mood at the Last Supper, constitute an edifice
of embarrassment and humiliation I seriously doubt they would have
wanted to experience again.

The Eucharist we celebrate, modeled on that Maundy Thursday
Passover Meal we call the *Last Supper*, became a Sacrament of the
Church sometime after the legalization of Christianity. Every wing of
the Church Universal that celebrates the Sacrament sees it in essentially the same way. The 'Words of Institution' are taken from New
Testament Scripture, using the words of the Apostle Paul from his
letters to the Church at Corinth. Some church traditions accept the
elements of bread and cup as symbolic or representative of the body
and blood of Jesus. Others see the elements as being miraculously
transformed into the actual body and blood of Jesus. Either way, the
Sacrament has deep meaning for Christians across the centuries and
around the world. As such, it should be respected and revered as a
worthy meal for repentant communicants.

In this treatise we will explore the roots of what might have been
an alternative Eucharistic practice in the period prior to 313 AD, that
is, the period beginning during the lives of the Apostles and continuing through the period of persecution. The only evidence for this
alternative possibility is seen on the walls of the catacombs in Rome
and in a few early documents of the Church.

Numerous frescoes referred to as Eucharist exist in the burial
chambers of Rome. When confronting those Eucharist art works in
the catacombs for the first time in 1974 several questions struck me.
Why is the cup, which the Church associates with the blood of Jesus,
missing from the table so often, nearly half the time? Why is the plate
of fish on the table when there are no New Testament accounts of the
Last Supper that mention fish as part of the meal? I proceeded with
the hypothesis that the meal being portrayed was not based on the
Last Supper where the cup is critical and the fish is absent.

Bread and Fish appear on the table in every catacomb Eucharist
fresco and sarcophagus. The presence of the Bread is not unusual as

it is also part of the Last Supper sacramental meal we celebrate. But the question is, 'Does the Bread represent the body of Christ as in our sacramental Last Supper?' The answer may lie in the post-resurrection Emmaus road account found in Luke, chapter 24. Two followers of Jesus, Cleopas and his unnamed friend, were returning home following the crucifixion of Jesus. Perhaps they had been waiting since that ugly Friday for a chance to escape Jerusalem without being arrested by the Roman authorities. On their way to Emmaus a stranger appeared and questioned why they were downcast. It was the resurrected Jesus, but they didn't recognize him. They asked if he was the only one in Jerusalem who didn't know what had happened during those terrible days! The Stranger began to explain their Scriptures to them, giving a new interpretation to the prophecies regarding Messiah that Judaism had misinterpreted. As they stopped for something to eat they recognized the Stranger accompanying them as the risen Christ when he took the bread, broke it, and gave it to them. Note the sacramental tone with which Jesus offered the meal:

> When he was at the table with them, he took bread and blessed and gave it to them. And their eyes were opened, and they recognized him. (Luke 24: 30-31 ESV)

The words of verse 30 are reminiscent of Jesus' words at the Last Supper four days earlier (Luke 22:19), where he equated the bread with his body which was to be broken. However, this encounter with Cleopas and his friend follows the brokenness of the crucified Jesus who now appears in his newly resurrected state. We must hold this thought as we continue.

After Jesus broke the bread with Cleopas, Scripture says he 'vanished from their sight'. Immediately the two ran back to Jerusalem to tell the disciples, still gathered in fear, what they had seen. Scripture tells us they didn't believe this second report of a confrontation with the risen Lord. Then Jesus himself 'appeared' in their presence in the upper room. Still disbelieving 'for joy', the disciples recognized the 'ghost' who appeared among them in that upper room Sunday night as the risen, flesh and blood Christ when he ate a piece of broiled fish in their presence.

The Eucharistic frescoes in the catacombs all point toward a single type of meal where, in addition to the bread, fish was included—the two post-resurrection meals mentioned above serve as the model. The *Fish* and *Bread* mainstays of catacomb Eucharistic portrayals seem to indicate that the meal depicted is more closely identified with the events of Easter Sunday and the risen One—the Emmaus Road 'breaking of bread' and the Upper Room eating of fish—than with the Maundy Thursday meal with the about-to-be-crucified Jesus. Given the two meals recounted in Luke 22 and 24, the first filled with sorrow, the second with joy, and given a choice between them as a foundation for Ritual, which seems the more likely to have been chosen in the afterglow of the death and resurrection of Jesus?

The book of Acts tells us that Jesus' followers continued to 'break bread' together. 'Breaking bread' appears to be a Eucharistic phrase. While Jesus 'broke bread' with his disciples at the Last Supper, isn't it interesting that the words also were part of the Emmaus road confrontation with the risen Christ recorded in Luke 24, and are used again in the post-resurrection meal prepared by Jesus, as described in John 21! Further, the Gospel of Luke, which provides the Eucharistic foundation, and the *Acts of the Apostles*, which establishes and perpetuates the post-resurrection Eucharistic tradition, are thought to have been authored by the same person. *Bread*, almost always portrayed with the *sign of the Fish* in catacomb art, is never identified in those chambers with the broken body of Jesus; it only and always points toward fellowship with the risen Lord.

As we have suggested, *Fish* points us toward the resurrection. Jesus is said to have eaten fish with his disciples three times; all three occasions follow his resurrection! The *sign of the Fish*, then, must be considered much more than just a Christian sign. It should be acknowledged that *Fish*, or *Ichthus*, was the earliest sign of the risen Christ.

We must take a moment here to understand the Greek word

*Ichthus* and how it became an acronym for an early Christian creed. The first letter, *I*, stood for *Iesu*, or Jesus, the son of God's earthly name. *Ch*, in Greek *X*, pronounced *Chi* (key), was short for *Christ*, a resurrection title. *Th*, the Greek Theta, was the sign for *Theos*, or *God*. *U*, *unigenite*, means *only begotten Son*. And the final letter, *S*, was for *Soteris*, or *Savior*. Taken together, the *Ichthus* creed reads: *Jesus Christ, God's only begotten Son, Savior*.

The sacramental meal in catacomb art where *Fish*, or *Ichthus*, is always on the table may very well be a joyful feast with the resurrected Jesus who has been validated as both Lord and Christ (Acts 2, Romans 1) through the resurrecting power of his Father.

The tradition of the cup is of importance also, even though it is absent almost half the time in catacomb Eucharist portraits. We know that in the practices of the early Church the cup was not always wine. On occasion it was water, and sometimes water and wine mingled. When Eucharist followed Baptism—in itself a death-resurrection sign—the cup was milk and honey mixed! Without going into great detail, it must be suggested that honey appears to be a sign of life; more specifically, honey is a sign of that life which comes out of death. In other words, honey is used as a resurrection sign. Several New Testament translations of Luke 24 (including King James) say that Jesus ate fish *and a honeycomb* Easter night when he revealed his risen Presence to his disciples.

One need only go back to several events in the Old Testament for the roots of this sign. The manna that sustained life for the children of Israel in the wilderness was said to taste like honey. When Samson killed the lion and ripped open its carcass, *'He saw a swarm of bees in it, and honey'* (Judges 14: 8). This story appears in a catacomb fresco and suggests that out of the bitterness of death comes the sweetness of life: good news for those given over to death at the mouths of lions! Finally, when God intervened on behalf of the children of Israel and delivered them out of the bondage of Egypt, he led them to the promised land of *milk and honey*. Out of their death-like existence under the Pharaohs they had been 'resurrected' to the land of sweetness. The symbolism of honey was clear to the early Church: new life out of death.

Here is a recipe for re-enacting a Resurrection Eucharist: take the bread of the Emmaus road experience and couple it with Jesus' words in the Gospel of John, *'I am the bread of Life'*. Then add the cup of milk and honey, a sign of deliverance from death into the sweetness of life. Remember that Baptism—the event preceding the milk and honey cup—was in itself a sign of death and resurrection: being buried with Christ symbolizing his death, and being raised with Christ symbolizing his resurrection. Place on the table the sign of the *Fish* signifying the presence of the risen Christ. The Eucharist which results is very different from the one in which the key words are, *'For as often as you eat this bread and drink the cup, you proclaim the Lord's death until he comes'* (I Corinthians 11: 26).

The sacramental meal I have described is the only type depicted in catacomb art. As such, it gives ample visual evidence to support the thesis that a Eucharist existed in the early Church that was based on the resurrection meals with Jesus.

We might at this point raise the question regarding the ways we refer to the Sacrament of Eucharist. Is it the *Last Supper* or the *Lord's Supper*? Do we use these terms interchangeably? In our minds do they mean the same thing? Or is it possible they were originally attached to different meals? To answer that question it is necessary to define the use of the title *Lord*. This title was used in *Apostolic* times as well as in the early Church as a reference to the risen One. Remember Peter's first sermon preached in Jerusalem (Acts 2: 36) and his concluding words: *'Let all the house of Israel therefore know for certain that God has made him both Lord and Christ, this Jesus whom you crucified.'* In other words, Jesus has been validated as *Lord* through the resurrection. If we accept *Lord* as a resurrection title, that renders the phrase 'The Lord's Supper' a reference to a meal with the resurrected Jesus. The Eucharist scholar Lietzmann (whose interpretation follows shortly) would concur, as he supports the existence of two distinctly different meals in the early Church. Oscar Cullman, another scholar who doesn't fully agree with Lietzmann though he agrees in part, raises the question of the possibility of two meals in the title of one of his treatises: *Last Supper or Lord's Supper?*

To this point in our treatise evidence supporting a *Resurrection Eucharist* is meager, based solely on catacomb art, a few passages of Scripture, and a cursory interpretation of the psychology of the disciples. If all we had to go on was the art of the catacombs it would be inadvisable to make too much of it. However, a number of very reputable scholars (Lietzmann, Cullman, Higgins, Vöörbus, and others) have devoted much of their lives to the question of *Eucharist* and seem to be of the opinion that a *Eucharist* different from the one we know and celebrate may have existed in the early Church, perhaps existing side by side with the Maundy Thursday type, perhaps preceding it.

Hans Lietzmann suggests there was a second type of *Eucharist* in the primitive church—a joyful meal looking toward the second coming of Christ. Both he and Rudolph Bultmann are of the opinion that the *Eucharist* was not instituted by Christ at the Last Supper. Joachim Jeremias opposes that view, seeing *Eucharist* as an eschatological meal instituted at that last Passover meal with the about-to-be-crucified Jesus.

> *In any case, clearly contradictory views of eminent scholars cannot all be correct. Bultmann's theory that the Eucharist is a sacramental meal originating in the Hellenistic [Greek speaking] church cannot be reconciled with Jeremias' thesis that the Eucharist is an eschatological meal instituted by Jesus at the Last Supper [a Jewish Passover meal]. Lietzmann's conclusion that there were two types of Eucharist in the primitive church is not compatible with the position expressed by Oscar Cullman, namely, that there was one Eucharist which included both characteristics.*[1]

Unaware of Eucharistic art in the catacombs, Lietzmann's evidence supporting a second practice is taken in part from an early document discovered in 1873 called *Didache.*

> *The Didache is ranked by common consensus among the most precious discoveries of the [19th] century in the area of early Christian literature. It is an ecclesiastical manual dealing with catechetical, liturgical, disciplinary and pastoral matters and, as such it is a mine of wealth.* [2]

> *The data point to Jerusalem as the original home of the prayers of the Didache, and to some time between the years AD 30 and 70.* [3]

Not all scholars agree with that early date for the *Didache*. Some argue that it was written closer to 150 AD, while most would place it between 90–100 AD. However, all believe that whenever it was created it was putting into written form practices and prayers that were already in existence, thus placing them into the lifetimes of the Apostles, men who would have shaped the Eucharistic tradition. Chapters 9 and 10 describe *Eucharist* and its prayers.

> *…what kind of ritual meal does the source exhibit? Is it the Eucharist? The answer in the affirmative has been given by A. Harnack, P. Batiffol, J. Weiss, K. Volker, H. Lietzmann, K. Lake, and others. Others believe it represents the Eucharist in part and the Agape [an actual meal to satisfy physical hunger] in part…. Still others assert that these prayers constitute only the framework for the communal meal of Agape which was followed by the Eucharist…. This last explanation has inspired clouds of speculation…. It is simply not credible that the document—which was designed to deal with the matters concerning the life, worship and ecclesiastical practice of the Christian community, and in which everything else of the cult and life of the congregation is registered—should neglect such an important cultic act. That the source would deal at such length with the Agape yet*

*ignore the central act [Eucharist], in the worship of the community, that indeed is unbelievable. [4]*

The author goes on to say that the language of the prayers is not ordinary language. In his opinion the language appears *sacramental* and contains a *Eucharist tone.* He writes,

*The prayers have the rubric: 'About the Eucharist'.[5]*

The liturgical texts in *Didache* contain no reference to the death of Jesus, his broken body or shed blood. There is no thought given to Jesus' sacrifice, nor is there any reference to the cross.

*...the Eucharistic imagery does not show any relationship between the rite and death of Jesus. There is no question of a memorial of the death of Jesus, and no reference to the broken body or the shed blood. Not a single word is used to mention the fact of the death of Christ.... Indeed, the Eucharistic prayers do not even hint that the sacred ritual is related in any way to the tradition of the Last Supper celebrated by Jesus with his disciples.[6]*

The Eucharistic imagery in *Didache* singles out *Life* as its central theme, and the elements—bread and the cup—are representative of the gathered, worshiping community.

The prayer over the cup, which comes first, states: *'We give Thee thanks, our Father, for the holy vine of Thy servant David, which Thou hast made known to us through Thy Servant Jesus'.* The phrase, *'holy vine of David'* was Israel's way of referring to itself as the chosen people of God.

*Actually of Canaanite origin, the metaphor of the vine became deeply imbedded in the Israelite tradition.... The 'vine' became a favorite metaphor, a popular way of describing Israel under the figure of the vine.... It developed*

*into a symbol for salvation history, a standard emblem for*
*the elect people...*[7]

'Holy vine of David' in *Didache* seems to suggest that those who
believe Jesus is Messiah or Christ are the *new* chosen ones of God,
that is, the new '*Holy vine of David*.'

> *This image was destined to play an essential role in nascent*
> *Jewish Christian theology. In fact, it became essential for*
> *the self-understanding of the new Christian community. It*
> *learned to see itself as the fulfillment of the ideal Israel, the*
> *new Israel replacing the old...*[8]

The cup in *Didache*, then, is a sign of our being chosen by virtue
of our faith in the risen One; it is not a symbol of Jesus' blood.

The prayer over the bread begins: '*We give Thee thanks, our*
*Father, for the life and knowledge which Thou hast made known to us*
*through Thy Servant Jesus*.' We have been given, the prayer says, the
incredible gifts of life and knowledge. When the prayer continues it
speaks of those gifts in terms of 'immortality' and 'eternal life'. We are
in possession of those gifts at this very moment, which guarantees our
being gathered at the end of time. The prayer continues: '*As grains of*
*wheat have been gathered into one loaf so the Church, though scat-*
*tered around the world, will be gathered into one loaf in the presence*
*of the living Christ.* 'The loaf is the sign of our gathering, now and in
eternity; it is not a symbol of Jesus' broken body. The image of the
'gathered loaf' in the *Didache* prayer,

> *...was the ground of the hope of resurrection of the whole*
> *man and of the consummation of union with Christ at the*
> *Parousia when the church would be gathered into God's*
> *Kingdom.*[9]

We must bear in mind that the earliest Gospel, Mark, was written
no earlier than the 50s AD, perhaps as late as 65-70 AD. The Gospels

of Matthew and Luke were written before 70 AD, and John's Gospel perhaps as late as 98 AD.

John's Gospel seems to corroborate and validate the earlier dates suggested for *Didache*. Where *Didache* uses the metaphors of *bread* and *vine* as the spiritual gifts made known by Jesus, John transforms those metaphors:

> ...the Fourth Gospel equates the eternal bread with Christ himself: 'I am the bread of life'. Again, in the Didache, the term 'vine' is a metaphor for the spiritual gift of God revealed through the servant Jesus whereas the Fourth Gospel identifies Christ himself with the vine: 'I am the true vine'. 'Life' in the Didache is an imparted gift of God made known to the congregation by the servant Jesus; in the Fourth Gospel, Christ is proclaimed as the life: 'I am... the life'.... The Fourth Gospel seems to depend on the Didache for its tradition. [10]

The circulation, acceptance and understanding of the Gospels, which contain the earliest written accounts of the Last Supper as well as the post-resurrection meals with Jesus and his disciples, took time. It is hard to imagine that no Eucharistic rites or memorials existed prior to their circulation, that is, during the interval between the ascension of the risen Lord circa 28-33 AD and the earliest date for the written Gospels circa 50-55 AD, an entire generation! Practices most certainly grew out of the experiences of Jesus' first followers. In all the fragments of Eucharistic liturgies extant from the first century (with the exception of Luke's Gospel) no words appear linking Eucharist to the suffering and death of Jesus or to the Last Supper. The early Church could indeed have been commemorating and continuing the essence of the meals the Apostles had experienced with the resurrected Christ, as recounted by Luke with Cleopas and his friend eating bread with the risen Lord on Easter afternoon, and with the disciples in the Upper Room that same evening when the risen Lord ate a piece of broiled fish. It would have been natural for them to do so. John's Gospel continues the theme of *bread and fish* in chapter 21, where the risen Lord prepares a meal for his disciples. All the Gospels concur—the only *bread and fish* meals that Jesus ate followed his resurrection. The feeding of the four and five thousand with bread and fish make no mention of Jesus eating the provisions, only that his miracles provided the food for others. The *Multiplication of the Loaves and Fishes* miracles are very frequently portrayed on the walls of the catacombs, and it is thought that their popular use was due to their association with *Eucharist*. As has been stated, there are no *Eucharist* frescoes in the catacombs that bear an association with the Last Supper meal. *Bread* and *fish* are always on the table, just as *bread* and *fish* are the major elements in the multiplication miracles of Jesus and his appearances on Resurrection Day.

Jesus' words at the Last Supper, *'Do this in remembrance of me'* appear in only one late manuscript of Luke and in none of the other Gospel manuscripts. Paul's words of institution in I Corinthians 11 date to shortly after 50 AD Neither of these texts is referenced in *Didache*, and neither is modeled in the Eucharist frescos of the catacombs. Taking into account the latest date ascribed to Jesus' ascension, 33 AD (it could have been as early as 28 AD), and the earliest possible date for Paul's letter to the Church at Corinth (which preceded the writing of the Gospels) around 50 AD, we are left again with an entire generation of believers not privileged by what we now call the New Testament scriptures. Are we to assume that they did not celebrate commemorative meals based on either the Last Supper meal or the post-resurrection meals until Paul told them how to do it? They surely must have continued in the spirit of the meals they had enjoyed with the risen Christ.

The word *Eucharist*, a Greek word, contains other clues we should heed. The first syllable, *'eu'*, is a prefix that always suggests something positive and good. At the time of the Last Supper, and preceding the day of resurrection, it is inconceivable to think such a prefix would have been considered in creating a word to characterize that event.

The second syllable, *'char'*, is the root syllable for many Greek words. Among them are:

- Chairo - greeting, rejoice
- Chara - joy,
- Charis - grace, gift, favor, pleasure
- Charisma- gift
- Charitoo - a favor
- Charizoma - I give, I forgive

These words seem to be more easily associated with a meal focused on the risen Christ than with the somber event of the Last Supper. Given the strong resurrection emphasis of the New Testament, particularly the *Acts of the Apostles* and the Epistles, and in light of the later evidence in catacomb art as a whole, it is hard to believe that an early Christian Eucharistic practice commemorating the Last Supper could stand outside the mainstream of their resurrection-minded theology, isolated and alone.

Much more could be said on this subject. We could also speculate or call into question what Paul meant in I Corinthians 11. If he was instituting a Eucharistic practice for the first time, why had there been no celebration for an entire generation? If this was meant to be a *new* practice focusing on the death of Jesus, what was the character of the one it replaced? If Paul was intent on establishing a new and definitive *Eucharistic* practice, why did he write of his ideas concerning *Eucharist* only in his letter to the Church at Corinth and never to anyone else? We could ask the question how his *Eucharistic* words, which seem to focus exclusively on the death of Jesus, fit with his total theology that places the resurrection of Jesus at least equal in importance to the crucifixion, and perhaps in a position of supremacy over it. Remember that the title *Lord* refers to the risen One. Could it be that Paul was attempting to correct a practice in Corinth that had become so lopsided in its resurrection emphasis that it had lost all sense of the sacrifice that preceded it? Was he in effect saying, *"When you eat this bread and drink this cup, don't forget that our risen Lord also suffered and died?"* Such a solution to the dilemma would be in keeping with Paul's interest in fusion and balance between the death and resurrection of Jesus.

If, indeed, the early Church celebrated a *Eucharistic* meal based on the meals with the risen Lord, what happened to that meal, and how did we end up with our single commemoration based upon the Last Supper meal? Answers to this question, if it can even be considered a valid question, remain clouded in obscurity. Again, one can only speculate.

Perhaps a contributing factor was the Church's response to the *Arian* dispute over the divinity of Christ. The *Arian* argument was that Jesus was only and fully God, not man. Consequently, the argument goes, it was not the Son of God who died on Golgotha hill. It could be posited that in order to destroy the *Arian* heresy it was necessary to emphasize Jesus' *human* nature. He *was* flesh and blood, he suffered, he bled, and he died. He was both God *and* Man. What better way to establish his dual nature than to emphasize the very thing the *Arians* denied—his human nature—not to ignore his divine nature, but merely to refute the heresy which refused to acknowledge Jesus' humanity.

Running parallel to that movement perhaps was the concurrent idea that a sinful humanity could not sit in the presence of a sinless, triumphant Savior. The early Church had expected the rather immediate return of the risen Lord. When it appeared that might not take place in their lifetime they began to look at our fallen world, possessed of suffering, sin and death and found it easier to identify with a Jesus who, like them, also suffered and died. It was easier to relate to the One who truly understood their suffering. However this may have played out, in the 4th century following the end of the Roman persecution of the Christians there appears to have been an increasing tendency, not present earlier,

> *...to speak of a 'change' of the elements, by consecration, into the body and blood of Christ.* [11]

*John Chrystostom [c. 349-407 AD] calls the Eucharist 'a table of holy fear', 'the frightful mysteries', 'the mysteries which demand reverence and trembling'. The consecrated wine is called 'the cup of holy awe', 'the awe-inspiring blood'. The Eucharist is the 'awe-inspiring and terrible sacrifice', 'a fearful and holy sacrifice'.[12]*

Post-legalization, 4th century *Eucharistic* practices became completely different—in tone, in symbol, in meaning—from those posited sacred practices of *Eucharist* based on the post-resurrection meals with Jesus. The fish, *Ichthus*, had both figuratively and literally been removed from the table—the last vestige of the risen One no longer was a silent participant. Over the centuries even the symbolic *bread and cup* changed character.

*How far Eucharistic theory has really moved from the Patristic teaching is indicated by the confession imposed on Berengar by Nicholas II's council of 1059 AD: 'Bread and wine which are placed on the altar are, after consecration, not only a sacrament but also the true body and blood of our Lord, and are sensibly, not only in a sacrament but in reality, handled by the priests, broken, and crushed by the teeth of the faithful.'[13]*

## Conclusions

As we conclude our discourse on *Eucharist* it is once again important to remember that our current practice is a *Sacrament* of the Church; it is accepted as such by almost every wing of Christendom and has been for centuries. We must not change it. This *Sacrament* is a constant reminder of the overwhelming sacrifice Jesus paid to cover our sin. We need that reminder.

Should the contemporary Church consider a celebration of a *Eucharist* meal based upon the resurrection meals Jesus had with his disciples? I leave that decision to the reader. However, it should never replace the *Sacrament of Eucharist* we now celebrate. It may be an experience we want as a reminder that we fellowship with a risen Lord. Perhaps it could be part of our Resurrection Day celebration. (*A model liturgy for a Resurrection Eucharist appears in another appendix*).

One thing is clear—it is not enough, nor has it ever been enough to single out the death of Jesus, his sacrificial offering, as all-sufficient. Unless Jesus was raised from the dead his sacrifice would mean nothing. The apostle Paul said it clearly. If we do no more than round out our current *Eucharist* with Easter words and the promise of Life, that will at least be a step in the right direction. We can do no less. Gustave Martelet has said it very well:

> *Suppose that for a moment in our minds we withdraw the risen Christ from the Lord's Supper, what remains of the latter? The table is immediately bare; it has been cleared; no dish remains to supply our needs; there is no Presence; the table is no longer sacred, and we can leave it without regret. This is what we are told by faith: without the risen Lord Himself, His supper is nothing. In that supper, then, it is He who is everything. It is not that the guests are of no importance, but their value here comes from the Person who invites them and receives them.*[14]

The *Eucharist* is the *table and the supper of the Lord*. It is there, says Martelet, that he himself, and he alone, illuminates us by his word, initiates us into his resurrection, communicates to us his Presence in the Spirit, and, loading us with his love, incorporates us into his Body. Without all these blessings,

> *…would the Eucharist—if indeed it still existed—be anything but the feast of the Lord's absence, the liturgy of an imaginary gift, the rite of men who have no kingdom,*

*and the empty forms of disillusioned hearts?.... Between the Eucharist and the resurrection perfect unity exists, so that we must either retain them both together, or reject them both. If, then, as we have seen, the resurrection still holds good, theologians must, from their side, show how the Eucharist rests entirely upon the resurrection or say goodbye to it forever.*[15]

# End Notes: The Resurrection Eucharist

1. Vöörbus, Arthur, *Liturgical Traditions in the Didache*, Else, Stockholm, 1968, published by Estonian Theological Society in Exile, p. 25
2. *Ibid.,* from the Forward
3. Gibbins, *The Problem of the Liturgical Section of the Didache*, Journal of Theological Studies, Oxford XXXVI (1935), p. 381
4. *Op. Cit.,* pp. 63-66
5. *Ibid.,* p. 68
6. *Ibid.,* pp. 133-4
7. *Ibid.,* p. 125
8. *Ibid.,* p. 126
9. *Eucharistic Theology Then and Now*, Clements et al. The Society for Promoting Christian Knowledge, London, 1968
10. *Op. Cit.,* pp. 153-5
11. *Op. Cit.,* p. 51
12. Kilmartin, S. J., Edward J., *The Eucharist in the Primitive Church*, Prentice-Hall, Inc., Englewood Cliffs, N.J., 1965, pp. 151-2
13. *Op. Cit.,* p. 58
14. Martelet, Gustave, *The Risen Christ and the Eucharist*, translated by Rene Hague, A Crossroad Book, Seabury Press, N.Y., p. 119
15. *Ibid.,* p. 120

# An Introduction To The Celebration
# Of The Resurrection Eucharist

AS WE HAVE just concluded, roots for the *Resurrection Eucharist* reach back to the first century of the Christian era. The celebration of the Passover meal on Maundy Thursday became the model for the traditional *Eucharist*. But the risen Christ also ate with the disciples following his resurrection, the first occasion in the Upper Room on Resurrection Day. Later it was the first recorded full meal of the risen Christ, where Jesus prepared a meal of *bread and fish* for his disciples (John 21: 1-14) that became the model for the *Resurrection Eucharist*. Outside the New Testament the only extant liturgies for *Eucharist* from the 1st century make no mention of the suffering and death of Jesus, or of his broken body and shed blood. In the early liturgies 'Life is the central image.

The Fish-Cross on the altar points toward the moment on Easter night when Jesus revealed himself as alive to his disciples by eating a piece of broiled fish in their presence. As 'Death was swallowed up in victory' (I Corinthians 15), so in this symbol the cross, a sign of Jesus' sacrifice, is swallowed up in the fish, an early Christian sign of the resurrection of the risen Christ.

The cup contains milk and honey. These elements were always used when *Eucharist* followed Baptism, which in itself is a Death-

Resurrection sign. Milk and honey represented Israel's deliverance from their bondage in Egypt to their new life in the Promised Land of milk and honey. In Hebrew texts the phrase *Holy vine of David* referred to the children of Israel as the chosen people of God. In the ancient Christian prayers, *Holy vine of David* referred to the new chosen people of God—those who believed the risen Jesus was the promised Messiah. In this *Eucharist* the cup, then, is a sign of the 'chosen-ness' of his followers, not of his shed blood.

The bread is not associated with the broken body of Jesus. Rather, according to the ancient prayers, it was a sign of the body of believers, scattered around the world, who would be gathered into one loaf in the presence of the risen Christ at the end of time.

The introduction to the 'Lord's Prayer' includes the words, "… made us bold to say". Their use is intentional, as it was the resurrection of Jesus that turned the fearful and dejected disciples into bold witnesses for the risen Lord.

As we celebrate the *Resurrection Eucharist* we not only celebrate the risen Christ, but also our 'chosen-ness' and our 'gathering' into the presence of the Savior. We declare that we will bear witness to the risen Christ, just as the early Christian community in the book of Acts 'witnessed to the resurrection of Jesus'.

This Resurrection Eucharist liturgy has been compiled from early fragments and documents from the first five centuries AD Chief among these is the *Didache,* a manual for Church practice that describes how *Eucharist* should be celebrated. Dating back to the end of the 1st century or the beginning of the 2nd, it is reflective of a practice already in existence, according to the scholars. Also included are Gospel and Epistle texts as well as texts from non-biblical sources. The existence of an early *Resurrection Eucharist* is verified in catacomb art, where every portrayal of *Eucharist* includes the *Fish* on the table, thus linking the sacramental meal with the risen Christ.

# Options Preparatory To The Celebration Of The Resurrection Eucharist

## Meditation Before the Celebration of the Traditional Eucharist

Judas betrayed him. Peter denied him. The others abandoned him. What have we done? Do we have a little of Judas in us? Peter? Are we among the nameless who simply flee from him?

Whatever we've done, wherever we are, Jesus invites us—all of us—to taste his forgiveness—his forgiveness and his grace we so greatly need yet so blatantly don't deserve.

This is the table of forgiveness and God's abundant grace for sinners who recognize their need for cleansing. Let us worship together with gratefulness to the Lord who so lovingly forgives and pardons us.

## Celebration of the Traditional Eucharist

*(At the conclusion of this Eucharist,
sing a verse of a communion hymn)*

## The Stripping of the Altar

**Minister I**: And as Moses lifted up the serpent in the wilderness, so must the Son of Man be lifted up, that whoever believes in him may have eternal life. (John 3: 14-15 ESV)

*(While the previous passage is being read,
Minister II removes the cross from the altar,
turns toward the congregation, and exits out the center aisle.)*

**Minister I:** O Lord, God of my salvation; I cry out day and night before you. Let my prayer come before you; incline your ear to my cry! For my soul is full of troubles, and my life draws near to Sheol. I am counted among those who go down to the pit; I am a man who has no strength, like one set loose among the dead, like the slain that lie in the grave, like those whom you remember no more, for they are cut off from your hand. You have put me in the depths of the pit, in the regions dark and deep. (Psalm 88: 1-6)

*(While this is being read the plates of bread
are removed down the center aisle.)*

**Minister I:** *(After the bread is removed)* Is your steadfast love declared in the grave, or your faithfulness in Abaddon? Are your wonders known in the darkness, or your righteousness in the land of forgetfulness? But I, O Lord, cry to you; in the morning my prayer comes before you. O Lord, why do you cast my soul away? Why do you hide your face from me? Afflicted and close to death from my youth up, I suffer your terrors; I am helpless. Your wrath has swept over me; your dreadful assaults destroy me. They surround me like a flood all day long; they close in on me together. You have caused my beloved and my friend to shun me;

my companions have become darkness. (Psalm 88: 11-18 ESV)

*(While this is being read the cups are removed down the center aisle.)*

**Minister I:** Yet a little while is the light with you. Walk while you have the light, lest darkness come upon you: for he that walks in darkness knows not where he goes. While you have light, believe in the light, that you may be the children of light.

*(While this is being read another Deacon/Elder takes the single lit candle, faces the congregation until the passage is finished, then exits the center aisle.)*

*(Minister I then folds the altar cloth and exits the center aisle.)*

**Hymn:** O Sacred Head Now Wounded (vss. 1 and 2)

# Meditation before the Celebration of the Resurrection Eucharist

**Minister II:** The table is empty. All that reminds us of Jesus has been removed—his body the bread, his blood the cup, his cross the sign of his sacrifice for us; even the candle which reminds us that he is the Light of the world. And soon, the two candles which represent his deity and his humanity will be snuffed out.

Life is barren without him. But he has not been abandoned by God, nor will God abandon us.

The Light will re-enter our darkness. The table will again be full, for wherever the risen Christ is, life is full, joy is complete, and power is available: power to overcome our darkness, power to live in a threatening world, power to bring Christ's love to others, power to carry us to the daily awareness of Christ's presence.

This barren table will become the rich, sumptuous feast of empowerment—a foretaste of the joyful heavenly banquet reserved for those who profess Jesus to be the risen Christ, the Son of God.

So, even now, as we enter the darkness and barren-ness symbolic of a life without the living presence of Jesus, let us with eager anticipation wait for the coming of the risen Lord.

*(The reader blows out the remaining two candles,
removes the altar cloth, and leaves via the center aisle.
Now proceed to the Celebration of the Resurrection Eucharist)*

APPENDIX **IV**

# Celebration Of The Resurrection Eucharist

*(From the back two women bring a white altar cloth from the back to the altar, place it on the altar, and return to their places. Minister I follows after they have placed the white altar cloth on the altar and places the Fish-Cross on the center of the altar).*

**Minister II**:…on the first day of the week, at early dawn, they went to the tomb, taking the spices they had prepared. And they found the stone rolled away from the tomb, but when they went in they did not find the body of the Lord Jesus. While they were perplexed about this, behold, two men stood by them in dazzling apparel. And as they were frightened and bowed their faces to the ground, the men said to them, "Why do you seek the living among the dead? He is not here, but has risen. *(Luke 24: 1-6 ESV)*

*(After reading, Minister II enters with the lit center candle, lights the two altar candles, moves to the center, faces the congregation, raises the center candle, and proclaims:)*

**Minister II**: Christ is risen!
**Congreg**: **He is risen indeed!**
**Minister I**: Death has been swallowed up in victory!

**Congreg: Death, where is thy sting? Grave, where is thy victory?**

**Minister II**: The Day of Resurrection! Be illumined, O ye people! The Passover, the Passover of the Lord! From death unto life, and from earth to heaven, has Christ our God brought us over, singing a song of victory, trampling down Death by death—upon those in the tomb bestowing Life!

*(While Minister I reads the following, Minister II places the lit center candle on the altar in front of the Fish-Cross.)*

**Minister I**: He arose from the dead and cries: 'I freed the condemned, I made the dead to live again, I raised him who was buried...I am the Christ, I am he who put down death, and triumphed over the enemy, and trod upon Hades, and bound the strong one, and brought the dead safely home to the heights of the heavens.

**Hymn**: *(A resurrection hymn will be chosen)*

*(Minister II introduces the reading of the Scripture lessons that recount the Emmaus road appearance of the risen Christ.)*

## The Lesson

**Reader I**: Luke 24: 13-32
**Reader II**: Luke 24: 33-43
**Minister I**: We pray in the Name of him who has made us bold to say:
**Congreg: The Lord's Prayer**

*(After the Lord's Prayer two Elders/Deacons bring the cups of Milk and Honey to the altar)*

## Thanksgiving for the Cup

**Minister II:** We give thanks to you, our Father, for the holy vine of

David, which you made known to us through your servant Jesus; glory to you forevermore. *(Didache, chapters 9 and 10)*

**Congreg**: **We give thanks to you, our Father, that through His resurrection Jesus has become our hope and our deliverer.**

**Minister I**: For you alone, Lord Jesus, are the root of immortality and the fount of incorruption. *(Acts of John 109-110)*

# Thanksgiving for the Bread

*(1 or 2 Elders/Deacons bring the bread to the altar)*

**Minister II**: We give thanks to you, our Father, for the life and knowledge which you made known to us through your servant Jesus; glory to you forevermore. *(Didache)*

**Minister I**: As this broken bread was scattered over the mountains and when brought together became one, so let your Church be brought together from the ends of the earth into your Kingdom; for yours are the glory, the power through Jesus Christ forevermore. *(Didache)*

**Congreg**: **What praise, or what offering, or what thanksgiving shall we name in the breaking of this bread, Lord Jesus?**

**Minister II**: We glorify Thy Name that was named by the Father;

**Minister I**: We glorify Thy Name that was named through the Son;

**Congreg**: **We glorify Thy resurrection shown unto us by Thee.**

# Charge Over the Cup

**Minister II**: *(Lifting the cup)* He asked them, 'Have you anything here to eat?' And they gave him a piece of broiled fish which he took and ate before their eyes. Remembering his words, we lift the cup of deliverance, and in drinking, make our sacrifice of thanksgiving.

## Charge Over the Bread

**Minister I**: *(Taking the loaf and breaking it)* He took bread, and blessed it, and broke it, and gave it to them. And their eyes were opened, and it was revealed to them that the stranger was Jesus in the power of his Resurrection. This we do in remembrance of him, and make our sacrifice of thanksgiving.

*(Minister II holds the cup for Minister I, who dips a piece of bread into the cup, then eats. Minister I holds the cup for Minister II, who eats, and says:)*

**Minister II**: When you do this, you become witnesses to the Resurrection of Jesus.

## Procession of Witnesses to the Resurrection

*(The congregation moves row by row down the center aisle toward the altar. Each Minister serves the bread and cup to those on his side of the aisle. Each participant takes a piece of bread from the loaf, dips it into the cup of milk and honey, and eats, then moves to the side aisle and back into the row from which they came. At the discretion of the worship leader the congregation may accompany the 'Procession' in the singing of resurrection hymns.)*

*[The following is optional, but effective: After eating, each participant takes a small candle from their side of the altar, lights it from the side candle, and then returns to his seat.]*

## Prayers of Thanksgiving and Praise

*(Members of the congregation are encouraged to offer prayers of praise and thanksgiving for the resurrection power available to us through the resurrection of Jesus Christ, or to pray for guidance in living a life informed and inspired by the risen Christ.)*

## The Charge

**Minister I**: As Christ was raised up from the dead by the glory of the Father, even so we also should walk in newness of life.

**Minister II**: For if we have been planted together in the likeness of his death, we shall also be raised in the likeness of his Resurrection.

## The Benediction

**Minister I**: Blessed be the God and Father of our Lord Jesus Christ, which according to his abundant mercy has begotten us again unto a lively hope by the resurrection of Jesus Christ from the dead, to an inheritance incorruptible, and undefiled, and that does not fade away.

**Congreg**: *(Sings a Benediction hymn)*

# V

# For The Resurrection Eucharist

## Set-up:

- Altar
- White altar cloth
- 2 side candles and holders *(white)*
- 1 center candle and holder *(white)*
- Fish-Cross *(Altar piece in shape of the Fish, with the sign of the Cross on its face)*
- Advent candles, *(optional, one for each participant)*
- 2 chalices *(or more depending on the number of participants)*
- 2 plates *(or more depending on the number of participants)*
- Milk and honey *(2 parts milk for 1 part honey, mixed)*
- Round loaf(s) of white bread

## Participants:

- 2 leaders (Pastor(s) and/or Pastor and Elder/Deacon)
- 2 women to bring altar cloth to altar
- 2 readers for Scripture lessons
- Deacons or Elders to bring chalices to altar
- Deacons or Elders to bring plates and bread to altar

*(Altar in the front. Begin with 2 side candles and advent candles [optional] on the altar. Everything else is brought to the altar during the Eucharistic liturgy.)*

# Author's Biography

***Gregory S. Athnos***
Professor of Music (retired), North Park University
Chicago, Illinois

GREGORY S. ATHNOS served as Associate Professor of Music for thirty-two years on the North Park University faculty as director of choral organizations. In his second year he founded the popular Chamber Singers and toured extensively with them throughout the United States, Canada, Scandinavia, Russia, Estonia, and Italy. In 1975 he was founder and first conductor of the University Orchestra, continuing in that position until 1982. In 1986 he was appointed conductor of the University Choir, and led that organization in concert tours across the United States, Poland, Hungary, Sweden, Russia and Estonia. Altogether, he organized and led thirty domestic and foreign tours for the ensembles of the music department, conducting over 1000 concerts. Mr. Athnos also appeared as conductor in Minneapolis Orchestra Hall on six occasions, in Chicago's Orchestra Hall twenty-five times, and as guest conductor for the Chamber Orchestra of Pushkin, Russia, and the State Symphony of Estonia.

In 2007 Mr. Athnos was asked to be the conductor of the Majesty Chorale, which was invited to participate in the 2008 pre-Olympic Festival in China. Most of the singers were Chinese-born Christians.

They sang nine concerts of Sacred Music in Beijing, Tsingdao, and Shanghai.

Mr. Athnos was one of the most respected teachers on the University campus; often his classes had waiting lists. 'Innovative',' enthusiastic', 'provocative', and' challenging' were terms often used by his students, who called his lectures 'lessons in life'. He has also taught in the national Elderhostel program (now Road Scholar) on two campuses, Wisconsin and New Hampshire, where his 152 weeks of lectures on a variety of topics related to the arts have garnered rave reviews from his participants. One adult learner wrote of him, 'He is the Beethoven of lecturers'. In 2005 he was honored by Elderhostel International as one of its most highly praised instructors.

Mr. Athnos received his degrees from Northwestern College in Minneapolis, Minnesota, and the University of Michigan, where he was elected to the National Music Honors Society. He has also studied Norwegian folk music and its influence on Edvard Grieg at the University of Oslo. He has had 20 articles and poetry published in *Pro Musica*, the Music Journal of the former Yugoslavia, the *Mennonite Journal*, the *North Parker*, the *Covenant Companion*, and *Christianity and the Arts*. Mr. Athnos was recipient of the *1990 Sears Foundation Award for Teaching Excellence and Campus Leadership*, and the *1992 Honorary Alumnus Award*, conferred by the Alumni Association of North Park University, an honor granted only rarely in the school's 100+ year history.

He has traveled throughout North America, Europe, Japan, and China as conductor, guest clinician, and as lecturer in music and theology, the latter emphasizing the theological significance of the Art of the Roman Catacombs.

Mr. Athnos retired from university teaching in 1998, and has kept a busy schedule of lectures and seminars for arts organizations, Elderhostel/Road Scholar, museums, conference centers, and churches. Mr. Athnos also organizes and leads foreign tours concentrating on the arts.

CPSIA information can be obtained at www.ICGtesting.com
Printed in the USA
267815BV00002B/1/P